D1610333

Stanley Spencer at War

overleaf
Stanley Spencer in the R.A.M.C., 1916

STANLEY SPENCER
AT WAR

RICHARD CARLINE

FABER AND FABER

LONDON   BOSTON

First published in 1978
by Faber and Faber Limited
3 Queen Square London WC1N 3AU
Printed in Great Britain by
BAS Printers Limited, Over Wallop, Hampshire
All rights reserved

British Library Cataloguing in Publication Data

Carline, Richard
Stanley Spencer at war
1. Spencer, *Sir* Stanley, b.1891
2. Painters—England—Biography
759.2   ND497.S75

ISBN 0-571-11028-2

Contents

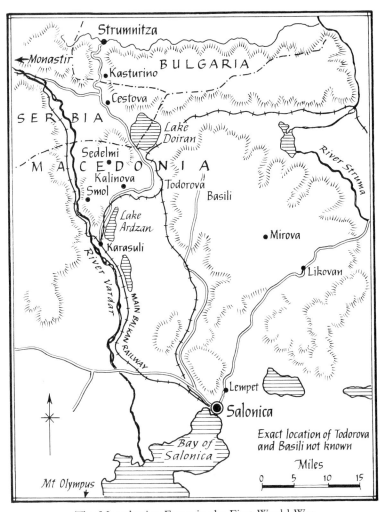

The Macedonian Front in the First World War

Introduction

In planning this book, I did not expect to write a biography of
Stanley Spencer; I had intended to confine it to a selection from
his early writings. Nor did I propose to write about him or his
beliefs, beyond providing a few notes, knowing that he had
opposed anyone but himself doing so. When in 1928 he asked me
to write about his work at Burghclere and I read to him, a couple
of years later, my preliminary draft, he was most disapproving. 'All
this about *my* ideas', he commented in exasperated tones. 'I can
write about them myself. I wanted you to write your own
impressions of my work.' But to write about his work without
delving into his ideas or the events that influenced him seemed to
me impossible. So on that occasion, I felt I must abandon the task,
to his regret as well as mine.

When Giles de la Mare of Messrs. Faber and Faber who had
agreed to publish this book pointed out to me that Stanley's
writing, despite being so expressive in itself, often lacked
continuity, especially when only extracts could be included, I
agreed that a biographical narrative to link these extracts together
was necessary.

Stanley Spencer's writings fall into three categories. There are
his letters; and there are his numerous notebooks in which he
constantly wrote; and lastly there is his autobiography, or
reminiscences as I have described them. I think my abandoning the
project of writing about Burghclere prompted him to write his
own account of his war experiences which had inspired his
Burghclere paintings. He began this about 1936, basing it on his
memory of the lost notes made when convalescing in Salonika in
1918, and continuing it intermittently, particularly while in

Glasgow between 1941 and 1944, and at Cookham Rise in 1945. He addressed this autobiography to his ex-wife Hilda, my sister, in the form of letters, hoping that she would edit them with a view to publication as a book, and she was in touch with his friend Gwen Raverat; but her own illness precluded her carrying out Stanley's intention. The task of editing would in any case have been considerable since his writing was very discursive, even rambling, and it was interspersed with personal messages to her: 'As I have gone along writing', he wrote, 'I have been seeking a place where I could feel a love that would comprehend all I am . . . a place for my wishes to live in. I was home-hunting.' Moreover, the autobiography extended far beyond the events of his life: 'I felt a need to write this book to and with you', he told Hilda. 'This autobiography I wish to be a novel of married life.' Although not continued beyond 1918, it reaches nearly 100,000 words.

When ill in 1959, and a few months before he died, he told his elder daughter, Shirin, of his wish to continue his autobiography and to see it published, and sought her help, but his final collapse prevented this intention being carried further.[1] Some years of uncertainty had to elapse before it became possible for me to undertake the task of collating and preparing his mass of writings for this publication.

Several distinct phases can be recognised in his letter-writing. His very early letters before he joined in the First World War, of which few survive, were chiefly to his brother Sydney and Henry Lamb and a few of them to me, and are very brief compared with later ones, in barely legible, immature hand-writing without punctuation, odd in grammar and spelling, though very vivid and expressive. Those he wrote during his War service were mainly to his sister Florence, with some to his friends Desmond Chute, Henry Lamb and James Wood. His constant reading of classical literature made his writing much more mature, and he had become more aware of grammar and spelling. After his return from the War, his letters were addressed almost entirely to Hilda but with some written to Lamb, myself and others, and they gradually became increasingly long—one to Hilda being described by him with pride as his 'hundred page letter'—very prolix and full of repetition. He found relief in thus committing his thoughts to paper, spending many long hours in doing so. His letters to Florence, Hilda or myself tended to be intimate and spontaneous, some to Hilda being harsh and acrimonious as well as lengthy, whereas to his friends, such as Lamb and Wood, he was much more circumspect, even deferential. It has been estimated that all this writing during some forty-five years until his death in December 1959 amounted to more than two million words.

Some of his 'jottings' in his notebooks are of a very private and personal nature and it is thought that he intended much of this material to be destroyed; he would not have anticipated that some of these private confessions might be used in other publications as they have been. His letters to Hilda contain much of a purely personal nature. I have tried to exercise discretion in omitting such passages or statements which I feel sure that he would not have wished published, without detracting from the truth.

In a book of this nature, the extracts from Stanley's writings are necessarily brief—more so than I would have wished. As far as possible I have preferred to use the letters written when the relevant events occurred, but I have drawn upon his autobiography especially for descriptions of his war experiences, about which he could not write so fully at the time under wartime censorship.

I have not deviated from the text, except in adding punctuation, the absence of which makes it difficult to follow. But I have had to omit words and sometimes sentences, here and there, for the sake of clarity as well as brevity, but only where their omission does not in any way change the meaning, as where he has diverged from the subject. Sometimes unnecessary words, such as 'this picture' or 'the fact that', are repeated constantly. All omissions have been indicated in the usual way, as have the few insertions of words which were not his but are added for clarity. I have also corrected his misspellings wherever possible.

I have confined the book to the first twenty years of Stanley's adult life, beginning with his student days and ending with the completion of his Burghclere paintings, which coincided with the break-up of his marriage with Hilda. I felt that the whole of his work during this period led up to and culminated in the painting of his war experiences—Burghclere being, in my view, his greatest achievement. It was during this First World War period that I first met him, and I was with him frequently after the War—being now,

I believe, almost the only person apart from his brother Gilbert to remember him at that time.

But I have also limited the period covered by this book for the further reason that his work underwent a great change in character after the separation from Hilda. It was after this, in the mid-thirties, that it changed dramatically in subject and intention, emphasising distortion and differing in his use of colour. He then began his self-revelation in painting self-portraits and nudes, and was compelled to accept many commissions to paint landscapes to supplement his inadequate income. His figure composition was frequently concerned with his early recollections but seldom captured the intense conviction that inspired his early work, in which form, tone and colour always formed part of his basic conception.

In writing, as in conversation, Stanley was always confident of being understood. In Yugoslavia in 1922, he would explain some abstruse idea to peasants who could not understand English. His gesticulation and the expression on his face seemed to suffice. I am reminded of a visit I made to a theatre in Japan, having been assured that my companion did not speak English. This would not have deterred Stanley, but I felt I had to try my few words of Japanese. 'What do you do?' I managed to ask him. 'Teach', he replied. 'What do you teach?' 'English' was the surprising answer, and my embarrassment was all too apparent. People may understand more than they admit. Stanley took this for granted.

Stanley's attitude towards women has been widely discussed since his death, and his work interpreted in the light of possible or imagined sexual aberrations. I should stress, however, that his writings during the period I have covered—and I have read most of what has been available—have revealed no indication of preoccupation with sex, nor have they shed any light on any subsequent attitude he may have adopted towards it, when he obviously suffered from his solitary mode of life and consequent sexual frustration.

In preparing this book, I have had the full concurrence of my two nieces, Stanley's daughters, Shirin and Unity Spencer, and I owe my thanks to them and to Dorothy Hepworth for permitting me to use and quote from his writings and reproduce his work for this publication, to Jack Martineau, Stanley's sole surviving executor, and to David M. Robson and, especially, Richard Elsden of Messrs. Dawson and Co., his solicitors, for clarifying and facilitating this permission. I am also grateful to my nieces for reading the manuscript and checking any mistakes. I am indebted to the Trustees of the Stanley Spencer Gallery at Cookham for the loan of the letters to Desmond Chute, and particularly to Geoffrey Robinson, Alec Medwin and Joan George, Chairman, Trustee and Honorary Secretary, respectively, of the Gallery, not only for the use of the letters but for access to other relevant material in their custody. Alec Medwin and his wife, now owners of Stanley's and Hilda's former house, Lindworth, have given their time in locating places where Stanley worked and enabling me to meet the occupants, among whom I should mention Kathleen Emmet, friend of Stanley's early tutor, Dorothy Bailey. I am particularly grateful to Marjorie Metz, Chairman of the Friends of the Stanley Spencer Gallery, and Philip Metz, who have been so very helpful during my frequent visits to Cookham, and to other friends who knew him.

I have had the unique opportunity of using Stanley's letters to Henry Lamb, and I am indeed grateful to Lady Pansy Lamb for allowing me to retain them so long and to quote from them. Stanley's letters to his sister Florence (Mrs Image) were passed on her death to their brother Percy Spencer and later given by his widow and daughter to the Tate Gallery for their archives, where the notebooks and the autobiography had also been deposited by Stanley's executors and heirs. Although I already had copies of much of this material, I have felt especially grateful to the Director of the Tate Gallery and to its Archivist, Miss Fox-Pitt, for allowing me to study the originals, for giving me much of her time in sorting out this mass of written material, and for providing photographs of hitherto unpublished material.

I must thank the staff of the Slade School at University College, London, and Mrs Lightbaum, the Archivist, for allowing me to inspect the school records and for sending me photos of work in their possession and permission to use them. I am also grateful to Miss Mitchell Smith for permitting me to quote from Adrian Allinson's autobiography (not as yet published), which refers to Stanley's student days, and to my life-long friend, and equally of Stanley, Kate Foster (later Mrs Kurzke),[2] for providing me with copies of her diary entries concerning Stanley and allowing me to quote them. I thank Christopher Cash, art master at Bedales School, for information about Stanley in connection with the school.

I also thank the Trustees of the Imperial War Museum and Joseph Darracott, Keeper of its Department of Art, in particular, for sending me photographs of Spencer work in the Museum and allowing me to reproduce them; also Duncan Robinson, Keeper of Paintings and Drawings at the Fitzwilliam Museum, Cambridge, for providing me with a photograph and allowing it to be reproduced, and the Director of the City Art Gallery, Rugby, for permitting me to use a photograph of the portrait of myself. I am also grateful to the Courtauld Institute of Art, University of London, for allowing me to reproduce their photographs of four drawings and paintings in my possession.

I am especially grateful to Peter Spencer Coppock for all his generous co-operation and professional skill in photographing drawings, letters or existing photographs for use in this book, which has entailed a visit to Burghclere Chapel and the Spencer Gallery in Cookham. In this connection I must also record my thanks to the National Trust for permitting us to take photographs in the Chapel and providing a colour photograph.

It would have been Stanley's wish to thank my mother for her generous hospitality whenever he came to stay with us, which he so frequently did. After her death in 1945, our dear housekeeper, Ellen Arnfield, was equally generous in continuing this hospitality.

But most of all, I must express my thanks to my wife, Nancy, who has patiently read through the draft of my text, giving me much needed criticism and advice and constant help in the preparation of this book.

I would like to dedicate it first and foremost to the memory of my sister, Hilda, as I feel sure would have been Stanley's wish, but also to my mother, Annie Carline, who helped him during many difficult periods and crises in his life. I would like to associate with them, my mother-in-law, Mona Higgins, a devotee of art, who of course also knew Stanley.

INTRODUCTION

Notes to Introduction

1. To the best of my belief, he never gave his consent to anyone else writing his biography.
2. Her death in October 1977, since this was written, has alas prevented me from showing her this text.

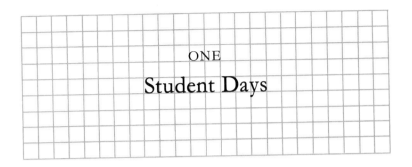

ONE
Student Days

'IDON'T THINK I have changed at all but increased and grown on what I started with', Stanley Spencer wrote after his return from the First World War. He was completely single-minded in pursuing his goal, which had become clear to him, even as a student. Writing in red ink on the page of a notebook, and thinking back to his two pre-War years, he continued: 'This is why those early stages of development were, to me, so important. I particularly wished my life to attain to a certain atmosphere, which, if not attained to this day, is and was tangible and clear. I thought I was right in thinking that no more convincing and emphatic medium could be found for expressing this particular quality of life and atmosphere than painting. I could see clearly that painting could bring the whole of that into life.'

Always wanting continuity in his work, he questioned whether he could retain or recapture his early inspiration, and added: 'What I did before the War, as a result of the impetus to effort this gave me, I have never done since the War.' Was his apprehension justified? His work during his first twelve post-War years reveals little change in style or objectives from his earlier work. It was after the completion of his war paintings in 1932, when his domestic life collapsed, that his work changed so completely, almost as if he had acquired a different personality.

That Stanley should ever have taken up art is one of the extraordinary aspects of his career. He had no artist antecedents, and the character of his home-life at Cookham when a child, with art seldom discussed and little understood, gave no reason to expect that he, the eighth child, would reveal an inclination to draw.

His father, William Spencer, organist and teacher of music, had a fondness for literature and would recite within the family circle passages from the poets and the Bible, which gave Stanley his early familiarity with it. The Bible was, indeed, his main source of inspiration, which was always related to home-life in Cookham. In this musical and literary family it came as a surprise to find Stanley, aged thirteen or fourteen, drawing illustrations to favourite fairy-tales and Bunyan's *Pilgrim's Progress*. Those that have survived reveal imagination and humour but little hint of artistic precocity.

Will, the eldest brother, and Harold, ten years older than Stanley, adopted musical careers, and their sister Annie played the violin.[1] Their father expected all his surviving nine children to become musicians like himself and his elder sons. Since Stanley revealed at an early age such enjoyment when they played and a precocious understanding of music, it was assumed that he would adopt it as a career.

William Spencer or 'Pa', as they called him, was perplexed when his son, age sixteen, announced his wish to be an artist. He asked Miss Dorothy Bailey who lived opposite to give him lessons in water-colour painting,[2] and A. J. Sullivan, the illustrator, in Cookham Dean, was consulted but gave no encouragement. It was decided to let him attend Mr Cole's classes at Maidenhead Technical School,[3] within walking distance of home. The school was plentifully supplied with casts of antique sculpture but provided no living model, and teaching was limited in scope. Stanley, whose only general education had been in the classes held by his two sisters, now gained his first experience of working with other students, and his year at the school left a lifelong impression.

Some thirty years later, about 1932, he made a sketch in his notebook of the 'Roman Gladiator' on its circular pedestal with students drawing, while the Mayor of Maidenhead in chain of office began his inspection by placing hat and gloves between the Gladiator's feet (Plate 1). In 1938, when living in Hampstead,[4] he recorded his recollections of a day at the school. 'I walk past the modern church and modern graveyard and up into Marlow Road. . . . The thought of Miss Burrell's finished "stippled" drawing of the Corinthian capital and of the "Laughing Fawn" comes to me and pleases me. Outside the big windows, but too high to see out of (which is what I like), I hear the shouting of the football match in progress in Kidwell's Park. I remember the strange effect in my mind of seeing one of these highly finished "stipple" drawings of the "Gladiator" taken from its most foreshortened angle. I must one day do a picture of this room, as each statue and easel or chair or person had a meaning for me. I felt quite disturbed in my mind when the big "Gladiator" that lunged forward from the dark right-hand corner was moved, and I hope it is back there again now. . . .

'I love to think of the "Athene" heads that lived in shelves in the east end and the "Lorenzo Medici" head among the capitals and beyond the first curtain. . . . I could worship every hard-edged shadow the gas-light made on the casts. I was always a little awe-struck by them, and when I saw the way the master handled them in shifting them about I saw, somehow, that my awe was not the kind of attention I was meant to pay to these casts. . . .

'One of these spiritual elements of Maidenhead in the expressive form of a Town Councillor comes in and signs his name in the top right-hand corner of my sheet of drawing-paper. The edge of his great and important-looking overcoat slides down the side of my face with the intense atmosphere of Maidenhead he has brought with him. It was interesting to see someone, whose sermons I had sat for hours listening to at the local chapel, with which I was often impressed, suddenly open the door of the room and with the gaslight full on his face, which was stern with white hair and small white beard, give a sharp glance round at us working, and to realise that he was a very important man indeed in the town, being several times Mayor, a J.P. and a Governor of the school. . . .

'When I looked at the grey-green distempered wall behind the pedestal casts on the shelves and contemplated in my mind as I gazed at the dead still shadows, I felt that local angle; and the whole feel of the wall and shelf was not like the feeling you have about shelves and things on them at home. And so I made homes of them, namely sanctuaries, in my mind, so that the fact that these places were subject to inspection, periodically, and every cast and shelf and junction between wall and shelf and shadow on wall, all provided and paid for out of public money, seemed to enhance the little private liaisons I had with these nooks and corners.

'The tall thin chocolate-coloured curtains, each about fifteen feet high and nearly as wide, which divided this room into four

1. *The Mayor of Maidenhead Visits the Technical School*; recollection of 1907/8, pencil, in a notebook *c.* 1932. Tate Gallery.

compartments, are still in my mind. It was in the evening, when different classes were held, that they were drawn across, but never right across, and one could get all sorts of glimpses of the different classes. I felt Mr Cole must change into someone else when he left some students, who were far advanced in the throes of "stippling" some Greek cast, such as the "Discobolus" ... for someone behind the curtain who was doing a "still-life" of some flowers ... to hear him tinkling the water-colour brushes just behind and saying "Patience, patience!" But he was kind to me and I was thankful to have his "patience" said to me. But he seemed to look very askance when, at a late stage of my stay there, I began to wish to do compositions and illustrations to stories.'

When Stanley was nearing seventeen his father felt that further tuition was needed and he consulted his friend and patroness, Lady Boston, at Hedsor, who recommended the Slade School of Fine Art at University College, London. She would pay the fees, and meanwhile help him in water-colour painting.

Father and son went to London in May 1908, for an interview with Professor Brown and his assistant Henry Tonks. Stanley was accepted without the usual entrance examination, but Mr Spencer was so uncertain of his son's ability to fill in the entry form correctly that he did it for him, signing 'S. Spencer, Fernlea, Cookham, 27th May.'[5]

Over forty years later (May 1949), Stanley wrote in a notebook: 'To me these exterior happenings, such as going to the Technical School, Maidenhead, and later to the Slade, are hardly as much as barnacles on this "me" that makes this journey, but more just driftwood through which my ship went at that time. But even as such it indicates something of my whereabouts.' This statement runs counter to his description, ten years earlier, of a pen and ink composition, *Scene in Paradise* (Plate 2), a subject set at the Slade, in which he sought to combine his three main sources of influence:[6] 'I made the central theme of this composition a clothes-horse, which was a sort of house I liked being in when it was standing round the kitchen fire, and in front was a mother holding a baby, who was reaching out and taking hold of the long hair of two bearded old men, who are reading Bibles. On the left, there is a nude standing. It is significant to me that I have tried to bring the three experiences of my life together, quite unconsciously, namely the Slade with life

2. *Paradise*, pen and ink, drawn at the Slade School, 1911. Slade School of Fine Art, University College, London.

drawing (the nude is just a model), the life at home, and the feeling the Bible gave me.' These three sources of influence continued to inspire him thereafter, even during the War.

Working at the Slade introduced him, not only to a new environment, but also to contemporaries with quite a different background and experience. It taught him to contend with others, as he would have to do in the War.

During this first summer term, Stanley drew from the 'antique' under Walter Russell's tuition,[7] taking the 8.50 train from Maidenhead and returning by the 5.08 from Paddington in time for his tea. In one of his numerous notebooks, he recorded (December 1939): 'Going to the Slade from Cookham was similar to me to what I imagine it would be if it were possible to get into a book one was reading. The sounds coming in at the open upstairs windows of the long corridor outside the Antique Room, sounds that were coming from the somewhat removed streets, sounds of a barrel-organ playing something which I had heard a cousin playing, . . . seemed "no cousins here". It seemed that I and that music was a part of the contents of a book on the cousin's shelf in their house next door. I was so much in the "Life-Room" that I can't think of any of the students as people one could see in the street anywhere. . . . I liked the girls' paint-covered frocks and walls plastered with palette-knife dabs.'

Stanley's friendly and open-hearted manner made him popular despite his eccentricities and occasional outbursts of temper. With his Eton collar, Norfolk jacket or blue jersey, he looked younger than he was at eighteen. His musical, slightly high-pitched, voice with faultless speech, showed no trace of the Berkshire accent. He made several close friends, notably R. Ihlee and M. G. Lightfoot from Liverpool, whose subsequent suicide so distressed his student friends.[8]

New students arrived in the autumn term of 1908, including Mark Gertler, C. R. W. Nevinson, Edward Wadsworth and Adrian Allinson, who were among his particular associates. In the 'Life-Room', to which Stanley was now promoted, the model took the same pose every day for a fortnight from 10.00 a.m. to 3.45 p.m., with three rests of a quarter of an hour and lunch. At 4.15, short 'action' poses, lasting five minutes, were taken, but Stanley had to miss these to catch his train, and it may have influenced his lifelong disapproval of rapid sketching. His progress was slow at first and he was not among those awarded prizes in June 1909.

Constantly mentioning his home, he acquired the nickname 'Cookham', and he was easily teased. Allinson, with whom he shared the 1910 scholarship, described a trick, which went astray:[9] 'Though month after month', Allinson wrote, 'his [Spencer's] designs earned the highest praise, on account of their failure to illustrate the theme, he never received the award.' Allinson drew an imitation 'Spencer', which conformed with the subject set, and everyone took it to be a genuine 'Spencer'. When Stanley heard of it, he was enraged and informed the Professor. He could accept personal banter with good humour but took great exception to liberties that infringed upon his work. However, he showed no trace of grudge when he met Allinson a few years later.

Stanley's award of the scholarship involved evidence of an adequate standard of education and he had to sit an examination in general knowledge. 'Apparently I failed utterly', he wrote shortly before he died; but the rule was relaxed—'a kind of cheating', as Stanley described it, continuing: 'Brown [the Professor], in an outburst one day, shook me and said "You only got the scholarship by the skin of your teeth."'

Stanley, just twenty in 1911, had never stayed a night away from home, and Tonks, thinking it would benefit his general development, arranged with his friend Harrison for Stanley to spend a month at Clayhaden, near Taunton. Although he wrote subsequently that he 'was more or less bullied' into it, adding, 'I felt when I got back that I had lost caste; my work was never the same,' yet the one letter he wrote at the time to his brothers Sydney and Gilbert, gives the opposite impression: 'This man is a farmer, a writer, a keen follower of art. . . . I like him. . . . Of course, I can walk well-nigh everywhere, because well-nigh everywhere is his. . . . Nobody about! Old everything! Old house, with old fireplaces, old beams.'

The Slade made him increasingly independent. He would visit Lightfoot in Hampstead Road, and Ihlee. He seldom had occasion to write letters, and the earliest that have survived were addressed to his brother Sydney. Very characteristic is one dated 1 July 1911: 'I hope you will forgive me, Higgy dear [sic], but I've been and gone and done and struck a bargain with Ihlee; it happened like this: I was up at Ihlee's the other day and he gave me about 30 half-used tubes of oil paint. After that, he asked me to let him have that drawing of Dot Bailey for 2/6d., which I did. After that, he said: "If you give me the half-crown back, I will let you have the box as well as the paints." I walked away with about 15 shillings worth of colours and a lovely oak box. . . .

'I have had this term: Scholarship, box of paints, reproduction of Philip IV Spain (Velasquez) from Wadsworth, Dhurer [sic] head from you, extra prize of one pound (not even third), a prize divided between four—Gertler, Carline, Camilla Doyle and myself—£2. 5. o. each.'

A particularly close friend was Darsie Japp; he ate his sandwich lunch in the Life-Room with Stanley, who always brought hard-boiled egg sandwiches. Japp and Ihlee visited Cookham that summer. Stanley's letter to Sydney continues that they 'went bathing down Odney. Ihlee didn't go in. After we had our bathe, a punt, into which Ihlee and I jumped, went "tring-tringing" towards Odney Weir. Suddenly, Japp suggested that we should shoot the weir, to which Ihlee replied: "I feel game." Suddenly and some to my relief, Japp realised that the bars were down, and so we had to go without that pleasure. . . . And now I will say good day, Hingy, from your loving brer. P.P.S. I was a horrid swank yesterday at the College Assembly. It was very pretty to see the whole of the professional board troop in in their lovely robes. The Provost wore a flowing red one, a most gorgeous sight.'

Stanley drew compositions in pen and ink at home. For the *Fairy on a Water-lily*, he tells us, Emily Wooster, who was by no means slight as in the drawing, posed for him.[10] *The Girl Feeding a Calf*[11] was to convey, he wrote in 1939: 'a feeling of love bringing things together and thus fulfilling each thing's identity,' so as to achieve a unity which is called design. His description continues: 'I go with my cousin, who takes the milk round, down to Mill Lane Orchard, through the ten foot high iron gates with "acorn-design" railings, to help her feed a young calf. She puts her hand in the pail of milk and the calf sucks at her fingers. She tells me to have a go, and I was surprised at the strength of its sucking. I was never quick at understanding and did not realise that the fingers represented the udders.' In a lecture at Oxford in the 1920s,[12] he sought to clarify what urged him: 'I was loving something desperately, but what

27

this was I had not the least idea. I took the first thing I came to and proceeded to draw it.'

In *Job and his Comforters*,[13] he reveals the early fascination that rubbish and litter had for him. His description continues: 'I only made two attempts: [Firstly] a half sitting and half lying figure. . . . I remember being disappointed when Lightfoot said the position was not possible. . . . This was an impression I had from seeing heaps of turf of manure out in a field; these were large Christmas-pudding shapes. . . .

'A later attempt was to have Job sprawled across the great rubbish heap that used to be over in Ovey's Farm; . . . as children, it was our happy hunting ground. I was always scrambling about on it and looking hopefully towards the farm gate for another barrow-load to come barging through. The Farmer's wife always allowed us to take anything we liked.'

He visualised *Joachim among the Shepherds*, a pen and ink wash drawing, in a favourite place, which he describes in the same reminiscences: 'I liked to take my thoughts for a walk and marry them to some place in Cookham. The "bread and cheese" hedge up the Strand ash-path was the successful suitor. There was another hedge going away at right angles from the path and this was where the shepherds seemed to be. We had to walk single-file along this path and the shadows romped about in the hedge alongside of us. And I liked the hemmed-in restricted-area feeling in that open land—a happening of great consequence in a place of no note, but of great note to me. That endless path! Could nothing be done to 'jolly" it up? And then Joachim and the shepherds gave it their blessing, and saved me from getting bored.

'That endless path! Wearisome, but I loved its uneventful length. . . . And there was Joachim and the shepherds. Oh Lord, revive my work in the midst of the years; in the midst of this boring path, make known a wish to celebrate the joy I felt in this "nothing-ish" sort of place. . . .

'Its meaning became so tense and wonderful that it seemed near and "findable"—out in the street somewhere among Cookham happenings. I would see the daylight streaming through the coloured glass of the front-door on the wall-paper. It is in the magical out-of-doors, just beyond that coloured stained-glass robin.

'Oh yes, and I did rather fancy wet November under Cliveden, and mud and ivy that grows among the grass. It all seemed to be a groping for tangible reality, and these outside things seemed contact points, especially wetness and mud. But the May hedge won.'

Certain social functions were traditional at the Slade—the fancy-dress dance in December, strawberry tea after prize-giving, and the end of term picnic. Stanley could not attend, if he wished to, or he would miss his train. He had very little experience of social gatherings at that time, and never learnt to dance. At Glasgow (1945) he recalled these festivities with some acrimony: 'I used never to go to the dance—didn't know there was one. . . . I was against anything detracting from the men's life-room. . . . I just somehow did not feel I could bear to rejoice one little bit until I could draw. There was a book at home called *Winning his Spurs*, and I did not feel I could come upstairs [at the Slade] and out into the sunshine of the quadrangle, spurless and unsung. When I could draw—up then, on then and out into the heaven of the Strawberry Tea. . . . By the way! Don't say I can't draw. Eating strawberries and drawing badly! It doesn't make sense.'

Stanley's Slade training was confined to drawing. This was his choice. He never had lessons in oil painting. In a memorandum written during his last years, he confirmed: 'In the four years I was at the Slade, I did about three days painting from one model—three days out of four years! Tonks taught me drawing and was very critical of it.' Stanley taught himself to paint, oil being his favoured medium. He seldom used water-colour, beyond applying a sepia wash, but he sometimes applied oil on paper. His methods were purely personal. After 'squaring up' his canvas to correspond with his preparatory sketch, he would make a careful and detailed drawing in pencil and fill the spaces with paint, using small brushes and a tiny palette, beginning at the top left-hand corner, progressing downwards and finishing as he went. He seldom re-painted parts as most artists do. Feeling certain of the effect he intended, he could sit or stand close to his easel, without surveying his work from a distance. His earliest oils were more broadly painted than his later ones.

His first oil painting, *Two Girls and a Beehive*, of 1910 'marks', he wrote later, 'my becoming conscious of the rich religious significance of the place I lived in. My feeling for things being holy was very strong at this time.' The following year he painted *John Donne Arriving in Heaven*, which always took a pre-eminent place in his own estimation; he described it as 'more directly from my imagination than any I have ever done'. 'I have always loved reading Donne', he told his Oxford audience in 1923, 'though I understand only a little of it.' Referring to a sermon 'about going to Heaven by Heaven', he interpreted this to mean that 'Donne went past Heaven, alongside', and 'getting a broadside view of it'. He explained: 'As I was thinking like this, I seemed to see four people praying in different directions. I saw all their exact relative positions all in a moment. Heaven was Heaven everywhere, so, of course, they prayed in all directions.'

He wrote to his brother Sydney (18 May 1911): 'I took that painting and showed Tonks—"crit" as follows: "I don't like it as much as the drawing; it has no colour, and is influenced by a certain party exhibiting at the Grafton Gallery a little while ago" (Post-Imps)—the damn liar! However, I sold it to Raverat for six guineas, and Tonks is going to have my next. I am inspired of late. I hate people individually, but I glory in human nature; sounds paradoxical, but it's true.' There is no evidence that Stanley visited Roger Fry's First Post-Impressionist Exhibition, and he appears to have denied it.

Although Stanley did not attend Fry's lectures at the Slade, Fry saw the *John Donne* and, immediately impressed, included it in the English section of the Second Post-Impressionist Exhibition at the Grafton Galleries, autumn 1912. Fellow exhibitors included Duncan Grant, Frederick Etchells, Wyndham Lewis, Spencer Gore, Henry Lamb, Bernard Adeney, with Vanessa Bell as the only woman artist and Eric Gill the only sculptor. None of Stanley's fellow students at the Slade were included. This was the first and only occasion when he willingly showed with these 'avant-garde' artists, and he always refused to submit work to an exhibition jury. Nor would he have accepted Clive Bell's assertion in the catalogue that each exhibitor 'owes something directly or indirectly to Cézanne'.

Stanley's loyalty to Tonks, more than personal conviction, might have induced his rejection of Cézanne, which led to his unhappy quarrel with Mark Gertler.[14] He had told Mark that his

(Mark's) work showed him incapable of understanding Cézanne, which Mark took as an insult. Although Stanley replied that he did not mean to be insulting, Mark felt this made matters worse, meaning that Stanley's words were 'not insults but truths', as he told their mutual friend and patron, Eddie Marsh, with whom he had planned to visit Cookham.

Gertler had some justification for anger, since Cézanne's work meant everything to him, whereas Stanley never studied it. The visit to Cookham was cancelled. Not until April 1914, was the quarrel partially healed, when Gertler wrote: 'The evening with "Cookham" was most successful and inspiring. We got on very well together and had a long talk on art.'[15] But once broken, their friendship never quite recaptured its former warmth, though they often met after the War in my studio.

At the end of the summer term 1912, Stanley left the Slade to work on his own at ideas that swarmed in his imagination at Cookham.

Notes to Chapter 1

1. Harold recorded in a letter to Hilda (Stanley's wife) in 1949, that Will played Beethoven's 'Emperor' Concerto at the Queen's Hall, London, when only fourteen.
2. The youngest of four daughters of W. H. Bailey, living at Eldon Cottage in the High Street, Cookham. Not much older than Stanley, she had acquired some slight familiarity with water-colour from her father, an accomplished landscape painter in oil and water-colour and pioneer photographer of the Cookham environment. The Baileys were the accepted artists of Cookham when Stanley was a child. She painted flowers, but subsequently took up fashion design.
3. Subsequently the Berkshire School of Art and Design.
4. Constance Oliver, Hilda Carline's fellow student at the Slade, took him as a lodger at 188 Adelaide Road at her request. Stanley re-drew the scene in the Technical School four years later for his 'Scrap-book' series.
5. Some writers have incorrectly recorded the date, as David Sylvester has stated in *Drawings by Stanley Spencer* (Arts Council catalogue, 1955).
6. In possession of the Slade School, but hitherto unidentified.
7. Later Sir Walter, Keeper of the Royal Academy.
8. Student friends included W. L. Clause, J. M. B. Benson, F. A. Helps and Sydney Carline, all of whom gained prizes, and some, like Ihlee, became prominent in the New English Art Club.
9. Allinson wrote his *Memoirs* shortly before he died

10. Now in the Spencer Gallery, Cookham.
11. Given to his friend, James Wood.
12. At the Ruskin Drawing School.
13. Believed not to exist any longer.
14. Whether or not this repudiation of Cézanne reached the ears of Fry, Stanley was never welcomed by him. I recall occasions when Fry ostentatiously turned his back on him.
15. Written to their fellow student, Dora Carrington, published in *Mark Gertler, Selected Letters*, edited by Noel Carrington, 1965.

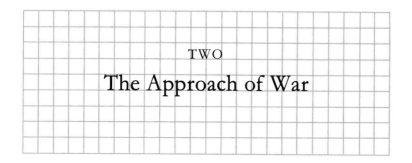

TWO
The Approach of War

STANLEY'S FIRST OPPORTUNITY to paint on a large scale, to which he attached great importance, came after leaving the Slade School in 1912. He worked at home strenuously, as if not unaware that he had not long before his world might be disrupted by war. This early work, together with the subsequent war paintings, were to establish his position as one of the most significant, and especially one of the most original, of artists in this century.

The subject set for the Slade Summer Composition Prize was the *Nativity*, and he began immediately on this, the largest work he had as yet tackled, its size being prescribed. Space being insufficient in the nursery at Fernlea,[1] where he and Gilbert slept, he was given use of the barn at Ovey's Farm, across the road.[2] When the picture was submitted, he shared the prize with Gilbert Solomon. The picture is particularly significant for its landscape setting, the first he attempted, of woods, haystacks and flowers. In 1935, he recorded his source of inspiration: 'The marsh meadows, full of them [the flowers], leave me with an aching longing, and in my art that longing was among the first I sought to satisfy. . . . [It] celebrates my marriage to the Cookham wild flowers. It is our way, of not only joining in the creation, but in a way sharing in the creation, because we, in a way, re-create.' (Plate 5.)

He always wished to relate his idea to a particular place. Even when far from Cookham in the War, he would endure hardships, or even court them, to be near the place which gave him inspiration. He explained his attitude in a lecture on Composition at Oxford in 1922:[3] 'I am very slow at assimilating my surroundings, but once they are, then they begin to have for me a

33

great meaning. Some artists think that meaning cannot be expressed. Well, if I thought that the only way to express what I know about Ferris Lane, . . . near my home, was to be done, as I have sometimes had to do it to passing motorists, by just shouting: "First on the right, second on the left", I should just burst. I shall do a picture some day with these words as a title. . . .

'It is always a great effort for me to describe anything tersely to a goggled motorist that is and is not all in a moment, and as I stand in that dazed condition, . . . I say to myself dreamily: "Second turning on the left; how strange I never realised that before." If someone were to direct me to Ferris Lane in such a way, I should never find it. At least I would and I should walk up it, and it would be to me "the second turning on the left", with the result, of course, it would never be Ferris Lane. All a motor-drive really consists in is just bearing to the right with an occasional turn to the left, just to keep the car from going round and round for ever in a circle.'[4]

His next important painting, *The Apple Gatherers*, was begun in autumn 1912, for the Slade prize of £25, available for fourth year students. This he won. It was visualised in an orchard behind the garden of Fernlea and visible from the 'nursery' window. He felt the people were the natural outcome of the place, like the 'divinity' that presided there. In 1936 at Lindworth, Cookham, he recalled the impression that such a view of nature made upon him: 'When at the end of each day, it had begun to get too dark to paint in the kitchen of "Wisteria" where . . . I was painting "Apple Gatherers", I used, sometimes, to stand on a little landing . . . and look from the cottage window to the still bare branches of some spindle-like trees which were hidden in a confusion of over-grown yew-hedge and other shrub-stuff,[5] and there watch and listen to a black-bird which could be just seen in the dusk, making a little darkness . . . among these few criss-crossing twigs and thin branches; the notes sounded more local and more immanent as darkness came on. And then an object passes diagonally down among the twigs into the inviting and homely darkness below.

'I look across to the left, where I see in the light of the slowly strengthening moonlight and the last pale influence of daylight Colonel Ricardo's chestnut trees standing at Lullabrook.[6] And as the moon begins to cast a faint gleam of its light in the dome-

there are three people pray

ing along the side of it

3. *Grape hyacinth*, watercolour 1918
   sent from Macedonia to Florence.
4. Sketch for *The Centurion's Servant*,
   oil paint on a letter to Henry Lamb, 1 October 1914.
   Lady Pansy Lamb.
5. Sketch for a composition, *c.* 1912 to 1914.

shaped tips of them, I listen and in a few moments the sound of owls hooting is wafted across to the window.

'Although it was only a few moments ago, while I counted ten sometimes, between the moments when the black-bird retired below and the owls began, yet in that moment the transition of one life to the other, of the evening and the verge and beginning of night, seems as great as the passing from this life to the next. . . . While two circumstances of my experience may be wide apart in their physical relationship and joined closely together in my mind, so I see in physical life examples where two moments in nature suggest to my mind a remoteness in their spiritual relationship.'

The Apple Gatherers, one of the very few of his early pictures unrelated to any incident in the Bible, was his homage to nature. It brought about an event scarcely less important to his future development than his entry to the Slade. This was his meeting with Henry Lamb (Plate 7), introduced by Darsie Japp, in June 1913. Although Lamb was intimate with members of the Bloomsbury 'set', having shown in Fry's Second Post-Impressionist Exhibition, it was his close friends, Augustus John, Boris Anrep and George Kennedy, who, henceforward, comprised Stanley's artist circle.

Lamb asked to buy *The Apple Gatherers* for £30, but agreed to release it when Eddie Marsh offered £50. The curious unequal proportion of the figures was explained when Stanley sent Lamb a preliminary sketch (8 December) with the information: 'The great size of the two central figures was unintended and accidental. As you see in this [the sketch], they are normal size, and better for that reason.' The disproportion doubtless resulted from his working so close to his canvas. He had also painted his *Visitation*, with the view of the garden (in Jas Wood's collection); subsequently he wrote on a sketch for the left-hand figure (in Richard Kennedy's collection): 'about 1912–13; Peggy Hatch posed for it in our Fernlea, Cookham, garden.'

In February 1914, he was working on his most ambitious painting yet of *Zacharias and Elizabeth*, and he invited Lamb to see its beginning (7 March).[7] He had conceived the idea the previous December, 1913, telling Lamb that he had a 'big square canvas': 'I am going to have it out of this canvas if it's the last act, as Brer Rabbit would say, and if I don't succeed, then Joe's dead and Sal's a widder, to quote Brer Rabbit again.' The scene was based on the view from the rear window of the staircase landing on the second floor at Wisteria Cottage, looking towards Cliveden Woods, though he did not paint any part from sight.

In the mid 1930s, Stanley wrote about this picture: 'What the places in Cookham had to tell me was nothing remotely connected with landscape. . . . I wanted to absorb and finally express the atmosphere and meaning the place had for me. . . . It was to be a painting characterising and exactly expressing the life I was, at the time, living and seeing about me. It was an attempt to raise that life round me to what I felt was its true status, meaning and purpose. A version of the St Luke passage, the gardener dragging the branch of ivy, and Mrs Gooden giving me permission to walk about in the garden of the untenanted St George's Lodge, resulted in this painting.' His love of texture was revealed in things half hidden in grass or foliage, a bird-nest, cobwebs or a person's hand, in this and other paintings.

Walls or fences, like the wall that recedes and bisects this composition, attracted him. They may lead the eye into the composition or separate one area from another, but Stanley liked them for their own sake. In a lecture in the early 1920s,[8] he explained the mystery he associated with them: 'I have always had a longing when I have come to a place where there has been a high wall, to want to see over it, to find out what was on the other side. Cookham was full of high walls. . . . As I was unable to see over these walls and could not climb over or break them, I set about mentally visualising what was there. I knew what I should desire to be there would be perfect, and I had only got to identify these desires and I should know what was spiritually there, though not, perhaps, what was physically there. Physically, it might have been a motor-garage. In fact, recently, I have been to Cookham and, owing to the introduction of motor-bus services, I have been enabled to see over the tops of many walls and found what I saw quite different from what I had expected. But what overjoyed me was that when I got down from the bus and walked along by the same wall, I found that my previous supposition was true and I could still enjoy the feeling of wonder at what was on the other side.'

At this period, 1914, he disclosed the wish, which one could never have expected, to embark on sculpture, revealed in a letter to Lamb (27 April), perhaps with his favourites Donatello and Ghiberti in mind: 'I am trying to do my Zacharias thing in "basso relievo"; is that what they call it? I am doing it with modelling clay, but I am going to do it with stone; I do not like clay. I itch to do trees in it, not damnable conventional trees, but trees as they are in my painting of this picture.'

A year later, he again told Lamb, 27 May 1915, that he wanted to make a bas-relief from a composition of which he sent him the sketch—three people on garden seats facing one another across a table with a laurel hedge behind. Whatever sculpture he may have begun has not survived.

Stanley's friendship with Lamb was stimulated by their mutual devotion to music and admiration of the work of the Old Masters. He sought Lamb's advice as he had previously consulted Tonks. He had received an invitation from Henri Breuil to become Membre d'Honneur of the Union Internationale des Beaux Arts.[9] Stanley accepted without fully appreciating the honour, and had asked Lamb (10 October 1913): 'Is this society any good? . . . I thought it would be nice if I wanted to exhibit in France.' But this was something he never did.

On one of his visits to Hampstead (30 October 1913) he wanted Lamb to take him to the National Gallery. In a previous letter (24 October) to Lamb, he indicated his antipathy to Hampstead, so surprising in view of subsequent events: 'Many people have tried to convert me to Hampstead Heath, but with all its fine trees, wonderful views, I always get horribly depressed whenever I go there. . . . I wish the National Gallery was in Cookham, but I have many reproductions of fine pictures of Old Masters, lent me by the Raverats.[10] They stimulate me; they quicken me. Do they not do so to you?' Stanley also knew the Old Masters through the pocket-size series published by Gowans and Gray. He chiefly admired the Florentine and Sienese Masters and asked Lamb (1 April 1914) to send him 'anything by Lorenzetti'. 'I am getting a very good collection of postcards', he added. 'I do not put them into a book; because I like to look at them separately. I take one out, according to how I feel, and put it somewhere in the room, so that I can look at it if I feel inclined. It sort of keeps me company and makes me work. . . . P.S. Do not forget the Lorenzettis.'

He indicated his intimacy with the great Masters, when he told me on one occasion that he had once dreamt that he was walking on Cookham Moor, where he met Signorelli standing like his figure of 'Anti-Christ' in Orvieto Cathedral. Signorelli greeted him with a smile, saying: 'Good evening, Spencer; I liked your picture in the New English.' Having written this down, I showed it to Stanley in 1929, but he took offence, crossing it out as a presumption. Doubtless, he recalled the crushing rebuke he received from Tonks after submitting a composition with the plea that perhaps he had been influenced by Masaccio. 'When competent to imitate Masaccio would be time enough to speak of influence', was Tonks's rejoinder.

Although Stanley seldom read the newspaper and took little interest in current affairs, he seemed to acquire, like many others, a lurking premonition of approaching war. He asked Lamb (27 October 1913): 'I am very interested in this "F. Rays" business. If it is true that it is impossible to prevent these waves from exploding things, what will become of war? We shall go back to the days of archery. I shall ask Japp about it; he knows everything; at least he told me he did.'

When war was declared on 4 August 1914, Stanley was painting his self-portrait larger than life-size, with its tightly closed mouth and penetrating anxious eyes, as if he wanted to ensure that his identity was preserved for posterity.[11] Eddie Marsh saw it at Wisteria Cottage, where Stanley had worked continuously,[12] and bought it for £18.[13] He asked Stanley why he had painted it so large and received the reply: 'Next time I start a portrait, I shall begin it the size of a threepenny bit.'[14]

The outbreak of war immediately concerned Stanley as it did most young men. His sense of security had vanished. He was inclined to enlist on the instant, as brothers Percy and Sydney proposed to do. Not fearful of danger for himself, he feared lest Gilbert might become a victim. He sought Lamb's advice at once: 'It is intolerable to be out of it; I cannot think. If you know of anything that either Gil or I could do, let us know. I expect it is rather selfish, but I am determined that Gilbert shall not volunteer for foreign service; there is not the least necessity. . . . He could simply put his name on the list of those to be called if required, so that he could get on with his picture. . . . There are other duties to do besides fighting. What ghastly things those Liège Forts are. There seems to be no sport in war now. . . . If I go to war, I go on condition I can have Giotto, the Basilica of Assisi book, Fra Angelico in one pocket, and Masaccio, Masolino and Giorgione in the other.'

Henry Lamb had been trained in medicine at Manchester before taking up art, and now with doctors in demand, his war-time destiny was obvious, but enrolment took time and, meanwhile, he visited Cookham.

The feeling that he ought to volunteer again assailed Stanley in November, when he wrote to Lamb, now at Guy's Hospital, (23 November): 'Do you know any decent regiment that would have me or Gil? We both feel it impossible to settle down, because to work at our job one has to enjoy things and I find that impossible. At least I can enjoy, but then there is the constant shock of realising what is on. . . . I think it is necessary for people like me to join. . . . I am quite sure I am as strong as thousands who are fighting, and the more beastly the stories become, the more I feel I ought to go or do something. Gil walks about like a lump of lead. I believe that with all the monotony of training, I should be happier doing that than here in Cookham trying to work. I wish they had mules in the Army: then I could be dressed up as a dwarf and pass as the Red Cross Knight.[15] . . . The one great drawback to our joining is our mother.'

They did not actually enlist—perhaps Lamb persuaded them to delay in case the War should end quickly, as many expected. However, they both volunteered in December for military training in the Maidenhead Civic Guard, with drill in Kidwell Park under Sergeant-Major Baldwin. Fancying the Ambulance as their best sphere of service, they attended the St. John's classes at Bray, four miles distant, ultimately acquiring the certificate.

In the reminiscences he was writing in Glasgow in 1944, he recalled the anxiety he felt: 'How could I continue gently putting myself among these mellow Cookham daily happenings? How could I stand in the cow-shed [in Ovey's Farm], opposite the house I was born in, and keep my eye on the wide crack of the door and warn Charley, the cowman, if and when Mrs Hatch, from bawling "Charley", showed imminent signs of coming down the yard? Or go down Odney and bathe in the midst of all its wild wonder and meaning and back home to Will and Schumann? How could all this be entered into whole-heartedly when war came? ... I was crushed and felt I would have to leave it all.'

With such anxieties as background to his thoughts, he involved himself in painting, feeling that time was limited. In September 1914, he had become engrossed in a new theme, *The Centurion's Servant*, more familiarly known as his 'Bed picture', and sent Lamb a sketch in oils (1 October) (Plate 4): 'It will be the first picture I have painted in a room.' He meant of course an interior.[16]

The concept of this extraordinary picture seems far removed from the passage in St Matthew, in which the centurion tells Jesus: 'My servant lieth at home sick of the palsy, grievously tormented.' Being so familiar with the Bible, Stanley must also have recalled the verse in Numbers (Chapter 32): 'Shall your brethren go to war and shall ye sit here?' Does the violent action of himself in the picture, as if running to escape, and sprawled across the bed, suggest his own dilemma?[17] Are the three figures kneeling by the bed, the middle one being himself, praying for his peace of mind?

Whatever his subconscious motive may have been, he explained to Lamb his intention to paint two pictures, one echoing the other which was to have been of Christ with the Centurion. In the 1930s, he recalled the associations which had prompted him: 'In our home ... there was an almost unknown place, namely the attic. This was the servant's room. ... At times, I heard converse going on and felt it might be the maid was talking to some angel. Later, the servants (our servant and the one next door) told me they could hear each other through the wall. ... The iron bedstead had the white porcelain knobs as seen in the picture. When our servant came down ... I would not have been surprised to see her face shine as Moses did when he came from Mount Sinai. ...

'The people praying round the bed may have something to do with the fact that in our village, if anyone was very ill, the custom was to pray round the bed. In church during prayer I sometimes looked round. ... I remembered every position. ... I thought of all the moments of peace, when at such moments this [scene] might occur. The figure turning his head somewhat away to the left seems to feel that there is some presence that has brought about the change.'

Lamb wanted to buy the picture and Stanley wrote to him (4

6. *Richard Hartley*, 1927.

7. *Henry Lamb*
by Gilbert Spencer, R.A.,
c. 1921.

December 1914) that he had been ill but 'I will send the picture to Hampstead as soon as I am well.' He wrote to him again (25 January 1915), having recovered—he had been ill with ulcers and delirious: 'Shall I send the "bed" picture to your place in Hampstead, or keep it here until your return from France?' The picture, however, had to remain at Cookham. Later, in Stanley's absence, Tonks arranged with old Mr Spencer to show it at the New English Art Club. This enraged Stanley when he learnt of it after the War. 'My father acted without having had any previous instructions from me at all', he wrote. His father, naturally, had thought he was acting in his son's interest, but Stanley was often indignant when some action was taken without his being consulted.

The picture gave Stanley his first notice in the press, Charles Marriott of *The Times* having pronounced it 'the most interesting picture there'. Stanley would read press comments with delight. He subsequently recalled an occasion in Bristol Hospital, when a patient showed him the words in the *Daily Mail*: 'Mr Spencer bids well to revive the now almost finished art of the subject-picture.' He immediately rose in the estimation of staff and patients. 'Due to my useful ignorance,' he commented later, 'I was never able to see when a critic was meaning to praise or dispraise; so I always took . . . whatever he said as being praise. On one occasion, when to my delight . . . a critic said that one of my pictures might, if it had been better drawn, have won a prize at the Salon;[18] my genuine delight knew no bounds; I had to tell my artist friends. I was astonished at being met with roars of laughter.'

Despite his assertion that he could not work amidst this war activity, he seemed to reconcile himself for a while and early in 1915 began a new concept of *The Resurrection*,[19] reporting it to Lamb on 25 January. He used two canvasses, one for the 'Good' and the other for the 'Bad', their shape being suggested by the spandrels flanking the chancel arch in Cookham Church. 'Not that I should ever do it in there', he wrote Lamb in February. 'No, if I did I might get depressed by it and never want to go into the church again.'

He wrote to Sydney (his brother) while painting it:[20] 'I am giving the bad ones a nasty time. I made the earth on their backs a lot thicker today. As to the one down in the bottom right-hand corner, he can't budge; I have got him absolutely set. I feel like God, when I look at him peeping out of a nasty gash in the ground. In . . . the "Good ones" coming out, there is an oldish man with a purple cape. His hands are feebly placed on either side of the split-open grave, out of which he has come half-way. He has kind of mutton-chops, but looks all the better for them.'

Having completed the two *Resurrection* canvasses in March 1915,[21] he felt the need to record his feelings about Cookham, epitomised by the cowls, while he still had time. His military training was drawing to an end, when he would feel that he must enlist. His *Mending Cowls* was to be his first large composition based, at least partially, on direct observation. When about to begin, he wrote to Lamb, now on the Western Front (24 March 1915), enclosing a pencil sketch and fearing lest it might not 'give the feeling of it being particularly the Cookham malthouses', but 'might be malthouses anywhere'. On 19 July he told Lamb that he had finished it.[22]

The cowls,[23] visible from the nursery, and behind Fernlea garden, constituted the chief link with Stanley's life, hitherto, in Cookham, and he recorded his feelings about them in 1944 at Glasgow: 'They seemed to be always looking at something or somewhere. When they veered round towards us, they seemed to be looking at something above our nursery window, and when turned away to be looking down. The earth by the base of these very big malthouse buildings was never visited by us, so that they were a presence in the midst of the maze of Cookham. From wherever seen, they were somehow benign. With their white wooden heads, they served as reminders of a religious presence.'

He felt a desperate need to put on canvas the ideas that were still teeming in his mind. He had already begun his *Swan Upping*, and he told Lamb accordingly on 24 March 1915. The scene was Turk's boatyard below Cookham Bridge. The idea came to him in church, as he wrote later in Glasgow: 'I could hear the people going on the river, as I sat in our north aisle pew.' But the actual theme was the collecting of swans by men of the Vintners Company for the clipping of their wings.

I first met Stanley in May 1915, through our mutual friend, Richard Hartley (Plate 6),[24] who was living at the Crown Hotel and usually joined Stanley and Gil at their early morning swim at

Odney. Hartley showed Stanley two of my sketch-books and when he expressed his liking for them, I wrote asking him to keep any of the drawings he liked, receiving his generous reply of 2 May: 'I should not take one except for the fact that I really want one, and since I do want one, I am going to have one, but only on this condition that if ever you feel you would like to see it or have it back, you will write and say so. . . . I know that if I had money, I would buy back every picture I ever sold. . . .

'I want to look at the "roundabouts" and "animals" again.[25] . . . In one you have drawn the base of the roundabout. . . . There is another which I think . . . is wonderful but does not move me like the one with the base, which is largely to do with the feeling I get from it. I believe you rather look down on these roundabouts drawings, don't you? . . . I understand them more; that is how it is. . . . I should want to make a very perfect finished picture of it. Why? Because I should want to. . . . They give me the most extraordinary feelings. Do you do paintings of these ideas? If you do, I shall come and see them. This letter is rather rambling, but then today is Sunday. . . . 4.30 And now to push my mother from Maidenhead to Cookham in her bath-chair up and down the switch-back like this [a sketch] in the blazing sun. . . . P.S. 7.15 Mar is pushed.'

Stanley revealed in such correspondence his capacity for recognising anything of interest for him in other work, however immature. When I visited him, as I recall, he was working in the attic of Wisteria Cottage, amidst the vegetables and straw, and lit only by a skylight at the back, and I was flattered to find he had copied one of my slight drawings of a leopard and had pinned it on the wall. 'It was very nice to have you to see my pictures', he wrote in a postscript to the above letter. 'You allowed them to look at you, which is a thing that hardly anybody ever does.'

Another letter followed in May: 'Two "roundabouts" ones, please. I have taken them out, and I shall mount them.[26] . . . Some people's studios ought to be like those old shops, where we used to have "H-penny dips"—a shop that is full of all sorts of things. I think how nice it would be if, instead of all this New English Art Club, London Group, Society of this, that and the other, we each had a studio and in front of the studio a little shop with a window full of all sorts of things, and someone behind the shop door to call "shop" when anyone comes in. That is why I like seeing old Clifton at Carfax & Co.'s place.[27] . . . I told Epstein that I thought his advertising himself was no good. "Well," he said, "if I did not advertise and exhibit, I should never sell anything." . . . If I took an "animal" out of your book, it would be as bad as taking a few bars out of a piece of music, so I shall not.'

This was my last news of him until we met again after the War. I was the first artist friend he made who happened to be some years younger than he. A few weeks later, in July, he enlisted in the R.A.M.C., having left his *Swan Upping* half finished.

Notes to Chapter 2

1. When the Spencers were no longer there, the name was respelt Fernley.
2. He revealed his liking for Ovey's Farm as early, so it is claimed, as 1906 when, barely sixteen, he made an elaborate and accomplished pen and ink drawing of the interior of the stable with a cart-horse on the opposite side of the yard from the barn. Both buildings have subsequently been demolished.
3. To students of the Ruskin Drawing School.
4. He was impatient of activities he could not share. His attitude towards motoring was modified in 1929, when he himself acquired a motorcar and learnt to drive. But following an accident, soon afterwards, when driving my mother, Hilda and me to Maidenhead, which made him nervous—it was his own error—he stopped using the car.
5. The spacious garden of St George's Lodge, now part of the John Lewis's Odney Club, lay at the back and a little towards the right behind Wisteria Cottage, which faced the main road and the Tarry Stone.
6. Lullabrook House, separating Odney Common and St George's Lodge, is now Odney Club.
7. From St Luke, Chapter 1. Incorrectly dated '1913' by Wilensky (*Stanley Spencer*, 1924), and as '1912' by Elizabeth Rothenstein (*Stanley Spencer*, 1945). A letter to Lamb, dated 7 March 1914, states: 'My big Zacharias picture just begun', and on 1 April: 'I am doing a small painting of it as well. I do this between 5 and 7 in the evening'—perhaps the one he gave to James Wood. He wrote to Lamb, 24 March 1915, that John Rinder had bought the composition, and, he hoped, would also buy the big picture which he wanted shown at the New English. It was bought by Muirhead Bone.
8. To students of the Ruskin Drawing School.
9. Professor Breuil, the acknowledged pioneer of pre-history.
10. Jacques Raverat married Gwen Darwin, Stanley's first and chief woman friend at the Slade. Both were fellow students there.
11. Wilensky (op. cit.) and Elizabeth Rothenstein (op. cit.) date it as '1913', as does Maurice Collis, more recently, in *Stanley Spencer, a Biography*, 1962. In a

letter to Lamb, dated 7 May 1914, Stanley states: 'I must stop now and go on with my portrait that is getting on at last.' There is no other portrait to which he could be referring.

12. Stanley was allowed to paint in Wisteria Cottage during these years by Jack Hatch and his family, coal merchants.

13. Stanley wrote to Marsh (20 April 1915) that he had cleaned the portrait and would ask Gilbert to deliver it.

14. Edward Marsh, *A Number of People*, 1939.

15. From *The Faerie Queene*.

16. Though dated by Wilensky (op. cit.) as '1915', repeated by Eric Newton in *Stanley Spencer* (Penguin Modern Painters, 1947), and by Collis (op. cit.) as 'in the first half of 1915', the dated letters to Lamb show that he had finished it in 1914.

17. In a letter to the *Christian Science Monitor* (probably never posted), Stanley repudiated the suggestion by Frank Rutter, the art critic (21 March 1927) that the picture was 'inspired by the experience of the war'. He could scarcely have evaded its influence, however, and it may have been unconsciously expressed.

18. This famous annual exhibition in Paris exemplified what was considered academic and therefore backward by Stanley's artist friends.

19. Dated by Wilensky (op. cit.) as '1914'; but Stanley wrote to Lamb, dated 'February 1915': 'I am getting on with the people coming out of the graves.'

20. His letter to Sydney (undated) must have been written in February or March 1915, as he states that Lamb was in France.

21. Subsequently bought by James Wood.

22. Incorrectly dated by Wilensky and by Newton (op. cit.) in '1914'. Stanley's correspondence reveals that he was uncertain whether Lamb or Wood had staked the prior claim to buy it. In the end it went to Mr and Mrs Behrend.

23. Later demolished to make way for houses in School Lane.

24. A product of Eton and Cambridge, Hartley was a fellow student with me at Tudor-Hart's art school in Hampstead.

25. They were drawn on Hampstead Heath and at the Zoo.

26. He had preserved them in his trunk full of sketches, left when he died.

27. The Carfax was one of the first galleries in the West End of London to show the more progressive and younger artists.

THREE

At Beaufort Hospital

'I HAVE NOT DONE any painting for a month now', Stanley wrote
to Lamb on 19 July 1915, 'because of the John Ambulance
exam. I have at last given way, though while I was painting, I stuck
to it manfully. But now that my Mar's attitude has altered and has
proved that she can do without us, without dying as she thought
she would, and also Cookham having become completely stripped
of its youth, I feel I can no longer stick living here, but must exist
somewhere else, suspend myself till after the War. I have finished
my Kowel [Cowls] picture and I have done a lot to the river-side
picture.

'. . . Gil went to a hospital at Bristol, an awful place and awful
hospital; I may go there. . . . Wherever I go it is bound to be vile,
but I am prepared for anything. I expect my duties will be cleaning
out lavatories and taking the "pan" round the ward.

'It seems such rotten luck that Gil and I had to do this instead of
being "tommies". I should have thoroughly enjoyed being a
private in the Berkshires. I mean I should have liked the training.
Mar has got an idea that the R.A.M.C. is not dangerous and that
one does not go to the "Front". I shall let her think that . . . July
21st: I have just heard that I leave for Bristol Hospital on Friday
morning (23 July). . . . It will be nice to be with Gil.'

Henry Lamb, who was expecting a commission, had suggested
that Stanley might apply to be his 'batman', but Stanley wanted the
offer made to Gilbert, who had meanwhile enlisted in the
R.A.M.C. Stanley even expressed a wish to serve in France, though
he could have had no conception of what 'trench' warfare meant.
Now aged twenty-four, Stanley looked very unlike a soldier, with
his slight figure, crimson cheeks, tousled hair, making gestures

with his fine, bony fingers. Yet, he was conventional as regards society, with a pride in being English. His love of a peaceful existence and hatred of strife was tempered by his sense of patriotism, and he was prepared for any dangers that came his way.

Years later, he wrote: 'I was very bad at drill and so was often in trouble.' But at the time, he had enjoyed its order and routine in Kidwell Park.

By nature he was not at all sentimental, and disliking emotional scenes, he intended to slip away from Cookham without bidding his parents farewell. He was always awkward over saying goodbye. Not knowing how he would feel, this being his first prolonged departure from home (apart from his brief visit to Somerset), he decided not to walk the usual way, as he explained shortly before he died, 'in order to feel I was not leaving' Cookham.

He described the occasion in his reminiscences, written in Glasgow in 1944, based, he states, on what he had written in Salonika in 1918: 'I had to meet a party of St. John's Ambulance men and to proceed with them from Maidenhead to Bristol by the 12 noon train. I should have gone from Cookham station to Maidenhead, but the day being a rainy July day and wishing to leave the village via Sutton Road and Widbrook Common, so that I could have one more walk over that Common as a civilian, I decided to walk it. I also felt that if I left the village at its eastern end, I should not get the rather melancholy feeling which I experienced when I left from the western station end.

'So in a summery suit and mackintosh I slipped away, called out "good-bye" to Pryce-Jones, the chemist, as I went round chapel corner. Then I passed and looked down Mill Lane, secret and peaceful, but not for me. When I got past Sutton Croft, I noticed a big thunderstorm brewing over in the direction of Cliveden Woods, and before I got to the red-brick wall, it was beating down. I kept as close up to the wall as I could, as it was sheltering me to a certain extent.

'It did not rain so heavily across Widbrook, but when I got to North Town Moor, it became positively vicious and quite upset my mental equilibrium which on that day, owing to circumstances, had become very shaky. . . . This storm gave me a kind of pre-vision of what I was to see and experience, and my thoughts became wretched and I felt very harassed.

49

'My straw hat was all limp and sticky. Why God should have put such a damper on my patriotic ardour, I could not understand; and then the very thing happened I did not want to happen: I met my father on Maidenhead platform with his cycle. He had cycled in from Cookham, so that he could say good-bye to me. I met our St John's instructor and he thanked us all for our present to him, which was a walking-stick with a dog's head on it. I do not know why I should have remembered this unless the fact that at the most important moments of my life, I generally remember the least important facts, is an explanation.

'I got into the train with several other recruits and, just as the train started, my father called through the carriage window to the man in charge of us: "Take care of him; he's valuable", which made me feel very awkward. . . . I thought, like those other young men, their "pa's and ma's" have not come to see them safely packed off! . . .

'On the journey, I could not help seeing the great fields full of ripe corn, wheat, barley, oats . . . and great spans of mustard round about. But it was all forbidden fruit to me and that is, perhaps, why it all seemed so extra sumptuous and tempting. I remember some malt-houses, . . . because being so accustomed to seeing only our own cowls on the Cookham malt-houses, any cowl different from those seemed deformed. . . .'

On arriving at Bristol, he continued by tramcar or bus to Beaufort Lunatic Asylum, taken over by the R.A.M.C. for war casualties. His story continues: 'I came to the gate leading into the Asylum grounds. (Plate 33) . . . This gate was as high and massive as the Gates of Hell. It was a vile cast-iron structure.[1] I love such things. Its keeper, though unlike that lean son of the hag who kept the Gate of Hell, being tall and thick, was nevertheless closely associated with that rapacious gentleman, being the man who had charge of all the "deaders", and did all the cutting up in the post-mortem operations. I could imagine him cutting my head off as easily as . . . cutting up chunks of beef. His eyes were beefy.

'But as soon as I had passed through that gate, and was walking down the drive, all my patriotic ardour, which I had struggled hard to retain, seemed again to leave me. A great clammy death seemed to be sitting or squatting on all my desires and hopes. Everything seemed so false. The day did not seem like day to me and the men did not belong to day. I felt that these beings, should they journey to where my home is, would evaporate into nothingness long before they got there.

'Even the trees and laurel hedges were affected; they were so deadly still; had someone been round in the morning and dusted them with a duster? A cobweb had been missed here and there. The ground was hard and had a ring of iron about it. The lamp-posts, sign-posts, railings and the trees seemed to be riveted to the ground. A steel-like uniformity prevailed and nothing could prevail against it.

'. . . We were escorted across a courtyard and along a kind of loggia or verandah—really a place along which all the food was conveyed from the main kitchen to the wards, and then . . . along a wide wall-papered corridor (very old-fashioned wall-paper) and at length into a ward—an empty one. . . . I looked at the pictures on the wall. They were of the Victorian Pears' Annual nature, and they have an associative interest for me. I cannot imagine anything more incongruous than the feelings I had on that summer afternoon, sitting on the spring mattress of one of the many empty beds—everything seemed to be directly opposite to what, under natural circumstances, it should have been. The ward seemed, with so many pictures depicting child-life, more like a nursery.

'A great hulking man was sprawling in the empty bed opposite—a man who had come straight from a corn-merchant's yard, a man used to carrying bags of flour about. I was not about to enter a life I had never lived before; I was actually in and living . . . in it. I was not aware of what it was . . . I ventured . . . into a smaller ward and then into the large corridor through which . . . we had come. . . . I looked out of the window below and there, in the middle of the paved court, . . . was a small octagonal open at all sides summer house. I noticed some consumptive case in a bed under it. The court seemed a sort of dreamland. . . . So much was I oppressed with the feeling of unreality that when at length one of the patients rose a little off his pillow, I experienced quite a queer sensation. . . .

'I felt pleased to think that with the advent of tea, I should have to take some sort of action to get it. And so "en masse" we four of us made our way with fear and trembling to where we had our food, which was in a large room having a long broad table in it.'

Back again in the empty ward with the other recruits, he found the pictures on the walls reminding him of home: 'How could I say to myself: "Well, it's alright; things are not so different after all; you've just come from your bedroom where you worked, and now you are almost back again in it." But . . . I had prepared myself for something different. What about that corn-merchant's man lying . . . on the bed opposite and Smith's book-shop youth sitting and writing at another bed? It was a case of . . . having discovered that we had each made some awful mistake and were in a trap, and the stupefied expression on each of our faces proclaimed this. . . . We had each to find our levels . . . in our own way. It was a case of every man for himself, and this instinctive feeling produced an atmosphere at once of unfriendliness between us. We each became to each other a symbol of our own helplessness. This consciousness, as those minutes dragged on, of a growing estrangement, was terrible, and all this to be happening in a big room rather like in feeling to the coziness of one's own bedroom at home.'

When Stanley found opportunities to draw, the patients asleep proved ideal models and sometimes the orderlies posed for him (Plate 27). He usually gave the drawings to the sitters. When the hospital was taken over at the outbreak of war, some of the mental patients were retained for domestic work. Stanley, as always, felt compassion for such cases. Moreover, his imagination was fired by their presence and the feeling of unreality it gave. He recalled his reactions in a notebook (undated), but written much later: 'The sunlight is blazing into the corridor just near the Sergeant-Major's office, and I say inwardly: "Oh! How I could paint this feeling I have in me, if only there was no war—the feeling of that corridor, and the blazing light, and the Sergeant-Major and his dog— anything as long as it gave me the feeling the corridor and the circumstance gave me." If I was Deborah, the lunatick who doesn't know there is a war, I could do it. His sullen face and shifty eyes—I envied him the mental agony of being cut off completely from my soul.

'I thought in agony how marvellously I could paint this moment in this corridor *now*. And if at any time this war ends, I will paint it *now*, that is with all the conviction I feel now, but it can only be done as long as I am assured that I am not suddenly going to be knocked off my perch. No! Not quite like that, because that can easily happen. No! Not that! But it was a belief in peace as being the essential need for creative work, not a peace that is merely the accidental lapse between wars, but a peace that, whether war is on or not, is the imperturbable and right state of the human soul; and that only is found in the peace of Christ.'

After some months (7 December 1915), he wrote to Lamb that he was 'horribly fed up' and wished he was in the infantry (Bantams): 'I get no exercise, drill and that is what I thirst for. I know what drilling is. . . . Ever since I have been here, I have done nothing but scrub floors.' Stanley had a respect for recognised authority but resented its imposition arbitrarily. There were the nurses who singled him out for teasing, and there was the Sergeant-Major, as described in notes written in 1929, who: 'walked about the ground, with his four fingers stuck into his two lower tunic pockets, . . . his fat thumbs stuck outwards. . . . He walked as one doubly guaranteed, whose soul was master-locked against anything but comforting thoughts, physical rather than spiritual. If nothing could prevail against the uniformity of which he was supreme architect, how could anyone prevail against him? and so the Sergeant-Major walked about.' Elsewhere in his re-miniscences, he describes the Sergeant-Major: 'He was quite terrifying enough, even though he did not wear puttees. If you did come anywhere near him when he did wear puttees, God help you.'

Stanley found the quarter-master, downstairs, much more likeable: 'This man had nothing to fear from the Sergeant-Major. If the [latter] was Mussolini, the Quarter-Master-Sergeant was the Pope, and the life he led in those stores was quite monastic.' He began to associate sunlight with the emergence of the Sergeant-Major: 'The bright sunshine seemed in some way a warning signal. . . . But it didn't warn. It always seemed to me to be ticking me off itself or urging the Sergeant-Major to do so, and if he did the sun would shine at its maximum. . . . How could I rejoice in his size and his shiny buttons? I know what I felt when I caught sight of the little crown . . . on his arm. . . .

'Once, for a second, I forgot . . . I whistled the Chopin I heard coming from some gramophone in one of the wards, and a Sister hissed at me: "Stop that whistling." . . . I was not simply dodging the Sergeant-Major. I never attempted to dodge any of the inevitable parades. My dodging consisted in not that but meeting

squarely all the innumerable un-analysable mental shocks that
continually beset me, such as catching sight of the pendulum
swinging in a clock inside the place where orderlies had their food
or suddenly becoming unbearably dispirited. . . .

'No doubt Satan hoped I was going to be idiot enough to stop in
my journey across the yard with my tray and actually smile at the
[Sergeant-Major's] dog's antics, but he was mistaken. . . . I felt all
apologetic, sort of saying to myself: "Yes, that's alright; I realise it
would be dangerous to be the least degree out of my slot. There's
the Sergeant-Major's dog, and although I am not the S.M.'s
orderly, I am working in a hospital that is his and, therefore in a
sort of way, I am part of him myself. I could not presume to be his
dog, nor yet his cuff-links, but he had a blue-striped shirt. . . . I can
remember his hands, their thickness. I might be one of the stripes
in his shirt."

'There now! I am feeling more comfortable and, as I cross the
courtyard, I feel I can hold the tray of bread, butter, sugar, monkey
brand etc., a little steadier. . . . I know that man could pick a
quarrel with a stripe on his shirt, and that stripe would be me. He
would pick me out anywhere. But he would be more likely to fall
foul of his trouser buttons, being very fat as he was. I would look
to the other stripes on his shirt anxiously to ensure that I looked the
same. . . .

'Why should I have been so sensitive to these things, I wonder?
Because, I had always been rather easily crushed and because I was
sociable, and loved human contact, when it was harmonious, and
horrified at any sign of hatred in anyone of myself.'

On evenings off, Stanley would go with other orderlies to have a
shave: 'The dense atmosphere, mingled with scented cigarettes
that the orderlies smoked, seemed to remove any feeling of
unfriendliness. . . . It was the feeling that one has when a
thunderstorm has been a long time gathering and there have been
dreadful flashes and ear-splitting crashes; then, at last, comes the
rain . . . .

'There was a lavatory seat which proved to be the S.M.'s special.
I don't know if Kings on their thrones are apt to be more terrifying
than when they are not—I imagine this is so—but the S. M. on his
lavatory seat was . . . quite the contrary. . . . It was the only time
that he became friendly.'

One of Stanley's duties concerned the beds: 'Everything in this hospital was so instant and so quick . . . that every bit of change, no matter how slight . . . would be felt, and the arrival of a convoy— two hundred or more [patients] would arrive in the middle of the night—was the most disquieting and disturbing change in this respect. One had just got used to the patients one had; had mentally and imaginatively visualised them. . . . Thus, there are four beds that way and in that little recess one bed. Numbers one and three of the four beds are occupied and so is the recess bed. They are now familiar entities. . . . I remember the names—Good, Riddle, Courtney, Hines. . . . Each is inseparable, in my mind, from the beds they respectively occupy. They are significant, . . . and so are the beds which are unoccupied. . . . And what are the unoccupied beds? As yet my unborn creations—a new sort of spiritual limb. I am going to grow in the night . . . What will the world be like tomorrow? What about Courtney and Hines, when the beds between them are filled? That significance will remain . . . but another God creation takes place during the night, and I will find it in the morning.'

He had to move patients with their beds from one ward to another or perhaps to the theatre: '"Courtney must go this time", says Sister, and a trolley must be bagged—there were only a few to go round. . . . One was expected to be smart or cute and quick and know all the dodges, and none of these things could I be or know. Every second lost meant another trolley lost, another place in the theatre's gangway "bagged"; and there was the chap lying helplessly in his bed in the ward—a cosy scene . . . but a disturbing one, when you knew you had got to have all that shifted to the front row of a crowded theatre at the far end of the hospital and that in fifteen minutes time.'

Stanley managed to stand up to the ward Sister, difficult though this was at first. 'There is a Sister here', he wrote to Florence in 1915, 'and she goes hunting, she hunts for dust under the lockers. She is a crotchety Scotch woman. She told me that she never would allow an orderly to rest once during the day.

'Sister: "Tell Chorge I want him."

'Me: "Tell who, Sister?"

'She: "Chorge." Me: "Chorge? You mean George."

'. . . She said to me the first day she was in the next ward to mine:

"By Jove, boy, I'll put you through it the first day I get you under me." Lo and behold, the next day I was "under" her. She began by standing over me and lecturing to me on scrubbing, while I scrubbed. I let her go on to the end; then I looked up at her, and asked her if she could see what she was doing. She smiled as I said: "I've got you now; there you are, standing on the piece of floor I have just scrubbed, and now I suppose you will walk down the ward with filthy shoes after George has just polished it." '

The Sisters treated him with more respect, when they learnt he was sufficiently important to appear in the newspapers, but this led them to remark: 'Orderly. When are you going to get that commission?' He did not aspire to promotion. In fact, throughout his three and a half years of military service, he never rose above the rank of private.

There was a bathroom in Ward M.1, where he enjoyed working, as he records in his reminiscences: 'Now and then, I was hired from [Ward] 4A to scrub this stone-floored bath-room and I used to enjoy it rather. The orderlies might give me a bit of cake . . . and the Sister would condescend a little. I liked the surface of that floor and the colour was very good—some parts faded india-rubber red, and some more ochre and some peach-like. (Plates 8 and 34.)

'The bath-room of [Ward] 4B was quite different. It was more jolly and matter of fact and had a deal-board floor and free and easy entrance and exit. It was the way through to the lavatories, so that there was continual passing through. . . . Yet here in 4B bath-room, the more noise, the more men and general washings and bathings took place, the more a certain atmosphere and special character became enhanced. It was the hospital in its most robust form.'

During his first few months, Stanley could enjoy little or no congenial conversation with fellow orderlies, nurses or patients. He regarded the latter in a purely objective way: 'When I looked at the patients, I could never believe they had been ordinary soldiers. To have seen any of them submitting to discipline would seem very extraordinary, a kind of shock. I know there might have been some quite ordinary things that could account for this, such as the fact that this mysterious "deity" was only, really, a pathetic little chap, possibly an organ-grinder, but to me it was inconceivable. . . . A patient, when he had completely recovered with his new khaki suit issued to him, at once seemed to lose caste. He was no longer what he was in that hospital. To me, both young and old patients seemed not to have been wounded in this war, but in the Boer War or Crimean War. . . . I could not imagine them before they were wounded. . . . to be wounded seemed to be a profession.'

Stanley's ever-ready smile and disarming demeanour made him liked by those with whom he worked, and he could not fail to make friends, despite the impression of loneliness and of being the victim of persecution that he has given. He acquired at this time one friend from outside, whom he was to value greatly. This was Desmond Chute, still in his 'teens, an ardent Roman Catholic and, as Stanley described him subsequently, 'with all that spiritual outlook and vision that I, myself, loved and longed for'.

Chute's mother was a friend of the colonel, and, as Stanley explains in a notebook of 1948, her son could 'sneak away into the wards to find me . . . as usual swathed in sacking and scrubbing floors. When he first approached me and I looked up from the floor and saw him approaching me, much as he would approach an altar, I felt his love and regard for me. I felt here . . . is some sort of deliverance.' Chute gave Stanley a copy of St Augustine's *Confessions*: 'There is a glorifying God', Stanley has recorded in his reminiscences, 'in all His different performances. This struck me very much. . . . "Ever busy, yet ever at rest. Gathering yet never needing, bearing, filling, guarding, creating, nourishing, perfecting, seeking though thou hast no lack!" And so I thought "bearing, filling," coming, going, fetching, carrying, sorting, opening doors, shutting them, carrying tea-urns, scrubbing floors, etc. Yes, he was a friend indeed. I never disliked doing any of these things; . . . Sweeping up had become part of the performance of painting the picture afterwards.'

No concept influenced Stanley's thoughts, thereafter, so much as this of scrubbing, but all the hospital work inspired him, as described in his letter to James Wood (Plate 24) (26 May 1916):[2] 'I think doing dressings, when you are allowed to do the things in peace and quiet, is quite inspiring. The act of "doing" things to men is wonderful.' Referring to the words of St Augustine, he continues: 'I do not think of those words but I feel those acts. . . . What a subtle thing is the change from one thing to another, no matter what it is. . . . Now I am sweeping; now I am cleaning dishes; now I am polishing. There is such unity and yet variety in it. I think this feeling is in those things (bass reliefs) in the Giotto Campanile. . . . After my days work at Beaufort, I have wanted to draw a picture of everything I have done. But why . . . I could not say.'

He referred to these ideas in his reminiscences in 1936: 'When I used to push Ma about in the bath-chair, I could look at things with the impersonal eye of an animal, and, when returning with the chair empty, I felt oh superb; I felt as light-hearted and free as the sky and clouds. I felt like a case returned empty . . . If and when I was called upon to do any job that . . . was not my work, I was always glad when the work was such as to allow for the free wandering of my thoughts. . . . Every portion of floor scrubbed was, because of all I contemplated as I did it, a kind of work completed.'

The sight of blood or entrails held no terrors for Stanley, all being part of God's creation and, therefore, fully acceptable. He thought of litter, the contents of a dustbin or, indeed, dirt in general, as part of nature and similarly holy. This recognition of reality, whatever form it took, was revealed in the fascination he felt for surgical operations. The first he witnessed at Beaufort is described in an undated letter of 1916 to his sister Florence: 'Operations had a terrible influence over me. I remember when it was eventually decided that they would have to operate on a patient named Hawthorn—an elderly man with a sweet nature. . . . The abscess, which was a big one, had burst and flooded his body. . . . I had always felt excited to see some of the internal organs. He went in at 10.30 and came out at 1 o'clock and all that time was a strain. . . . Dr Reynolds, while Dr Morton was scrubbing his hands, sat on a high chair and to anyone who went by . . . would say: "Fetch so and so; don't touch me; do so and so." . . . He is so complete, so compact. I wish I could draw [him] sitting on a chair in a perfect state of sterility. I saw other operations, but none so exciting.'

He long retained this powerful impression, as indicated in a letter to Desmond Chute, undated but probably written in May 1916: 'I should love to do a fresco of an operation . . . and have the incision in the belly in the middle of the picture, and all the forceps radiating from it [a sketch]. . . . How mysterious the hands look—

wonderfully intense. There was something very classical about the whole operation . . . What is so wonderful, also, is the stillness in the theatre, and outside the swift, silent steps of those "fetching and carrying". I would like to do a figure on either side of the operation, of a nurse and a man with frock bringing sterilisers. This does not sound much but leave it to me.' Though seen so vividly, this was one subject that he never painted though he included it in a sketch (Plate 25). It led him on to his first contemplation of a series of frescoes, anticipating his work at Burghclere, and he wrote to Lamb (4 July 1916): 'I wish I could do a picture of each different thing I had to do in the hospital, so wonderful in their difference.'

He amplified these ideas in a letter to James Wood (27 July 1916): 'I am still thinking about the hospital, which the more I think about, the more it inspires me. I am determined that when I get a chance, I am going to do some wonderful things—a whole lot of big frescoes. Of the square pictures, there will be the "Convoy"—(I have that alright). The operation (and that). Then the narrow panels—a nurse (Oh such a beauty for that), an orderly (very good). . . . Think of the different things there are in a hospital, a storesman, an engineer, a carpenter, a surgeon—(I have that and it exasperates me not to be able to do it). . . . What will be wonderful . . . [are] the places where things [were] going on, and all is still and quiet and then, outside, all tumult and hurry. I am too hot to write, and the smell of meat for our dinner is sickening.' It is strange that despite this feeling of urgency, he did not attempt to paint these scenes until several years after he had returned from the War.

Notes to Chapter 3

1. In 1929, he wrote to me: '. . . these gates would never properly shut; they always reminded me of how the Gates of Hell in *Paradise Lost* rolled back with mighty clang and remained open for evermore.'

2. A Cambridge graduate, Wood became a close friend both of Stanley and myself. The author of several books (co-author with C. K. Ogden and I. A. Richards of *The Foundations of Aesthetics*), he devoted himself to painting, after studying under Tudor-Hart, and had several one-man shows, at the Leicester Galleries and elsewhere in London.

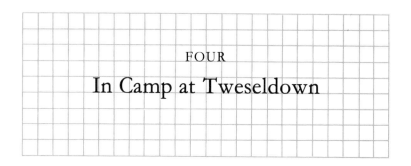

FOUR
In Camp at Tweseldown

STANLEY HAD APPLIED at Beaufort for service overseas and was at last posted for field training. He left Bristol on 12 May 1916. 'I swept the ward out . . . with George Saunders. I felt a bit sad. Poor old George was so upset.' He wrote thus briefly to his new young friend, Desmond Chute. Stanley had been at Bristol over ten months.

He arrived, first, at a converted naval hospital in Devonport, and wrote Chute at once of the unfamiliar scene: 'It was an extraordinary sight to suddenly see the sea. I have only seen it once before in my life, and that was only for a few minutes.' At Devonport, conditions seemed scarcely different from those at Bristol, and Stanley, naturally, felt apprehensive. In the reminiscences he wrote in Glasgow, he records his first encounter with the sergeant-major, 'a great burly old chap'. 'He said: "There are two Sergeant-Majors here." Then, with almost a look of amusement on his face, confidingly and somewhat whisperingly: "Have you seen him? Sort of new kind of God-head, two in one, not one incomprehensible but two incomprehensible."

'I remember in a dim way standing stiff in the company of hundreds of men out on the vast plain of green lawn in front of the building and noticing the great span of white steps . . . lined either side with men—sergeants, N.C.O.s or men. At last a single figure trim and neat, gloves, sam browne, appeared on top step in the centre, a smart-looking young officer apparently. He began to descend step by step leisurely. I noticed with a shock that his uniform, though similar to an officer's, was not so. He carried, as far as I can remember, a sword by his side, but possibly it was only a highly polished baton or cane. The officers were as terrified of this as we were.'

Stanley proceeds: 'There was difficulty about getting food there. We were not apparently placed on the ration list, were not "indented" for, so the only thing to do was to queue up, wherever one saw a queue, and try and get dished out with something without letting the man issuing the ration notice you. He was usually bending down and kept his eyes on the little canteen one held out under the sacred flow of tea. But I, being short, my face or some part of it came below the rim of his hat, and also something possibly un-Devonportish in my movement, seemed to make him pause and an altercation would begin, and I and others would be shunted to another queue. . . . If there was anything left we had it.'

Two days later, Stanley was moved to Tweseldown Camp in Surrey, whence he wrote to Chute (16 May 1916), giving his address as: 'No. 3 Hut, D. Lines, W. Coy, R.A.M.C., Tweseldown Camp, near Farnham.' 'It was a relief to me to come here', he adds. '. . . When we got to Fleet, we got out, and had to walk with full kit (kit-bag and all) for nearly three miles along a straight road. We were just pouring with perspiration, but it was great fun after "ward" work. . . . There is no hospital work here. It's field ambulance work. . . . I saw one go out today. It was a wonderful sight—wagon after wagon and the thick-necked horses. *Later*. Lights out just sounded. Here we are, rows, two long rows of us, in the usual hut—just lumps on the floor [a sketch].

'*Wednesday*. First thing this morning, we were out on the parade ground in our shirt sleeves and slippers, doing swedish drill. After that with a roaring appetite, we sat down to a big bowl of tea, and some bread and butter, and bacon and tomatoes—very good. After breakfast, cleaned up for parade at 8.30; paraded and then were told off to several large wagons, which we begin to shove and haul along. It was perfect. I felt as if my soul would bust for joy. It is extraordinary how these experiences quicken my whole being.

'[*Later*] Yesterday, we went for a ten mile route march. A whole company ("W" Coy) in one confounded lump, moving; in front, one man (captain), like those egg-laying insects with a little head and tremendous body [sketch] . . .—over sandy, bumpy ground, and then gorse and fir trees. It all seemed just right. . . . At length we got to the road again [a sketch] over a little hillock, and down into the road, arcaded with beech trees, making the sunlight green, because the light we got was coming through the leaves. . . .

'Practically all my hair is off, clipped right close like a criminal. In fact, I feel like a rejoicing criminal.'

He continued the letter, again, the next day: 'It's lovely the way the sergeants talk: On the heels *rise*, on the knees *bend*, and all said so horribly mechanically. But this swedish drill is not bad for you; in fact, it is good for you, but it is ridiculous. Can you imagine what it is to me, after going to the wards in the early winter morning, when all is dark and close and stuffy and lazy, and then getting up the same early hour and going out into the country lanes with just slippers, and trousers and shirt on, . . . then a double and then this drilling, which very stiff, and that shows it is wrong? We are always in the open and that is just what I longed for. . . . On our route march, we were marching under the beeches; their shadows simply poured down the soldiers' backs.'

He wrote to Chute a week later that there was to be 'another long route march with full packs', and added that 'that will mean some more reading under the tall pines.' Almost for the first time he was feeling inspired by the landscape, telling Chute in the same letter: 'I would like to draw the land and trees and tents here, but I doubt if I should be allowed to[1] . . . The camps and tents make me want to do a big fresco painting.' He wrote in similar vein to James Wood (familiarly addressed as 'Jas'), who was now a gunner, on 26 May: 'The trees are wonderful about here and it makes me mad not to be working. I must try and get a portable paint-box and canvas. The canal here is quite wonderful. You can hardly call it a canal; it is so overgrown with trees of all kinds. There is a place where we bathe in the evening, which is a plot of ground surrounded with young black poplars and behind that fir trees, and in the centre . . . is a palm-tree in bloom. All the grass is long and tangled in this little bit of mud and somehow adds to the wonder of this tree being where it is.'

Stanley was mainly anxious for books. He was virtually educating himself in classical literature, and he thanked Chute for sending him a translation of Homer, which, as he told him, he could carry in his haversack and read 'during the intervals of drill', adding: 'It is a part of my day— . . . the "doing" part.' He also had Giotto and the Church of St Francis of Assisi; 'So that even Giotto is dragged into this drill.' Jas had sent him books on Donatello and the young sculptor, Gaudier-Brzeska, recently killed on the Western Front.[2] In his letter of thanks, he told Jas apologetically: 'I wrote several letters to you, but always forgot to post them. But if I remembered to post letters, I fear I should forget to write them. . . .

'This life greatly quickens the soul. . . . We sleep on straw sacks, and you know how fine it must look when all are in bed. It will be "Lights out" in a little while, so I will cease.'[3]

He felt inspired by such scenes, writing to Chute, later in June: 'The men are sleeping this afternoon [a sketch]. One man had his head in a wonderful position. Another man slept with his hand mysteriously appearing behind his head [another sketch]. It is so wonderful to see all these things in actual life.' He found that constant 'straining after something' usually ended with the desire to paint or draw, which, he realised was out of reach.

His restless state of mind combined with his constant reading made him feel very undecided in his religious beliefs. While retaining his fundamental convictions, his loyalty to Chapel or Church in which he had been raised, was clearly shaken by the Roman Catholic doctrine which Chute regularly emphasised. He told Jas (26 May) of his dislike of the Church of England Church Parade. He thought he might put up with it if held in 'a church of ancient build'. 'But', he adds, 'we just have to crowd into a hut and try to recollect what we are about, whether we are at Mass or Kit Inspection.' He could not communicate these religious doubts to his family when he had weekend leave early in June; and he hesitated to tell his favourite brother Sydney, on leave from the Western Front, who hoped, ultimately, to take Holy Orders. This was Stanley's first visit to Cookham for several months. 'I had been quietly longing to see my brother Sydney', he told Chute (10 June) and, 'I opened the door and there was Sydney. We embraced one another, while my "Par" stood wondering when my brother would introduce me to him. My hair being cropped close like a convict's, my Daddy did not know me.'

He wandered round, revelling in familiar scenes. From the window of the house opposite, he looked at the signboard of the King's Arms and his 'precious cowls appearing' above. He was visiting the Wooster girls: 'And then these girls!' his letter continued, 'I felt I could hardly dare think that all this really was . . . All my earliest compositions were influenced in a certain way by these girls.'

All too soon, he was back at camp, and while it was quiet, with the men asleep after dinner, he could continue his letter: 'The hut door will open and a voice which frightens will cry: "Fall in!" I will stop. I hear the sergeant's cane on the neighbouring hut doors.' He found the drill very wearisome, and he continues his letter: 'This afternoon, we have had hell. There are a few dull and a few "don't cares" in our company, and that means we shall go on doing squad drill for the rest of our lives. You march along and in right-wheeling, one man does not keep his "dressing". That section of four is taken out and put into the backward squad. They make a slip there, and they are in for fatigues and C.B.' Next morning, they were 'doing right and left inclining—awful'.

In mid-June there was the memorial service for Lord Kitchener, with 'over a thousand men on the parade ground' [a sketch]. A general inspection followed, and Stanley reported that his section had 'come off well'.

'I shall be glad when we get to the manoeuvres . . .,' he tells Chute (19 June), 'especially when there are night ones and one has to go out and search for wounded, which are previously distributed over the country . . . Now is latrine building, which is not bad.' Continuing later, he adds: 'Yet another day and I feel as different a person as if yesterday had been a year ago. I am going to do a composition, I believe. Somehow I feel I can here.'

After more than two months in camp, however, Stanley was now wishing more than ever that he might be sent overseas. The uncertainty was depressing. Towards the end of July, he told Chute: 'I was watching the sun helmets coming in, and the lovely cool "drill" suits . . . for the hundred men going out of our company, and thinking . . . that their dull training had come to an end. They are going to Salonika. I have heard that two hundred are wanted for Mesopotamia.' He had been on another route march— 'too hot to be anything to me, except at moments', and had soaked through two shirts. He heard a church bell ringing, and adds: 'I was not contemplating on anything; I was just contemplative.' Gas helmets had recently been distributed, and Stanley reported to Chute (24 July): 'They give you a sick headache; the smell is so sickly. We look most "bonny" with them on [a sketch]. But truly aren't they devilish? They horrify me.' He finds letter-writing and reading difficult in the hut, telling Chute: 'It is impossible to concentrate . . .; there is a continual noise . . . There are thirty men present when I write these letters.' Again, he is depressed over the long delay, and unburdens his feelings to Chute: 'I feel so disturbed, unsettled and sometimes desperate about what I am going to do. . . . When you are told you will be away in ten days, you can't settle down at all. But I know what you mean, that a man can live in perfect felicity under any circumstances . . . but I can't do it yet.'

In another letter to Chute (undated), he tells him more about the training: 'We go into the trenches and bring the wounded out. We have to keep our heads down, because the Captain tells off a party to pelt us with stones if we show ourselves. . . . The communication trenches are so narrow that the "gassed" man, we are carrying in his overcoat, gets wedged.' He did not resent the discipline and welcomed the officers' approval, while critical of those fellow soldiers whose efforts were insufficient. Despite his slight physique, he was determined to play his part successfully. But he was agitated by the behaviour of the sergeant, which he found threatening, and he told Chute (24 July): 'He has a proper red-hot Irish temper and when he loses it, he walks slowly towards the offender, swishing his cane up and down in front of him. Just before he stops . . . he brings his cane up with a sweep over his shoulder.' He aired his complaints to Lamb, now an officer in the R.A.M.C.: 'The men here do not seem to care when the sergeant bullies them, but I do. . . . I am not brazen-faced and the army will not "make a man of me", because I do not intend it to.' But he found congenial company among the men. One especially, whom he described to Chute in July as his friend, was 'cross-eyed, gets drunk and always puts an "I did" on to the end of any of his achievements. He comes from "Middlesboro, he does" and there "isn't a better place in the world, there isn't". . . . You think of mallets and chisels when you look at his face.' And he adds: 'In these "disgraceful characters" is the true power of forgiveness. . . . When he closes his eyes, you can't see where they are closed, because his eyelashes are the same tone as the flesh.' Stanley felt so amused by this man, that he described him again in an undated letter to Florence: 'When he returns from leave, he comes rolling in, knocks everything over, wakes everyone up, keeps all the hut in uproar and when he has arrived at his bed and all is once more still, he announces in a low apologetic mumble: "I've come, I have." When he goes to Middlesboro, he brings me a long stick of Middlesboro rock. In the same grumbly voice: "Here's the Middlesboro rock, it is, Stanley!" . . . Last time he came back, he had brought some clay pipes with him for his mates. . . . He looked very doubtful, as he felt for them, as much as to say "If they aren't broke, then my name's not Clarence." '

It was a relief to Stanley when he was sent with the water-cart to the Basingstoke Canal, describing it to Chute in his letter of 24 July: 'The horses have thick fat necks and short ears set back. As they lurch forward to pull the heavy water-cart, their glossy skin wrinkles upon their backs and buttocks. They have wonderful bow noses.' At last there are rumours that they will be sent to Mesopotamia, 'but', he adds in a letter to Chute in July, 'I think that we shall never go at all.' In August, however, he was able to tell his friend that departure was really imminent; 'I am now ready, even down to having made out my will, which I did this morning . . . Of course, we shall be in hospitals, but I shall stick it alright, though I wish it had been a field ambulance. I went home for four days leave and saw no one except Pa and Ma and sister, and Henry Lamb came . . . to see me on . . . my departure.

'I have been reading St John's gospel a lot lately and it is great. . . . How it sets my mind in order.' He adds that he has sent his large Shakespeare home, being too heavy, but is taking *Canterbury Tales*, some Gowans and Grays and, if possible, *Crime and Punishment*.

With training over, he wrote a brief note to Lamb (11 August), now addressing him as Henry: 'It seemed almost too good to be true when I saw you coming down the street. I felt that those times were over.' There was still another ten days of waiting, and he just had time (23 August), to write to Chute: 'We are going early tomorrow morning for the Far East. Reveille goes at 2.30, breakfast at 3 or thereabouts. Rather dramatic, isn't it? . . . We sleep on the bare boards tonight, as everything has gone back to the stores, except the blankets.' He was one of three hundred men leaving Tweseldown on 23 August 1916.

In his Glasgow reminiscences he records his departure: 'All night, we were, as is often the case when soldiers are going off early in the morning, up and some playing about and generally excited. At crack of dawn I liked going through Fleet and seeing the streak of dawn and heads silhouetted against it. The women of the houses lining the railings outside Paddington Station waved, and waved pith helmets also. I think the docks were Port of London Docks — much sound of steel repairing of ships; lascars in white scurrying about.

'We dribble on to the boat "Llandovery Castle",[4] a big hospital ship. . . . I feel the different consistencies of what I stand on. There is no food and we are there for two days. No doubt that those in charge of us wanted to ensure us being on the boat in good time and ceased to draw our rations from Tweseldown, imagining we would be rationed as soon as we were on the boat. But we were not rationed until the boat left.

'The wedge widening as we moved away from the quay-side, the throwing of letters to be posted to the "be-ostrich-feathered" Cockney women come to say "goodbye", . . . the seagulls swinging and swirling about the masts — all this was enhanced by the sudden appearance of food. Up until then, the sailor crew had taken us to their focastle and were sharing their own rations with us as best they could.'

They were quitting the Royal Albert Docks, and Stanley was just able to write a postcard to Florence: 'If I do not soon throw this overboard to some kind stranger to post for me, it will not be posted. We have nice wards to sleep in. Tonight, we shall go from here to, I believe, Southampton, and then I do not know where we shall go.'

Notes to Chapter 4

1. He never painted the landscape at Tweseldown. Hitherto he had treated landscape as the background to figure compositions.
2. He told Chute, 'I hated Gaudier when I knew him', but he found him 'extraordinarily certain and true in his drawing'.
3. Their correspondence mentions two drawings, one of a seated woman with child comforting her, called *The Widow*, and the other of a family with boy leaning on a table near a staircase, but their present whereabouts have not been recorded.
4. He saw this vessel again in Glasgow in 1944 'going up and down the Clyde'.

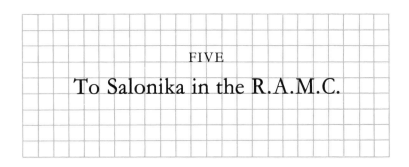

FIVE
To Salonika in the R.A.M.C.

S TANLEY DID NOT LEARN that Salonika was his destination until
they were at sea: 'We did not know where we were making for',
he wrote in his reminiscences.[1] 'We sang *Marseillaise* in the star-
light of the Bay of Biscay, the mast now and then eclipsing [the
stars]. . . . Here so big are the rolls, that one sees "places" in the
sea. One can understand the phrase "the trough of the sea". Our
ship was all lit up along the sides; it was like a cruise. The sea goes a
pale delicate green, as it shallows a little before the Straits of
Gibraltar, then, as one is through . . . the sea goes dark blue lapis
colour. To look west, as the sun was setting, a blood-red band is
seen.'

Stanley's reading of Homer made him interested in Greece, just
as Italy came to interest him through his study of its artists. Later,
he would deride 'foreign travel', claiming that he only travelled
when persuaded to do so against his will. Yet his few visits abroad
made a great impact, producing some of his most memorable
pictures, and he became intensely interested in Asiatic cultures,
especially those of Islam, India and China.

He began a letter to Chute in the Bay of Biscay, in August 1916,
continuing it intermittently: 'I am looking at Africa, the Moroccan
coast, and smoke is rising from behind one of the peaks. I have got
my *Odyssey* . . . and I am thinking about Cyclops. . . . I really did
not think it was going to be so just what I wanted. It is like
discovering yourself. I want to post this at Gibraltar. It makes me
tremble down in my inside, every time I look at yonder coast. We
are just opposite a huge African rock, which is just the colour of
pumice stone and *feels* like pumice stone.

'*Later*. We have passed the Cape of Gibraltar, and Africa is almost out of sight. On the African side is a big sailing ship, full of sails, absolutely Shakespearian [two sketches]. I am thinking of the Jew of Malta, and him looking down at his ships coming into the harbour. I think we must be off the coast of Tunis, as this is the nearest we have been to the coast of Africa.

'It is not mountains now but great rolling sandy hills that of course go up to a great height. Each hill is peculiarly rounded and dome-like, and gives a slight hint of what Egypt is like. It is dotted all over with white buildings that look like palaces or MOSQUES. . . . Out to the left, the hills rise to a great peak, on top of which is one of these large white buildings and the sun, which is nearly set, is shining full upon it. These hills are peculiarly wrinkled, like the wrinkles on the back of a bullock's neck—most wonderful.'

Salonika had been assigned to Greece after the Balkan War of 1913. A city of ancient Greek origin, with a population of about 150,000 mainly Turks, Greeks and Jews, it lay in an amphitheatre, backed by mountains to north and east. The Ottoman occupation of five hundred years had given this essentially Greek city, as I recall it, an Asiatic aspect, with numerous minarets, tall and slender, mingling with its Byzantine churches, and its streets with their tramcars generally dilapidated.

With the outbreak of war, the Allies (French and British) used the port for landing munitions in support of Serbia's defence against the Austro-Hungarian invasion. Bulgaria's participation as Austria's ally in 1915, coincided with Britain's withdrawal from the Dardanelles. The reinforced allied troops immediately began to push their way north up the main Balkan railway line, but a Serbian collapse compelled their retreat back to Salonika, where they formed a defensive line thirty miles north of the city. Further reinforcements in the summer of 1916 made this the largest allied force overseas.

The British army, under General Milne, about 150,000 strong, faced a force of Bulgars and Germans of similar strength along the Struma valley. In September, the British were trying to push eastwards across the Struma and westwards across the Vardar river. In overall command was the French General Sarrail, who inspired no confidence, and constant reverses ensued, followed by a stalemate. The rank and file could scarcely learn what transpired at higher levels, but Stanley like his fellows, must have felt that morale was low.

'As the boat swung on its anchor', his reminiscences record, 'the Turkish town slowly seemed to move round it, with its lights at night and minarets just visible in the blue darkness. . . . In the lighter, we were a jumbled mass and on the quay, when we were lined up, the sergeants seemed to find their voices again. I had been all the time at Bristol, very friendly with Lionel Budden, who was very musical—is now a school-master somewhere—and we two had managed to keep together until we were on this quay. Then, may-be because of the laws of the army, one of which is "tallest on the right", "shortest on the left" in single rank size, we were separated beyond all hope. It was our only difference. So we were marched off to different camps. We grinned, as we solemnly marched past to our several destinies. . . .

'In the train I think from Lembet, to which we were, after a few days, marched, I sat on the wooden seats, and was entranced by the landscapes from the window, low plains with trees and looking through them to strange further plains or fields, and here and there a figure in dirty white. It was not landscape; it was a spiritual world. I would go there again if I could. I was hungry and a man gave me a couple of Horlick's Malted Milk tablets. I did not think, at the moment, he had given me much, but when I had had one in my mouth some time, I began to express my thanks. . . .

'I felt that the front was miles away', he continues, 'and it all seemed as incredible and unlikely as it did in England. . . . I liked the look of the marsh land away to the North-West that disappeared in low-lying mists that lay between Mount Olympus and ourselves. The Vardar could be seen wandering up the wide plain. At night we were in tents and the sociable lights of our candles and the talk going on mixing with the general hum of conversation from the other tents made everything very cozy, and I liked the feeling that the darkness, that seemed to have a reddish glow, had a Bulgarian feeling in it.' A man had arrived at camp from another sector, and Stanley proceeds: 'If he had been Hermes straight from Olympus with messages from Zeus, I should not have felt more moved. . . .

'For about five days, a sort of sandstorm was blowing in from the sea direction, so that I was unable to gaze across to Olympus until this ceased. . . . As the sun rose, it was grand, . . . in shape rather symmetrical, a sort of wounded eagle shape, wings out and flopping on the ground. In the centre, just a small peak and the great shoulders reaching out either side; there were one or two stratas of mist that obscured the base; the upper bands were a pale emerald green, then blue-red and then the main widest band was magenta of a warmish tinge. . . . In the midst of this would suddenly appear, softly but there, what looked like a star, but which really was the early morning sunlight catching the little peak, that rose from the shoulders and left the rest in dusk. But I longed to be up that Vardar valley. . . .

'Somewhere in the valley, I saw some thin trees and, behind them, what looked like a small bridge and I thought I saw some Macedonians, but the impression on me was alright. It began in me a course of longing for something "findable" in that country, which lasted for the two and a half years that I was there and for years after. It became the goal and place wherein, spiritually, I was wanting to find the redeeming and delivering of myself in all the activities, unexpressed, [that I] had lived through and in.'

The 68th Field Ambulance, to which Stanley was posted, as he records in his reminiscences, was at Corsica (Plate 9), near Karasuli, some forty miles north of Salonika on the Belgrade railway and about ten miles, as the crow flies, from the frontier, where the Bulgars were entrenched. Between them and Karasuli lay Lake Ardzan, five miles long. 'It was . . . in this Field Ambulance that the deepest impressions were made . . . the quiet atmosphere, muffled; the oxen and their swaying from side to side, heads stretched forward under their yokes; the sleeping on the side of the hill above Lake Ardzan and the grass fire looking like a huge dragon stretching the length of the lake and reflected in it; the wild dogs . . . the wolfish symposiums at night. I saw that lights were out. . . .

'I had got out at Karasuli', he continues; 'and with a small group of field ambulance men were assembled on the little road track, similar to the one that goes along the bottom of Cockmarsh Hill [Cookham]; I thought: . . . Along this track, which wandered along the foot of some line of hills . . . from Karasuli to Kalinova, most of what was vital to me in Macedonia was felt. Whatever the number of kilos it is, 10 or 20, each one is a part of my soul.

When I think of the places along it . . . to describe each item is to describe something of myself. The other side of this line of hills was unknown to me. . . . Some way along, there is now a cemetery, the first graves of which were dug by a corporal and one or two men, including myself. . . .

'It was dark when we arrived, and I had the feeling of not knowing what world I should wake up in. . . . I thought as I lay there: "I will be an active part of that, whatever it is, at the back in the hillside darkness." If . . . I was to be metamorphised into being one of the animal inhabitants of the hill, I could not have felt more curious. I saw the little glows coming . . . from the bivouacs, and a few nights afterwards, I was seeing to it that they were put out at nine o'clock. I was now that special being—a soldier "on active service"—, though . . . where the distinction fell on all about one, it was difficult to feel it. Like [in] Gilbert and Sullivan: "If everybody's somebody, then no one's anybody.". . .

'At Corsica Camp, I used to go with parties of about ten or twenty men with stretchers to . . . the Sedemli ravine, which was a river bed sometimes with river and sometimes dry, to where one met the regimental stretcher-bearers'[2] (Plate 11).

Stanley's duties included handling the mules used for transport, which was to prove such a lasting experience. 'The mules and the ears thereof gave a certain feel to the place', was his comment.

The 68th now moved nearer Kalinova, the uninhabited shell of a Greco-Turkish village, probably destroyed in the Balkan Wars (Plate 37). 'Here I shared a bivouac', his account continues, 'with a youth the same size as myself. . . . We found we had other things in common, besides being the same height. This height was convenient because it left a certain space at the foot of the bivouac to put things. We carried out extensive improvements. . . . We, casting our eyes over the landscape one day, saw something shining in the sun away towards Lake Ardzan. It proved to be an old petrol drum. This we . . . buried at the foot of our bivouac. . . . It formed a cupboard, which took our equipment. We also built a little fire-place and a mantel-piece and a chimney stack. . . . As I describe this, I think what a different "me" it was to the "me" at Corsica.'

During these first autumn months of 1916, Stanley was backward in writing letters—one or two to Florence, as always

8. *Scrubbing the Floor and Soldiers Washing, Beaufort Hospital, Bristol,*
probably a sketch for the proposed mural in Steep village hall, 1921.
Fitzwilliam Museum, Cambridge.
9. *Troops out for a Rest*, Corsica Camp, Macedonia, 1919.

anxious for news, and a couple to Chute. Stanley had been hearing a description of the frescoes in churches in Malta, which prompted him to comment to Chute (28 October): 'I could not help thinking what a glorious thing it was to be an artist, to perform miracles. . . . If I see a man putting a bivouac up beautifully, I want to do it myself. And when I read of Christ raising the dead, I want to raise the dead myself.' Then he adds: 'I am starving for music.'

He had been reading Ruskin's *Modern Painters*; he also needed art materials. He was developing his education almost feverishly, as if he had no time to lose. To Florence, he wrote (undated but in 1916), giving his address: 'Private S. Spencer, No.100066, 68th Field Ambulance. I am very well off for clothes. This is me [a sketch] with all my clothes on, which consists of two vests, three shirts, one pair shorts, one pair trousers, two pants, one tunic, one leather jerkin, one overcoat and one mackintosh, one cap with ear flaps and mackintosh cover for it, one pair woollen gloves and one pair of leather sort of boxing gloves. The mackintosh cover to my hat is rather too big for me, as you notice in the accompanying drawing. Of course, I don't go about with all these things on at the same time. It is only just to show you what I could wear if I liked.'

Early in December, he had an abscess on his shin, caused by a new over-tight puttee, which put him in the casualty clearing station near Karasuli and thence to the 4th Canadian Hospital in Salonika. There he developed malaria, which confined him until the first week in January 1917. Convalescence for another month gave him the longed-for opportunity to draw his fellow patients, 'nearly life-size', as he wrote Florence, 'on the only paper I had, namely the pages of a Sister's autograph album'.

He had written to Florence, soon after being admitted to hospital (14 December 1916): 'There is a cockney man in our lot, and he is a real delight to me. I loved drawing him. I pictured what he would be like in "civis" in London. I saw the blazing many-coloured neckerchief and the tremendous buttonhole. It was all there. And he has such a humorous face, and quite a gentleman to speak to, though to look at him, he would positively frighten you. He used to dress my leg and his hand and his manner were as gentle as a mother's. We have another cockney in this ward; he is one of the "law love a duck, gaw blimey" type; bless him. You would marvel at the splendid spirits that our men possess.'

10. *Travoys along Sedemli Ravine*, Macedonia, 1919. Imperial War Museum.

11. *Soldiers at a Well*, Macedonia, 1919.

A week later, he wrote her again, asking for books, drawing paper and pencils: 'In *David Copperfield* I have come across parts . . . comparable only with Shakespeare in dramatic power . . . quite unconscious in Dickens, whereas it is conscious in Shakespeare. That is how the Greeks appeal to me—their conscious and obvious art.'

In November, he had written to Chute, of a new and unexpected passion: 'I am going to do something about the sea. My love for home and my love for the sea seem both to stimulate my thoughts.' Later (4 January 1917), in hospital, he adds: 'I wish you could see the sea here on a sunshiny day, the deep blue sea, all ribbed, like in a "Claude Lorraine", and the gleaming froth along each "rib", and the shadows of the ships on the surface of the sea, . . . and the hills beyond all bronze with the sunlight.'

Even after he had left Salonika, this enthusiasm for the sea remained, as in his letter to Florence of 12 May 1917: 'I feel still that I do not want to talk about anything else. I think after the War, I shall be a sailor. I used to feel, when looking over the side of the ship at the sea, that I could live for ever doing so. To suddenly see a narrow, crinkly strip of gold in the distance and say to yourself: "That's land"; and then you get a little nearer and you can just see a row of sailing boats, all with their pure white sails moving along the coast in even procession. Such a feeling of peace it gives you.'

This love for the sea was not sustained, prompting the question: Was it a fantasy born of the War? To the best of my belief, he never painted a seascape, though he had opportunities, nor included the sea in any of his main compositions, such as those at Burghclere. Later, any suggestion of a visit to the seaside would arouse an angry rejoinder.[3]

His letter to Chute in January continued with his description of hospital life: 'I do anything for these men . . . I cannot refuse them anything, and they love me to make drawings of photos of their wives and children or a brother who had been killed. A diary of a man, who was killed, chronicled the weather day after day, and as you read these monosyllables, it gives you an intensely dramatic feeling. . . .

'I could not help thinking of St Francis' reply to the robbers that met him in the wood, when I was speaking to an Irishman . . . he asked what I thought about the "after-life". I said that as the very

76

being of joy exists in that it is eternal, it is only reasonable to suppose that life, which only lives by joy, must necessarily be eternal. If these men have not gripped the essential, there is one grand thing: They are part of the essential.'

After convalescence, Stanley was assigned to the 66th Field Ambulance, though he had hoped to rejoin the 68th. He was anxious to have his brother, Gil, transferred to his unit, and was disappointed to learn that Gil, meanwhile, had obtained a transfer, which took him to Egypt. With the drawing-paper Florence had sent him in February 1917, he could draw fellow orderlies, and even the Sergeant-Major in his spare time. 'All those old feelings, I used to get,' he told her, 'about "wasting my time" are passing away. I feel more and more convinced that when I return to my work I shall be fresh to it, and though I have done nothing for the last sixteen months, I have improved in my work more than if I had actually been at my work all the time; that is my belief. . . .

'I often think it would be interesting to get together all my best chums since the War began. A good half the number would be drunk. . . .

'You ought to hear the wild geese out here. They fly over us night and day, and it is mysterious to hear them in the night. I was once looking to the horizon . . . at the little clouds, and I suddenly noticed one do a sort of serpentine dive and then it would roll itself up and then out again, then disappear altogether, and then appear stronger than ever. This was not a cloud, but a huge number of starlings, which you see in great solid masses that would nearly cover Widbrook Common, and these masses you can see miles and miles away, and when they disappear . . . is when they alter the direction of their flight, so that the light on their bodies and wings is the same tone as the cloud behind.'

He comments, with increased confidence, on the books Florence had sent him: 'I think that Dostoievsky would not suit you at all . . . I think you will only hate him, for a little while. . . . His books are unlike anything you will have ever read before. . . . All the time he writes, he seems to be going on, on, on and your head swims and you say to yourself: "For goodness sake, stop!" But you can't; you must hear this man out. You are like the people in the novel itself. You keep saying: "Oh! I must go"; and yet you do not go. No, you are certain that something is going to happen

77

and yet nothing does happen. . . . I did not understand the Gospel so clearly as I did after reading him. Shakespeare, also, greatly opened my understanding of the Gospel.'

The 66th Field Ambulance was at Corsica Camp, where Stanley had been before. He was employed there, at first, in the cookhouse, which he recalled in his reminiscences: 'Beginning early in the morning, I would cook rashers for sixty men—two each. On my left, as I knelt in a little groove cut in the ground for a wood fire, I had a wooden box full of cut rashers. On the fire was a dixie-lid in which rashers were fried. In my hand, I had two flat pieces of wood with which I picked out bunches of rashers.[4] (Plate 33) . . . The cook-house—a limber tilted up and a tarpaulin thrown over the shafts—had a cook called "The Black Prince", a grim-looking man, who kept away in some darksome dug-out place I did not go near and who, Arabian Nights genie-wise, usually appeared when one had done something wrong. One day, I was reading *Paradise Lost* and supposed to be watching a side of bacon that was simmering in a dixie. I smelt faint burning, but I was too late. He loomed out of the darkness with his big black dog, gave a kick at the dixie and sent the lid flying, and up went a column of smoke. . . .

'If I was on night patrol, just patrolling the camp, that was all, I would listen to the dogs higher up the hill where, in a clearance, they would sit round wolf-like and do their head-up whining, especially on moonlight nights. Now and then, the bivouac glows, one after another, would go out and appear again as one of these big sort of wild dog passed along for any possible tit-bit. . . .

'Some Cyprus Greeks, attached to the camp, used on some nights to do some of their dancing. Here there were jackals. One was . . . loping its way along among some low bushes and stubble. . . . Everything slid away as soon as I felt I was getting near. . . . Only a few hundred yards would be required to make one's own brother remote and intangible—more so than a foreigner.

'The Army Service Corps men in the plain below, who looked to the mules, were a people apart. The land they were on faded away, as a thing passes from one's recollection. . . . In the bottom of some [ravine] could be seen the white shell remains of tortoises . . . burnt [by] grass fires. They gleamed in the sun. I thought how I would feel if this were my native place and surroundings. I would see Bulgarian post-cards received ... when they occupied that part.... There was a stream and, here and there, a big stone boulder, which served ideally ... to scrub one's clothes.... One was in a world, where things happened, ... but at Bristol it was a "nothing-happening" place.... One night, it was so dark that the officer nearly walked us into the Bulgar lines.'

Early in March 1917, Stanley was again in hospital in Salonika, this time the 5th Canadian. Nasal catarrh developed into bronchitis and a return of malaria. During convalescence, he made twelve drawings of fellow patients. He was then posted, after a few weeks, to a different unit, the 143rd Field Ambulance, whence he wrote to Florence on the 25 March, delighted by the approach of spring: 'The flowers are out, primrose, violet, celandine and many other flowers unknown to me.... It is getting dark and I have no candles, and I want [this] letter to go tonight, so good night, Flongy dear. P.S. If you send me anything, send me some currant biscuits or bread and butter. We get bread and we get butter sometimes, but you know what a boy I am for bread and butter; and it is better to send that than these eternal tinned stuffs. Send me some of your own home-made bread, Flongy dear, and I will love you for ever.'

In a longer letter a couple of days later, he asks her for 'eatables of some kind', a sixpenny Gowans and Gray of Raphael, perhaps R. L. Stevenson, and adds: 'You must not think that I ask for eatables because I am not getting enough food. On the contrary, ... but I get so ravenously hungry up in these hills that I could eat a hayrick.... With the exception of the wonderful "Daily News Christmas Pudding", which I never got and I would like to know why, I do not think anything in that line has been sent to me ever since I left England.' To Chute, he wrote (8 April) in a home-sick mood: 'I *did* miss my hot-cross bun. I did not have one last year.... At home, we used to sit round the dining-room table, and each one of us had a big hot-cross bun for breakfast.... When I was about 6 years old, if I was not well, I used to sleep between my mother and father, who then slept in my room. You can imagine what lovely feelings I must have had.' He ends his letter: 'I should like anything like biscuits or cake or chocolate or anything *except* ginger-bread and seed-cake; I don't like that.'

He was now, more than ever, engrossed in his religious views and in the same letter to Chute he admitted his growing leaning towards the Roman Catholic doctrine. An enthusiasm, even temporary, could lead him to denounce his earlier beliefs, and the letter proceeds: 'I do not look upon the Protestant belief as an existing thing at all. . . . [Protestants have] lost the personal idea of God, . . . [and] that Christ said: "*I am*", and not "*in me*", is the way.'

Stanley's unit was moved in April 1917, to Todorova, nearer the Bulgarian line. He regretted leaving the neighbourhood of Kalinova, because, as he subsequently put it in his reminiscences, of 'the glimmer of hope I felt when under that wall', but adding the caution: 'I must be careful not to let things like a place, and appearance of walls and local surroundings arouse my hopes.'

The journey to Todorova occupied eight days: 'My job was among others', he continues,[5] 'to round up mules, young ones, fresh, alert-eared, that were here and there breaking away and striking out on their own. . . . (Plate 10.)

'When the objective is, as it was here, that one was going to no special place at all, only to where . . . one could contact the enemy, there is a sense of just wandering on, without objective, . . . through country apparently without habitation or name. Owing to heat, most of the marching was done through the night. The ground seems to melt away, walking after dark. But some nights, we would pause and be mushrooms with our bivouacs on some hill-side.

'It [Todorova] seemed to be a place right in the north or north-east of Macedonia. I think some of the flowers there were remains of private gardens from times when inhabited; no sign of it now, no buildings. . . . A rose-bush in the sun, I remember, and . . . a cloud of dust where it stood. The dust blew away and there was the rose-bush shaking a little—a "dud" shell.

'The sergeant would let me clear off up some ravine. Here I would sometimes see grass snakes or rock snakes. At night, while guarding the camp, the little Greek owls made me feel sleepy. What I thought might be nightingales were a bit monotonous nothing like the marvellous English ones. Also, the dogs at night moaned, . . . yelping or barking, a sort of "rer-rer-a-rer-rer" not quick, but . . . slow and deliberate.'

Of camp at Todorova (Plate 34), he records: 'As it sloped down to a shallow stream, the hill-side on which was our camp broke off into a few escarpments, the last one immediately by these shallows being a convenient height to stand one's glass, as one shaved. This stream[6] was sometimes nearly dry; then if a storm came, there would be . . . a pause and all at once a roar would come from the hills, and the stream would be a fast-rushing stream. . . . Basins formed by rocks further up in the hills would fill and we would bathe in them; it would be deep enough to dive into.

'At these times, I and the cook-house man and others betook ourselves to such places and tested depths and diving possibilities. I can remember this man so clearly and yet I did not know the man at all. Whether becoming a soldier made everybody just that and nothing other, I don't know. The cook-house here was close into the dark shadowy side of one of these small cliffs, and I used to like when I was on night patrol to sit and chat to him. . . . I can remember the idiosyncracies of him as I might of a horse. But those things—his diving his long length into the small basins of rock and not knocking against anything and the place where I went to see him were all one thing which had more meaning for me.'

Stanley still made portrait drawings, whenever he could, at spare moments, giving them to the sitters. In retrospect, he recalled three in particular, which expressed 'a whole something into which all myself comes, and each time manifesting a different me. God had a unique way of doing this by making man in his own image and thus saying Himself over and over again. Self or an image is meaning. . . . And so God says "Himself" in a number of varied images.'

Being recognised as 'the artist', Stanley was given the job, on arrival at Todorova, 'of painting the letters indicating men's and sergeants' latrines. . . . I made a big letter S for sergeants and painted some dog-roses round it.' With war activity still so sporadic, Stanley hoped, like others, that mere stagnation might bring it to an end: 'I felt that that hope', he wrote in his reminiscences, 'and the consequent constructive and productive results in me, [as in] my simple drawing of heads, the War would just melt away, like a snake charmer. The snakes would all forget. I had Gowans' and Gray's *Claude Lorrain* in my pocket, and a reproduction in it of his "Worship of the Golden Calf", a wonderful pastoral scene and . . . women and men dancing. "What has happened?" I thought. Why doesn't everybody chuck it and behave like this? Only a change of clothes and country dancing instead of shooting?'

The Bulgarian positions formed an arc running northwards along the Struma, westwards south of Lake Doiran, across the Vardar and west to the Serbian city, Monastir. The British faced the Bulgarian centre between the rivers Struma and Vardar. The total allied strength of about 600,000 was slightly less than that of the opposing forces.

The British began their advance, 24 April, after two days of artillery preparation. They were not helped by the unpropitious weather, with heavy storms in the mountains, as Stanley described in his letter to Florence on 19 May: 'I heard the sound of many waters, a distant roar, and the roaring got nearer and nearer. So I went down to the stream, and lo, it was quietly running over the stones between the rocks just in a "tomorrow will do" sort of way. But oh, there was such an 'orrible surprise in store for it, for up the stream a little and over great pieces of rock, came blustering on in great leaps and bounds the water. It goes at a terrific speed, as it is falling, falling, falling.'

The British objective was a short mountain range called 'Dub', a key position for the Bulgars, south-west of Lake Doiran. Supporting action by the French, Italians and Serbs to the west proved insufficient, rendering the British attack a costly failure, and it was called off a month later, 24 May, putting them once more on the defensive. The allied commander-in-chief, General Sarrail, was held to blame. It was this abortive offensive, which had put Stanley's unit on the move. Censorship forbad his describing it in letters, but he recalled events in his reminiscences in 1944: 'We went from Todorova to Basili, which was on a headland overlooking the valley. . . . The whole range or façade which, in its entire length, disappeared in a long cotton-wool snake of cloud and sloped out this and that way from under it into the long valley, appeared somewhat like the hem and bottom part of the skirt of some vastly huge deity. Here and there, I could faintly see smoke rising from Bulgar bonfires in their camps. . . . I liked the feel of the Bulgar. . . .

'From Basili another great trek, seemingly more towards the Struma Valley . . . to Mirova (Plate 13), where was a decoville railway and rail head. . . . The patients are put in the ordinary trucks and one stands by the buffer and puts the brake on at the corners. The mules haul them back. I was sometimes brakesman in these trucks, . . . also on the old ambulance wagon. . . . The rough jolting made . . . it difficult to keep awake.

'. . . At Likovan, I used to go with the ambulance to get a barrel of beer. One had to go early in the morning because the heat was feared in its possible effects on the barrel. It was very enjoyable but for this sleepy feeling, and the men riding the mules continually shouting to me. . . .

'Not being a drinker, I usually supervised the beer issue, which was nothing other than turning the tap on and leaving it on. . . .

'Now we did a vast journey; it seemed like going through the whole history of Macedonia. . . . It contained all those changes and completely different phases that Arabian Nights tales pass through, all in one tale. . . . Finally, we began to descend between near hill-sides; . . . soon we saw a valley streaming away below us—the Struma Valley. . . . So used had I been to digging the little drainage gutter round the bivouac to take the water away that I did the same here, when we camped—near Dragos.'

With the lines once more stationary, Stanley could write Florence (7 June) his thoughts and impressions off duty: 'The other day, I was having a rest after working in the sun, and I was thinking and thinking, . . . in much the same sort of way as our brother in distress, the tortoise. . . . He always is trying to do the most impossible things. Well, when I had not got any "think" left, I began reading Joshua. Goodness knows why! Well, I saw the High Priests and the mighty men of valour going round the walls of Jericho and blowing on their rams' horns, and then I heard the awful shout and sound of the falling walls and buildings. And then I saw the men rushing in on every side, massacring man, woman and child. Well, I thought: "this all seems very nice"; but something very nearly stopped me from getting to this "very nice" part. It was the part, where God commands Joshua to detail one man out of each tribe to carry a stone from . . . Jordan . . . to where he would lodge that night. "Oh! if God's going to begin detailing parties, I'll be one." Can't you just picture a swarthy son of a tribe of Israel writing to his girl: "Darling Zip! Sorry, nothing doing; clicked for fatigues"?' Three days later (10 June), he was writing to

Florence again: 'To go through a village and see the labourer returning from . . . the fields, you think of that part of Kings 11, the boy in the field crying to his father: "My head, my head." All that about Elijah and Elisha I think is so intimate and natural. The really inspired utterances come so suddenly upon you that their dramatic effect is intensified. . . . I have just done some washing. A shirt is an awkward article to wash. . . . First, I tell them off by sections, giving them the order: "Section number!" I do this to make sure that all the sections are there. This is how the old Greek women do their washing [a sketch]. The rain comes down in torrents; the woman works like one possessed all out in the rain, the mud splashing up all round her. The man stands majestic, contemplative, a far-distant look in his eye.'

Florence tried to satisfy Stanley's insatiable need for books and food, but military action had made their safe arrival uncertain. On 19 May, he had thanked her for books and biscuits, adding: 'In a few days time will come the Dickens and the bread. . . . Today, we all determined to behave like pigs and eat and eat and eat, just out of spite for the days we were unable to get canteen stuff. My esteemed comrade "Twister" said he would eat till he was like this, and he described half a circle with his hand.' Two days later, he thanked her for: '*Pickwick Papers, Bleak House*, a drawing book, two pencils, two pairs of socks, a Bible and indiarubber.' He was reading *Winter's Tale* and the historical plays, which prompted his comment: 'It is so beautiful how in Shakespeare's historical plays chivalry gives birth to chivalry. . . . I think that those nobles of the early "Henry" did well in placing their allegiance to their king before their own honour. Had they not done so, all would have been purposeless and chaotic. . . . P.S. "Cry God for Harry, England and St George." This is how I have been feeling all day long.' Later in June (undated), he adds: 'Although the War seems so horrible, yet it is nice to know that the same valour as was shown in King Arthur's most valorous knights has been seen in George Wallace, who used to clean our boots.'

Having learnt that Lamb, now a captain in the 5th Royal Inniskilling Fusiliers, was stationed near-by, Stanley hoped they could meet. He wrote to him twice, in July 1917, his first letter having gone astray. After listing all the ten authors and artists of whom he had books—he got his friends to carry some when they were on the move—his second letter (18 July) proceeds: 'I am reading Keats and Blake together. I think Blake is a great poet, but he makes me long for Marvell and Donatello. . . . There is something remote and secret about Andrew Marvell. I think Claude is very great. . . . Claude excites worship, not admiration in me. . . . Don't you just ache for Gluck, Mozart, Bach and Beethoven? . . . You did not get the chance of letting me hear much of Gluck up at Hampstead. . . .

'I think Raphael would have been a greater artist if he had kept to pagan subjects and not ecclesiastical ones. The "Council of the Gods" and the "Triumph of Galatea" are the only things of Raphael which move me in any way.' Claude was the only French Master whose work he greatly admired. Earlier in this letter he proceeds: 'Does not this country have rather a melancholy effect upon you? The sound of the Dardanelles has an awful fascination for me. . . . In England, we used to have mostly wounded and sick from the Dardanelles, and each patient had the same wonderful and majestic look in his face. It might have been my imagination, but it does not make any difference if it was.

'I have got all sorts of "feelings" to be made into solid matter when I return. But I think of the sea most of all, and Africa.'

On hearing from Lamb, Stanley wrote to him again the same day (20 July): 'I am a thousand times more determined to do something a thousand times greater than anything I have ever done before, when I get home; and am storing up energy all the time and would you believe that after I had more or less got over the horrible feelings I had when I was in the 68th, . . . about three months after I came out here, I began to feel not exactly happy but somehow something put something tranquil into me. . . .

'I no longer feel that most awful mental torture, that empty void, that awful and fierce wanting and yet nothing to hand to satisfy. In the cook-house of the 68th were some nice iron wedges and on the hill were some big pieces of rock, and I thought I would sit astride one of them and carve and carve and never stop. I did get some small and rather soft pieces of rock and cut heads out with a knife. But oh! how bitterly wretched I felt. My brain felt like a tin of marmalade that has been opened and fallen over and got full of flies and sand.' Needless to say, none of these pieces of sculpture made the previous year, could he carry with him. Thinking back again to 1916 when he was in the 68th, he adds: 'I asked the C.O., who gave me grand feelings, . . . if I could draw the hills and positions. He gave me plenty of material and told me I could have a mule and go all over the place. . . .

'I knew that at the Depots they were looking for draughtsmen, and I had faint hopes of our C.O. doing something for me. . . . But I think I am too much of a bloody artist and, of course, I know nothing about engineering draughtsman's job. Anyhow, he gave me all day to draw in and told the staff that I was to be excused duties.' This was the first indication of his having had either the wish or the opportunity for drawing the landscape. His transfer to hospital in December that year prevented its realisation. His letter to Lamb concludes: 'I think after all it has been for my good that I am in the R.A.M.C. and not infantry. I should never, I think, have been strong enough for that, though I can't help feeling that men who are always in the thick of the fighting in France must, in spite of the continual strain, find life more tolerable.' Despite this conclusion, he nevertheless applied for transfer to the infantry.

Earlier in the month, Lamb had arrived on horseback and the much desired meeting and exchange of ideas came about: 'We went and sat under a big tree', he reported to Florence some while later (2 September), 'among the big black and white sheep and two big shaggy goats, and talked about Claude, Mozart, Weber, Byrd, Keats and a lot about Blake, and he wants to send me a Chatterton.'

Notes to Chapter 5

1. Having lost the notes he wrote in Salonika, he had to rely on memory for writing his reminiscences in Glasgow in 1944, which he continued after going to live at Cliveden View in Cookham Rise in 1945.
2. His painting of *Travoys* (Plate 14) was a recollection of Smol, near Corsica.
3. 'You know for instance of my passion for the sea, and my itch to be always going away for holidays', he wrote Hilda 16 May 1930, in a very sarcastic mood. 'Ugh! I shudder at the thought.' But he painted the beach at Southwold (Aberdeen Art Gallery) when staying alone at Wangford, August 1937.
4. Painted on the long left-hand wall at Burghclere (Plate 33).
5. He records writing this 2 September 1945, at Cookham Rise.
6. Painted on the right-hand long wall at Burghclere (Plate 34).

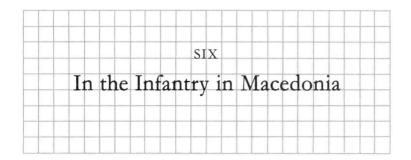

SIX
In the Infantry in Macedonia

THE INACTIVITY on the Macedonian Front during the summer months of 1917 had made Stanley restless, and he envied those who had greater opportunity for participation in the war effort, despite his pacific disposition. In August, he saw notices displayed at Mirova Camp (Plate 13) asking for volunteers for service in the infantry. He had learnt that the 7th Battalion, Royal Berkshire Regiment, was stationed near Kalinova, for which he had a nostalgic longing and he also supposed that eventual de-mobilisation might be quicker from the infantry than from the R.A.M.C. Having put his name forward, his transfer was confirmed in October, and he was returned to base. 'I had a difficult journey', he recalled in his reminiscences (1944–1945), 'on foot and on anything I could get on, back to the Depôt, outside Salonika somewhere, a journey of forty to fify kilometres over those Macedonian wildernesses.'

He did not mention this change of service when writing to Florence (2 September) with an enclosure to his father. He told her, mischievously, of photographs, received from Lady Ottoline Morrell, of 'Mr Morrell trying to use the scythe; in another, half a female is diving into a beautiful stream; in the other one, God knows why, is Asquith, . . . whom I do not know.'[1] He laid blame on Asquith, as Prime Minister at the outbreak of war, for his (Stanley) being in the Army.

Later in October, his infantry training began, lasting four months. He managed only one letter to Florence, giving his new address as 'No. 100066, Royal Berks, No. 3 Infantry Base Depot.' Only thus did his family first learn of his transfer.

On completing his training, which included bombing practice, he was posted to his battalion and wrote to Florence on 12 February 1918, telling her: 'I have finished training and am waiting to go up the line. . . . My candle is about to collapse.' He admits having had about forty letters from her during the previous two months, without answering them, but he had had time to meditate, and this revolved around the books he read and his religious convictions. He conveyed these also to his eldest brother, Will, and Joanna (12 February), mentioning having received a little book of Crashaw: 'It fits into my top left-hand pocket which, next to the poetry, is the best part about it. . . . Although I have had perforce to leave a lot of my "heavenly armour" behind in the Ambulance . . . yet I am still well armed with [these] poets [Crashaw and Milton] and Shakespeare. My "breast-plate" is a series of reproductions of Donatello's statues of St John the Baptist, St Mark and St George. Milton is the glittering spear. . . .

'I feel as truly happy as ever I have felt, in fact happier. At last I am back up the line. It is much colder, and the snow-covered mountains look ghostly white in the moonlight. As I walked along the road, I realised, as I do more and more, how God has given to the true artist His blessing. King David's Ark could not, I think, have been a more beautiful moving altar of praise than I was the day before yesterday night. I think the one and only perfect joy is the joy of giving perfect praise, and although I was not able . . . to give that living spirit of praise a "material body", yet it was every bit as clear in my mind.'

Stanley was assigned, later in February 1918, to C Company in the central sector, which was, as he had hoped, in sight of Kalinova, whence he wrote to Florence on 24 February in a delighted frame of mind: 'The mountains look beautiful, covered with snow. . . . I like the merciless wildness of this country. It makes one curse at times, but the cursing is a very fitting part of the "wildness". . . . I would not have missed seeing the things I have seen . . . for anything, but I do not want to touch any of these things until I can do so in the free time of civilian life.'

His arduous and rapid journey by foot, with one other man more experienced than he, gave him a foretaste of the strain ahead, for which his slight physique scarcely equipped him. In his reminiscences, he records the journey. 'I was worried at the darkness, the extreme roughness and the awful speed this man

12. *The Commandant Emerging from a Dug-out, Macedonia,* 1919. Imperial War Museum.

13. *Drinking Water, Mirova, Macedonia,* 1919. Imperial War Museum.

walked at. I was terrified of losing sight of him, as everything else in front of me seemed to be a whole mass of chaos and he the only fixed star to take one's bearings by. At last, we heard behind us some limbers coming along, forging their way through blackness and, like my man, seeming to know every inch of it. The man said: "Look here; these are the rations coming up; we'd better keep up with them." This meant that when they were past, we had got to hold on to the back and keep up, and as the mules were going it in good "non-stop" style, . . . I felt and dreaded the stitches in my side. . . . "How am I going to keep this up for miles and miles? But I must keep it up", and the dread of being left behind tightened my grasp. Sometimes the wretched drivers lashed the mules to a gallop and I just had to hang on. . . . At last, the mules . . . slackened their speed a little and we went silently forward, the riders on the mules just discernible in the darkness, looking spectral and awful.

'We were skirting round a road cut into a hillside . . . when suddenly a long clear shaft of light began to veer round towards us over the crest of the hill on the right. The mules started as the drivers pulled them silently to a standstill. I watched the shadow of the right-hand crest of the hill, over which the searchlight was just skimming. . . . The brow of the hill on the right just, and only just, concealed us from view but did just pick out the drivers' heads up on the mules. . . . We then hurried on until once again it came sweeping round but again missed us. . . . Then the limber wrenched itself round . . . and began to descend into greater darkness still and pulled up with a jerk. . . . The driver called out "C Company" and out of the darkness, and in a place, I thought that, but for this limber and its drivers and the man with me, I would be alone in the world, and at once, surrounding the limber, were men feverishly taking out the provisions. My companion then said to me "come quickly" and started to climb . . . a steep hill. . . I felt very tired and could not at first understand the hurry.'

Stanley now had to face the sergeant-major, who asked whether he had had any bombing practice, to which Stanley replied 'yes', and was told by his companion that he 'must be up the pole' for admitting it, as he would be detailed for a bombing raid.

'But I don't think to this day', is his comment, 'I could have said "no", when a special part of my training . . . had been bombing. It seemed a little less dark as I went along and looked at the dug-outs, all of which seemed different. I at last got to one I very much liked ... when I was told it was condemned and I reluctantly had to leave it and go to one which I did not like nearly as much.' (Plate 12.)

Recovering from this ordeal, he wrote to Jas Wood (3 March 1918): 'Up the line again, the sap of life has returned. I would far rather be out in the infantry than be working as an orderly in a hospital in England. . . . These mountains fill me with an eternal joy. . . . I think my period of service is not of degeneration but of being in the "refiner's fire". . . . Could you send me out a sketch book . . . (cartridge paper I like) some pencils also.'

Meanwhile Lamb's regiment had been transferred to Egypt, and Stanley wrote to him (18 March): 'I feel so much more alive since I transferred. . . . I think it is wonderful how men are a part of the spirit, the same as the corner in the wall or the slope of the land is part of it. . . . I enjoyed re-reading those parts out of *Paradise Lost*, where Milton is describing the "Hellish Army"; "The Imperial ensign, which full high advanced shone like a meteor streaming in the wind." . . . Can't you see that little pointed flame (the ensign) showing up against a background of dark mountains, gaping with great gloomy ravines?'

During these months, March and April 1918, the Front was relatively quiet, giving Stanley leisure for further reading and writing letters. He was for the time being particularly happy. 'The worst of the winter is over now', he wrote to Florence (7 March). 'Rich green grass shows itself under the dead, trodden-down grass of last year. There is one solitary tree—a very "Claudesque" tree— and it is dotted all over with hundreds of starlings, and they are all talking as hard as they can. . . . The rain is drizzling down and it makes one feel . . . [as] in "olden" days . . . in the nursery . . . and Agnes would be singing in a "sing-songy" voice: "Come in you naughty birds; the rain is pouring down." . . .

'Last Sunday a C. of E. padre . . . conducted a service under this tree. The rain came down, but we carried on. . . . I am sure that we would have stood out in the rain till Doomsday, rather than shorten the service conducted by such a fine little man.' Stanley felt he had to apprise her of his leanings towards Roman Catholicism, although aware that it would distress his orthodox Anglican father and chapel-going mother, adding: 'But do you know, Flongy dear, I hate the C. of E. I wish I had been born and baptised a Roman Catholic. I do not think a man can perform a pure act of faith through the Protestant religion. . . . I do not think our book of Common Prayer has any form. . . . But the order of Mass has a most perfect form; office follows office in perfect sequence . . . as a movement has in a Beethoven Sonata.'

The next day he felt he owed Florence a less controversial letter: 'This morning I went a short journey with a man who was very entertaining. . . . He smokes a pipe in a way that makes me think that there could never have been a time in his life when he didn't smoke. Before he would utter any sentence of importance, the index finger of his right hand would appear above the bowl of the pipe, bend forward and press the burning ash home. This would be followed by a few quick repeated draws, then a sigh, then: "You know, Spencer, this is a terrible war", uttered in that tone of voice as if he would say: "You know, if this war goes on much longer, it'll get serious." This would be followed with . . . : "Per–son–ally, I shall be glad when the whole thing's over." . . . Then, after a pause: "What a ter–ri–ble world we–live–in–to–be–shour."'

A month later, he quoted Milton to her: ' "Ten paces huge he back recoiled, the tenth on bended knee his massy spear upstayed." That's the sort of thing I live on, along with army rations. . . . When I come in in the evening, I wash and brush up and then I sally forth. . . . I have a few pieces of cardboard and I do a little drawing on them or else I contemplate the heavens.'

Ten days later, having received paints, biscuits and sketch-book, he continued his letter to Florence: 'The storks fly round, and I think of dear old Hans Andersen. . . . I had a lovely swim tonight in a lake, and the young rich dark green reeds growing up among last year's reeds, now dead and pink, were so luminous.' The receipt of paints enabled him to send Florence in a letter a sketch of grape hyacinths, the only work in colour by him that has survived the War (Plate 3).

As Private Spencer, No. 41812, C Company, he spent much of the hot Macedonian summer under canvas behind the lines, but in June 1918, he had a spell of outpost duty, living in a dug-out a few yards from the Bulgarian outposts on the mountain ridge. He had to get accustomed to shrapnel and sniping. The censorship forbade his describing these experiences in his letters at the time, but he recorded his feelings about the opposing soldiers in a letter to me in 1929: 'My feelings about the Bulgars were acted upon in a very remarkable way, owing to the simple fact that I *never* saw them, and yet they were only a few yards away. I felt that if I did see one, it would be more extraordinary than seeing a ghost; and can you imagine under such circumstances how fascinating it was to hear the sound of the gravel crunching . . . made by the wheels of their wagons?

'Of course, it is very difficult to express all the many wonderful feelings I had about the Bulgars, a number of these wonderful feelings resulting from the fact that they were the enemy. First, the "enemy" element gave me this feeling of remoteness from them — a feeling that they belonged to another planet. Also, it gave me the feeling I used to have about places, where the wall was so high that I could not see over into them. Secondly, there was the fact that we only went into "no-man's land" in the night, so that I never saw what that land looked like in the daylight. Everything had to be done in dead silence, and can you imagine the mystery when, on some pale Macedonian moonlight night, we were told to go into this unknown land, and we go and with all the feeling and wonder that one might experience in entering a jungle full of wild beasts?

'We, at length, arrive at a ravine which is full of flowers and ferns, not that one can see the flowers, but I could smell them. And all these scents and the just discernible shapes of the ferns and undergrowth, all somehow suggesting the presence of this fearful, yet wonderful mystery—the enemy.

'To call a big fat Bulgarian—a very homely sort of man—a wonderful mystery, is not what I do here. What is a "wonderful mystery" is that quality which a hill or a man or an animal or a ravine gets when it is to be feared. Who does not long to see a tiger in a jungle and not in a cage? . . . Is there not something that adds, imperceptibly, a feeling of mystery to the tiger, owing to the fact that one must not approach it? It therefore becomes remote. In this same sense a Bulgar became remote. . . . When you see some bird or animal . . . and are told that that bird or animal is extremely rare, it gives you a feeling that you are looking at one of the innermost secrets of nature. So with the Bulgar. The fact that he was only a few yards away and the fact that he was never to be seen gave him this feeling of "rareness" and the feeling of being a wild secret of nature.'

In his subsequent reminiscences, he expanded his description of outpost duty at this time: 'As the only contact with the Bulgars was during the night, I got the impression of their being a kind of beings which came from an essential and permanent night, and that each night, we, as midnight drew near, approached their dark abode and, as the morning came, descended and came away from it. I never felt that they like us, descended to their day as we descended to ours, but that somewhere further up in time in a place more midnight than midnight, they were in some way away in my mind still existing. Some nights it was extraordinary to me to hear the ground crunching under the wheels of some cart when I was told it was the Bulgars' ration carts coming up, just as ours brought ours up. No "Looking-glass" world was ever as intangible as that seemed to me.

'It seemed to me a queer arrangement that our activities consisted of outpost duty and patrolling the wire at night and in the day-time just doing odd fatigues, just outside our dug-outs. . . . We formed up, in the evening just before sunset, outside the dug-outs . . . taking two bombs each from a box as we did so. It was always suspected by the Bulgars as being the time to start a barrage. . . . The shells dropped uncomfortably near and I was glad when . . . getting to the outposts, we were able to take cover in a communication trench.'

Soon they had to follow a track along a shallow ravine 'full of undergrowth' and 'difficult to make out in the dark' to the outposts which were 'new-moon-shaped ruts in the ground'. 'I was very glad to scramble into them', he explains. 'One night, when shrapnel had begun before I had got to the outpost and was still on the Makikova track, I could not understand why the two men in front of me did not slip down into the gently sloping ravine . . . below such a high and exposed ridge. I thought: "Well, I can't stand this", and started off boldly down into it, but I had not stepped more than a few yards before I found I was walking in a mass of barbed wire. . . . I had to extricate myself very carefully and not get flustered and the feeling of being caught in every way was alarming. One of the men said something about: "You'll get yourself into trouble." '

Later in his reminiscences, he continues: 'Whereas in peace-time, tea-time was a happy time, when one could slack off a little and the day's work had been more or less mastered, here a terrible sinking feeling and loss of spirits assailed me, as I walked into the dark channel-like dug-out carrying my dixie of tea and portion of bread, because it was immediately after this that we had to "stand-to" outside our dug-outs and then the going into the outposts.'

He proceeds to explain how, one night, a piece of ribbon-wire had to be attached to the Bulgars' wire, describing it as 'a job about which one could say nothing polite at all'. 'When, after dark, we were assembled outside the Scout-Captain's dug-out to hear from him all about what we had to do, he talked about it as if it was the greatest joke ever hatched by the mind of man. . . . While I by no means felt the least contempt for my own natural cowardice, I did feel admiration for those men's courage and pluck. It was so absolutely right with them. . . .

'There was something intoxicating about this man. He grinned at us a big grin and said something about: "Are you frightened?" And then, "It will be quite alright; nothing to worry about at all; but all you have to do is not speak one word and hold the rivets well apart." . . . Somehow, his saying it would be "quite alright" made me feel it would be quite all wrong.'

Early in May, 1918, a letter from the Ministry of Information, signed 'A. Yockney', had given Stanley the startling news that he was appointed a 'War Artist' if willing to accept. It was, the letter stated, 'in connection with the scheme for utilising the artistic resources of the country for record purposes', adding that 'Mr Muirhead Bone, who takes a great interest in your work, has suggested that you could paint a picture under some such title as *A Religious Service at the Front*', or 'any subjects in or about Salonika, which could be painted by you before your return home'. Meanwhile, the War Office had been asked to release him.

Of course, Stanley was willing, nay eager, and had numerous subjects he could paint right away, given the opportunity. He had no need for suggestions. He now waited anxiously for the expected summons to Headquarters. He told Florence promptly, adding that he was not aware that Bone knew he existed. He formed ideas, which he explained to Chute (3 June): 'If I get this job, I shall be able to show God in the bare "real" things, in a limber wagon, in ravines, in fouling mule lines. . . . This place has a great hold on my mind. Mountains and mule lines is all my thought.'

Stanley wrote the same day to Henry in Egypt: 'I am aching to paint ideas I have for men asleep in a tent—that bivouac idea I showed you; of men at drinking water; . . . two pack-mule pictures; . . . a lecture on mosquitos; two mule line pictures; . . . one limber wagon bringing grub. I am as much influenced by this particular sector, as I was by Cookham in peace times, I do believe. I want to do some "ravine" picture.'

It seems tragic that the High Command's reluctance to release Stanley from his military duties of minor value, deprived us of these pictures he might have painted while in Macedonia. The suggestion of a religious service as a subject does not seem to have inspired him. In his letter to Florence (3 June), he indicated his readiness to begin painting: 'A little space of ground will be as it used to be to me, a universe. . . . I do not want to leave the Balkans until I have carried out some of my plans, though if I went to France I should, I dare say, find something there, as I have found something here.' Presumably the General Staff was reluctant to release men before the planned offensive. With the most dangerous service ahead of him, Stanley would be lucky to survive. His ideas for pictures had to remain stored in his mind, until some of them could be brought to life after demobilisation.

While waiting impatiently, Stanley romanticised about what he might do in the future, plans which he certainly never fulfilled and of a kind that he subsequently repudiated. 'After the War', he wrote to Florence (27 June), 'I can see myself doing some strange things. . . . I arrive home; . . . get in a train for Bristol, get out at Bath, stand on the railway platform and look towards a certain loathsome suburban church standing in the side of big hill; take notes and get back into train. Get out at Bristol, on tram up to Fishponds; go up a certain hill, a slummy street on left; small cottage; . . . on the window-sill, earthenware animals and flower pots; on the other side of house small cottage garden on a steep slope; . . . little orchard. Take notes and return to Cookham.

'Then off I would go to Plymouth, and from thence to the coast of Portugal, and there sail up and down the red-cliffed coast; then away again down the blue Mediterranean and see those great pillars of smoke rising off the top of the grey African mountains. Then up the Aegean Sea and gaze upon the isles of Archipelago, which now appear and now disappear—a rusty red colour from out of the thick purple mist in the East, as the sun sinks down behind some great Grecian mountains in the west.'

He then contemplates visiting Cornwall, Jersey, Belfast and even so far as America, for which 'Ballantyne is responsible' and photos he had seen of 'blue lakes and great trees, and shrubs and mysterious unknown mountains. Then I would return to Cookham and work and I would not stop working. I would be like one of my mates is with pick and shovel; you can't stop him. . . . A gleam comes into his eye, his face becomes set and he's off, and the only thing that would stop him would be to hit him over the head with a crow-bar. This man was a fire-eater in civil life, in other words he was a stoker . . . in the "Black Country". But I don't believe a crow-bar would stop me.' He would then go to Norway—'Chute gave me a wonderful description' of it—and 'to Weimar, the land of Goethe'.

After telling Florence in June that he had no news of his 'prospective job', but expected 'to hear in a few days', he wrote her again (16 September) that he began to give up hope. The same day he wrote to Chute, unaware that the final offensive, in which he would be heavily involved, had begun. Still unperturbed, he meditated, almost for the first time, about the issues which soldiers had been discussing since the Russian Revolution the previous year: 'I feel that the poorer classes . . . are not being given a proper chance to *live*, . . . their progress seriously impeded towards attaining a really high understanding of truth, purely through the fault of unnecessary, petty, material inconveniences. . . . I pray for the time when it will be accounted sin in anybody not to know the *Diabelli Variations*. There is no such thing as "individuality", "personality", "originality". Every man has the same "Name". His Name is the Resurrection and the Life. . . .

'There ought to be an equal distribution of labour. If any man is ignorant or a fool or a knave, you and I are largely responsible. I do not think this may be what is wanted, but it is just how I think.'

Stanley had been released from outpost duty earlier in September, as he relates in his reminiscences, and was glad to learn that instead of preparing a fresh attack they were to go down the line to be relieved by the Oxford and Bucks Light Infantry. Luckily, he was to go in a limber: 'I remember careering all through the night across Macedonia, as it seemed to me. . . . It was strange getting back to bivouacs, but I somehow did not like the place. It was like a very big shallow disused gravel pit, but all hard and bumpy. I was at once busy filling the mosquito-net pockets with sand and sewing each one up. . . . But first I tried to get water. In the inner slope of this place toward the cliff end of it was a tap and a collection of men near it. . . . I remember a . . . sergeant shouting that the tap was not to be used and a whole row ensued. . . . I felt there was something sinister in the cursed atmosphere of this tap incident. . . . After mid-day, I decided I would go to a place nearly a mile away where I had heard there was a big bath-house. Tired as I was . . . and beginning to feel more cheerful, suddenly there was a hubbub of conversation among the men, in the midst of which I could hear: "Yes you have", and "who said so?" and then I thought: "This sounds like those alarmist bits of news, which men so love to give to each other and which are usually false." But there was no doubt about it. A man came up to where I was and said: "Hey you, you'd better get back to your camp; they're packing up." I said: "What's up?" and someone said: "Going back up the line tonight and you'll have to be ready in about an hour." With a ton weight on my spirit, I dragged myself back and it was horrible as I approached to hear the infernal shouting of orders. . . . There were all those little pockets to be emptied and bivouacs packed. . . . We at last began to move and somehow . . . the shock began to subside.'

The offensive had begun on the Vardar sector to the west on 1 September, but was delayed on the British sector until the 18th, where they faced the best of the Bulgarian troops and the strongest fortified positions. Meanwhile, General Sarrail had been replaced by General Franchet d'Esperey since December 1917. Exhausted as the soldiers were, after being on the move all the previous night, Stanley's company had to set off back to the lines without rest, marching from three o'clock until nearly midnight. As they rested in the moonlight on the hill-side, letters were distributed for the first time in several months: 'Mine was from Mrs Raverat congratulating this bit of humanity, lying in the Vardar Valley, waiting for orders to enter what was called the Dome, on the

important appointment [for painting] I was supposed to have
got. . . . All the information I could have given her at that moment
was that the deliverer of the letter (a corporal) was telling us, as he
handed each letter, that they were to be destroyed as soon as read,
and that the sergeant-major was calling each of us to him and
asking us how many rounds of ammunition we each had.'

They could hardly rest, as they were to advance about two
o'clock that night. Stanley was handed an extra bandolier of fifty
rounds, but it was the anticipation of hand-to-hand fighting that
filled him with apprehension. He was informed that the last move
had lost a thousand men. He continues: 'As I thought what, in an
hour and half's time, I should be experiencing, it seemed to me
inconceivable what would or might be happening to me. . . . There
was the most glaring fact staring me in the face that the place where
yesterday, if I had shown myself beyond the second belt of barbed
wire for ten minutes in the dark, would have got a machine gun
bullet through me and where shrapnel was almost a continuous
occurrence. And here we were, we who for two and a half years had
not dared to make hardly one change at all in our front were going
to suddenly calmly tread over our wire and over the Bulgar lines
right bang in amongst them. Privates were usually not told
anything. I felt a kind of disagreeable gloominess and taciturnness
settle on my spirits as the night wore on. But 2 o'clock came and no
move; then 3 o'clock approached and no one seemed to be
preparing for anything. And I began to look about me from where
I sat on my ground sheet rather like a bird that feels morning is
near. Soon I saw men walking about, dividing in dark vertical
streaks the crack of dawning light. The disappearing night seemed
to take my dread with it. It was a clear dawn and I remember we
were all told if we liked to shave we could. My spirits revived as I
did so and as the sun rose. Then the whole camp began to get news
of what had happened. Apparently the Bulgars had fallen back, but
they were not at all sure how far. . . . I remember looking curiously
about at the ground in front of me, which I had only ever seen in
the darkness of night . . . The Bulgars were gone completely. In
one sense it was disappointing, but when I thought how ghastly it
would be if they turned and began to attack instead of retreat, I felt
very hopeful that we would continue to be disappointed.'

He had the opportunity to observe their barbed-wire, which was 'a thick mat of rusty stuff', and he wished there had been time or opportunity to 'see how they made their dug-outs'. After a long march, they halted by the Vardar and were allowed to bathe but not drink—they were short of water and thirsty. His narrative continues: 'All that tense and known and fixed routine life that had become our daily bread . . . that consciousness of the war and its awful immoralness seemed to belong to the past to another world. The War was still on, but something indefinable . . . was gone. . . . Having this sudden walk-over signified a change. One of the striking things in a war is its awful lack of variety. One's mind is all the time claimed and exerted and exercised by utterly boring things. . . . I began to feel in a sort of dream. Once, when we were resting mid-day . . . where there was some sort of grass and the usual lemon-thyme, I felt when we were all there as though some organ was being played and psalms were being sung. Purely imagined, it was just the dreamlike atmosphere produced by exhaustion and the heat and the soothing effect of rest.'

Although Stanley was still young—he had his twenty-seventh birthday in June 1918—and had abundance of energy, which he could sustain with comparatively little sleep, he was insufficiently robust to maintain the pace required; nor had he the requisite coolness and composure. He may have felt cause to regret his transfer from the field ambulance, for which he was suited, to become an infantryman, armed with bayonet and rifle. How could he expect to confront a burly Bulgarian peasant on equal terms? He felt no animosity towards his adversaries, nor any wish to be the instrument of death. On the contrary, he felt that the bond of universal brotherhood lay between them. 'On the second day of the advance', his reminiscences continue, 'we had wandered across one of these wonderful nondescript plains, amongst which the line of hills nosed about aimlessly, completely confusing one's sense of direction or whereabouts.'

That afternoon, his captain detailed three men, including Stanley, to scout over a line of hills. Each took a different gradient. He was proud to be selected for this assignment. He knew what was required of him, but as it transpired, it was to sour his sense of duty. While on the hill-side, before completing the task, he lost his water-bottle, so essential for survival, and while hunting for it in desperation he observed a platoon in the valley below and then one of its men detached to climb the hill, who on approaching, he records, 'said with his hand on the trigger: "I have orders to shoot you; I've got it cocked. . . . Go on! Get to the top of the hill or I'll shoot." ' Quite worn out, Stanley could only crawl back to his unit. When he explained the loss of his water-bottle, he appears to have been excused.

In retrospect, he saw this incident as an indication that the officers wished him 'well out of the way'. He could seldom acknowledge a mistake, either to himself or others. He had brought this on himself, but it produced in him a lasting grudge against his military superiors. His narrative continues: 'I arrived exhausted at a place in the evening, where we were rested and where for the night all I was called upon to do was to stand in a little dried-up ditch by some young trees and gaze out across the plains, and listen to the Macedonian owls. After such an ordeal, this was very refreshing.'

His suspicion that he was in for persecution was aggravated the next day. After a march of four hours across the plain, a fellow private was thought to be missing and the sergeant detailed Stanley to search for him. Some while elapsed without achieving any success, and soon Stanley feared that he had lost his way, while unprovided with food or water. He records: 'I felt very suspicious as to the true purpose of this errand, . . . seeing that it was very unlikely that the man was lost at all.'

When things went wrong, the suspicious side of Stanley's nature often asserted itself. As day wore on, he had begun to fear that he would be 'left to die', when he happened to observe an artillery column approaching. The major was compassionate, seeing that Stanley could barely stand, and granted him a lift on a gun carriage. On rejoining his company, he learnt that his fellow private had merely strayed into the wrong section.

A third incident during these few momentous days, proved quite different, revealing Stanley's readiness to face danger, when he understood the need for it. They were about to ascend a hill, which the captain, whom Stanley liked, thought he should reconnoitre. He called out: 'Come along'; but Stanley was the only one to respond amidst 'jeering remarks about V.C.s' from the other men. 'We went on up among little oak bushes. Then we ran across a plateau of long dried-up grass on the crest of this hill and down into another ravine and then began to go up the other side . . . among some more of these bushes.'

The captain now sat down to observe the other hill-side through field-glasses, telling Stanley to 'take out his map and writing-book' from his valise. While the captain wrote a note to give the planes and artillery the location of the enemy, he told Stanley to look through the glasses. 'It was like watching the movement of some sort of germs, through a microscope, that were extremely dangerous to human life, or seeing a tiger in a jungle—queer jerking marionette movements in which the foreignness of the men could be noticed.' Stanley carried the note to another soldier lower down and returned to the captain, who expressed surprise at seeing him again, since their position was very dangerous. An exchange of fire ensued, and 'the combing of bullets in the air wafted unpleasantly near', prompting the captain to advise: 'We are cut off', adding: 'We can't stay here; we must try and get back.' They had only gone a few yards, when the captain was hit and 'sank down to the ground'. 'His hand went up to his neck and I saw a gaping bullet wound in it.' Stanley bandaged the wound as best he could and then called for stretcher-bearers. 'Within about a quarter of an hour I heard men coming, and in a moment, he [the captain] was surrounded by men.' Stanley helped to support the wounded man, who was paralysed and heard him whisper to another officer: 'Understand, Spencer is not a fool; he is a damned good man.' While appreciating the compliment, Stanley wondered on reflection: 'What's all this? Who has been saying otherwise?'

Two days of marching had taken place before this incident occurred, during which they found a shelter which contained some of the 'never-to-be-forgotten German helmets', which reminded him of those they played with as children. 'These were real "Kaiser" ones', he comments, adding: 'I wish now I could have brought one, but I would not have carried a pin.' From a deserted dispensary, he took some bandages, which he preferred to his own, and a thermometer, but his companions suggested they might be poisoned. 'I felt less fascinated by all these discoveries, when a man pointed to a note written in English, which said: "We will be back soon."'

His narrative continues: 'I began to feel the terror of these wretched shells, which made us all cower in little places among the chalky sides of the hills. This eased off sufficiently to enable us to move a bit further on.' They rested in an enclosed dell, as evening approached. 'I was just hoping for a good night's sleep when I heard the ominous calls down among the mule lines of "load-up", and soon we were all off once again, as it was growing dusk across this plain. I suppose the fact was we were now under observation and could not have got across this in daylight.' They reached the foot of the next range of mountains in the dark. 'The air was being rent with the firing of our field-guns and the . . . officers bawling at the top of their voices among the din: "same target, same range, fire." ' They were ordered to sleep for one hour amidst this 'din', with its 'terrific echoing among the mountains'. 'Then we began to make a narrow track up into these mountains. As we got higher, it began to get cooler, and I was glad to fill my tin helmet from a little waterfall that gleamed in the moonlight.' Halting at the side of the track, the men were detailed to move off separately in the darkness. This was called 'connecting file', something which Stanley did not know and had not practised, and for a while, he lost his way, but managed, eventually, to locate his unit. His narrative proceeds: 'We continued until we reached the summit at midnight. It was terribly cold and we only had our scanty summer drill-shorts on. . . . I turned my flaps down and rolled my puttees . . . to make a covering of my legs.' They began the descent before dawn, past some villagers who were hastily driving their cattle 'and fleeing in all directions'. They were now in Bulgaria and assembled at 11 o'clock in a gully 'dried-up and full of broken rock'. He noticed the men were 'smoking' their bayonets. 'I knew some new cause for anxiety was afoot. Apparently in among the hills just in front of us . . . were some Bulgarians.' Ranked in extended order with fixed bayonets and told to keep in line, Stanley was warned by the sergeant of what would happen to him if he did not keep up. His plight was often aggravated by not knowing when a special effort was required, and blind obedience was not in his nature. It was now, however, when moving up over the hills that the incident with the wounded captain occurred.

He unwittingly strayed from his unit, and sought refuge in a recess in the chalk cliff. 'Everything was still,' he records, 'not a soul to be seen and only a deafening sound of a machine-gun.' At last, a man from another regiment came by, who indicated where

Stanley might find his unit; he might be taken prisoner if he remained where he was. He made his way along the river gulley and soon found his Company. Mounting guard that night in a small pit, he enjoyed the 'feeling of relief from the tension'. Before daylight they were on the move again. Soon they were on a country road, and Stanley was shocked when the man in front of him shot a dog for no apparent reason, and Stanley was met with abuse when he protested. 'I felt what a vast distance intervened between the minds of these men and my own. I was just thinking for instance how cosy and pretty it looked to see the early morning lamp-light in the cottages just by us here and this old dog and the fact that we had not seen any ordinary living people in houses or cottages for years, and then the whole scene blasted before my eyes.'

Bulgar shell-dumps were being destroyed, making 'a sudden rosy lightening of the sky'. He found the smell terrible: 'Two dead Bulgars lay in peculiar positions on the side of the road. . . . Further on was a horse and cart and the driver, all dead still. The driver was down between the shafts and horse. It was very difficult to breathe with handkerchiefs over our noses in the heat and great dust.' When they rested, Stanley found it increasingly difficult to rise again. 'I seemed to have become dazed', he explains. He was hardly aware of the 'cool wet sponge' that a stretcher-bearer put in his mouth, nor that the padre was asked to give up his horse, 'a biggish black mare', for Stanley to be laid across the saddle. A church bell was ringing and there was a town before them, with men and women coming out with jugs of water. 'This was Strumnitza', he records. 'I felt the blessedness of peace was drawing near. I wished I had been less exhausted, as I longed to talk or show some pleasure at meeting them.' Unable to dismount without assistance, he heard the loud voice of the colonel: ' "Who is that wandering round the camp as if the whole place belonged to him?" But I somehow felt that his day was over.'

Feeling partially recovered by the rest, Stanley was detailed to help carry blankets. Meanwhile an incident occurred, which struck him forcibly. He heard the regimental sergeant-major, whom he had not seen before, call out: "Expect you'd rather be painting, wouldn't you, Spencer?" This made him wonder. Had the War Office cabled for his release as a war artist and the instruction been ignored?

Again exhausted, he was carried on a stretcher to the shade of some trees, and later taken back by lorry. His feverish state was not helped, when they stopped at a crowded hospital, previously German, where he had to sleep on the ground. Having only cotton clothes, he was grateful when some Serbian soldiers let him share their straw mat and gave him tea. By the next evening, he was delirious and on the following day was put on a train for Salonika. It was the beginning of October, and the return of his malaria, and the War was over for him.

On the 16 October 1918, a Bulgarian staff officer arrived at British Headquarters, asking for an armistice, and three days later, the Bulgarian forces capitulated. Stanley's service in the infantry had lasted just over a year.

Note to Chapter 6

1. H. H. Asquith (later Earl of Oxford) was leader of the Liberal Party, to which Philip Morrell, M.P., belonged.

SEVEN

Back to Salonika and Demobilisation

'I LONG to *be*, to *live*', Stanley wrote Florence on the 3 October 1918, after admission to the 49th General Hospital in Salonika, adding: 'My only life-giver now is my Crashaw and a Tintoretto.' He told her that he expected to remain there 'only for a few days' despite feeling 'very weak'. He could now relax with reading and writing for the first time for several weeks. A week later, he wrote her again: 'I am going on well, though the slightest exertion makes me bad. . . . It would hearten me so if only I could get to do some painting.'

He was now anxiously following world events, and makes the comments in a letter to Florence (undated): 'All of us boys in hospital are excited about the acceptance by Germany of the Washington Note. . . . As Mr Wooster would say: "We've got'em on the run." ' He was reading Isaac Walton's *Lives*, including that of John Donne, who, as he told Florence, has 'influenced my whole artistic life'. In Crashaw, he found 'an almost pagan passion', enjoyed Swinburne 'in spite of his affectations', but thought Robert Browning 'hard to understand'. He drew the conclusion: 'But when are we going to get a really great poet like Milton? There seems to be some sort of "cult" running through the poems of modern poets. It is most insidious; no one seems to escape it.'

In a letter of 12 October, while recuperating, he tells Florence: 'In desperation, I am having to resort to *Daily Mirrors* and *Punch* . . . No matter . . . what you pick up, it is all war articles, war, war. . . . The only thing of interest . . . are my thoughts, and they just now seem like a row of dustbins. But one can find interesting and very nice things in dustbins . . . but I was thinking of a time

Kate Foster and Richard Carline at tea with the tray that he and Stanley had brought back from Sarajevo in Bosnia in 1922, in Richard Carline's studio at 14a Downshire Hill, drawn in pen and ink in 1926 for the Chatto and Windus *Almanac* for January 1927 (see p. 171), the only drawing of the studio Stanley ever made. This drawing (in the author's collection) is incorrectly described by L. Collis, quoting the second Mrs Spencer (in *A Private View of Stanley Spencer*, Heinemann, 1972) as 'showing the standard of cooking Hilda provided. Stanley and Hilda are about to eat or perhaps have eaten; on the table between them are a teapot and half a dozen open tins. . . . It was far from an exaggerated picture.'

when in poking about for cart-wheels and haddock's eyes, I disturbed a whole bevy of unopened tins of bully beef in good condition. The incinerator gave me a feed every night for a fortnight. But I honestly think that looking for treasure on dust heaps, where there is not too unpleasant a smell is a distinctly entertaining and elevating pastime.

'I used to love scrummaging about on Farmer Hatch's rubbish

heap. . . . I was almost always sure to find something that really satisfied my highest thoughts. . . . To think of those sweet spring afternoons when I could sit up in the front bedroom and with the window open, sit and read out of that big Bible the Book of Tobit, . . . so mellow, and the pages were just the right colour, slightly sunburnt round the edges. I have enjoyed reading about David. . . . Can't you picture Mephibosheth, who did eat continually at the King's table and was lame on both feet? . . .

'Oh dear! . . . Another dose of quinine? Good God! It was a tonic, dark colour, quite good stuff. The patient who gave it me says: "Here you are, Spencer, a drop of the best." ' He tells her of his wish to learn fresco. 'If Jacques Raverat's project holds good, we are going to build a church and the walls will have on them all about Christ. If I don't do this on earth, I will do it in Heaven.'

He had also written to Chute (5 October): 'My experiences seem to have quite unmanned me', and in a second letter, soon afterwards, added: 'In some of the awful moments, I have felt the need for greater faith and afterwards found myself asking the question: "Christ has been adequate to me in all things, but is he in this?" . . . It is an awful shock to find how little my faith stood in my stead to help me.'

Released from hospital on 21 October 1918, Stanley was sent to base camp for convalescence. He had made friends with the padre, which had replenished his religious convictions. In a letter to Florence, next day, he compared the 'heaviness and sumptuousness' of pagan life with the 'light blithe spirit of the Christian', its 'Fra Angelico feeling'. He likens the early Christians to children picking flowers in the meadows, and tells her that he means to make pictures of the Acts of the Apostles and is 'marking off passages'. There will be 'the apostles all dreamily gazing upwards and the two angels standing on the ground gazing at them', and 'all the good men doing good in different ways.' Recalling 'the awe-inspiring scenes . . . about which I have been able to say nothing', he assures her that he 'will be feeling more of an artist than ever'. 'I do not feel as if my life has begun, not my real life. I am getting ready to live, going through a sort of purgatorial schooling. But hope is stronger in me now than ever it was.' He adds that Crashaw says: " 'Thy generous wine with age grows strong, not sour." '

With returning strength, his environment was making an

impact. Referring in the same letter to some marquees on the hill opposite, he tells her: 'These marquees are white, and in the early evening, as the sun is setting and the moon rising opposite from behind the hill, . . . they look a delicate pink. Immediately behind the marquees are deep, almost black, warm black-green, trees, shrubs and poplars—the Lombardy kind—and behind the trees a rocky hill or mount, which appears fantastic, a light mauve colour, and above that the full moon which, the sunset still giving that peculiar twilight that we get out here, is surrounded by a halo which is a daffodil yellow colour, and the moon itself is a lovely silvery yellow. Nothing could look more romantic, just as if it was taken out of some fairy tale.' Such regard for colour supports the view, one incidentally that I have always held, that colour mattered to him in his early years, much more than in his later work.

Stanley had seldom written to his parents, communication with his sister being easier, but he wrote them on 28 October, though in a somewhat carping frame of mind: 'Not that I am unsociable, but I feel like Gulliver, when he visited the Houyhnhnms. . . . Not that these, my comrades, are like unto those horses, which were very learned and dignified philosophers, but in the way they regard me they are. I feel estranged from them. They like cigarettes; I hate them. . . . They like beer and rum; I hate it. They like sports; I loathe them in the spirit in which they are enjoyed. They like smart modern novels; I have never under any consideration read them. . . . They do not like Dickens and have never heard of Meredith and Hardy. Their knowledge of art extends no further than the Picture Palace. . . . If I can enter into these men's little interests and hopes, why can't they enter into mine? I read the Testament nearly all day, and because I do so, they presume I must be one of those priggish "holy" sort, whereas in many things I have paganistic sentiments. . . . So it is that I have in my conversation to remain silent and in my letters speak of the things that really interest me. . . .

'The War *is* coming to an end and that very soon, I feel sure, and don't forget . . . to have the old clothes-horse airing the sheets by the kitchen fire.'

One month later (24 November), Stanley was on his way back to England, travelling by sea to Taranto, thence by train up the east coast of Italy and across the Alps to Cherbourg—a slow and uncomfortable journey. Arriving at Southampton on 12 December, he had to proceed to the Royal Berkshire's Depot, before going home. Still in uniform, his arrival at Fernlea on the 16th was quite unexpected. His first enquiry was 'Where is Sydney?' He had not received his father's news of the brother killed in France in the last month of the war, after being awarded the Military Cross. Stanley's homecoming was a sad one.

Impact of home was overwhelming, and Stanley wrote promptly to Florence, now living in Cambridge:[1] 'Everything is so dazzlingly beautiful that I feel like the Disciples did at the Transfiguration. I believe I could even go as far as to kiss Colonel R. or Dr B., but I don't think they would quite understand.' On Boxing Day, he sought to share his happiness with Henry Lamb: 'I feel fit to burst with good health and just "lord" it about the village.' He had heard only then that Henry, now a Captain with the Military Cross, had been badly gassed after transference to the Western Front, and he wrote to him again on 4 January: 'I feel . . . kind of dazed and expect God to leap down and "snaffle" me with "no you don't",' adding: 'I feel like a blazing sun-flower' (recalling those they saw at the village of Kil-kut). 'Do you remember? I ought to see these places again.'

Stanley was due to return to the regimental depot to await eventual demobilisation there, but the War Artist Scheme came, for once, to the rescue, and Yockney obtained his release.[2] A commission to paint for the Imperial War Museum was now discussed. Having lost his sketches made in Macedonia—he had heard that 'personal property was put on a great heap somewhere', after the final advance—he had to draw upon his acute memory, and submitted five sketches of ideas for Yockney's approval.[3] The one of travoys arriving with wounded men at a dressing station at Smol, with its mules seen back view with their twitching ears, was the one selected (Plate 17). Before beginning work on it, he wanted to complete his *Swan Upping*, which was as he had left it, unfinished, when he joined the army.[4] He felt no compunction in continuing where he had left off, despite the length of time that had elapsed.

Stanley wrote to Chute (10 January 1919) telling him of his joy at being home. But his wavering religious uncertainty still troubled him. It reached a crisis with a letter from the sculptor, Eric Gill, at

Ditchling, an older man and ardent Roman Catholic, then at the height of his fame. At Chute's suggestion, he invited Stanley to visit the Priory at Hawkesyard on 20 January.[5] Gill reported to Chute on the visit: 'We are here and Stanley Spencer is with us having a fearful wrestle—chiefly with himself. He met us at Euston on Saturday, determined not to come after all, but we persuaded him, and he came just as he was with his hands in his pockets and no luggage at all. What will be the upshot of it, God only knows? He is in a curious mixed state of pride, prejudice, and humility and reverence.' Stanley gave, in retrospect, an entirely different account of this visit, repudiating any idea that he might have been considering embracing the Roman Catholic faith.[6] The truth may lie somewhere between the two versions. His natural independence and a certain obstinacy prevented him from committing himself in any direction. Indeed, the Army, then the New English Art Club and, still later, the Royal Academy, were the only institutions he ever joined and his only commitments apart from marriage. His deeply felt religious leanings remained purely personal.

Contact with Eric Gill ended abruptly, and his friendship with Chute, hitherto so intense, dwindled. Instead of his letters to Chute ending, 'your ever loving friend', the few letters henceforward ended 'yours ever'. Subsequently, in 1926, he wrote Chute at length from Wangford in Suffolk, including the astonishing admission: 'Yet I am not entirely in love with Christianity.' After this their correspondence ceased. When writing his notes in the 1930s, he had this to say of his beliefs: 'If one is sincerely trying to be a Christian, his work will be alright . . . but if he is like me, he will know of difficulties, real difficulties.'

In his Glasgow reminiscences of 1944, he sought to amplify these beliefs that underlay his work up to that time: 'My first outdoor anchorage seemed to be the Church. Somehow religion was something to do with me, and I was to do with religion. It came into my vision quite naturally like the sky and rain. . . . My early work was, as far as specified religion is concerned, nondenominational, but whatever was the direction, it was utterly believed in. It is just the fact that, as I said, it was nevertheless in harmony with known Christian religion and ideals means that whatever I love and have to do nowadays, if it is not in harmony with Christianity then I am still faithfully trying to turn and keep in the Christian direction. In other words there would be in such a case no clash. . . . I don't keep to the rules. . . . I dislike many of them and think them harmful to what I love and hope for in humanity. Nevertheless, these things, as I said, are an essential part of the Christian qualities.'

Stanley rejected the assumption that his picture of *Travoys* (Plate 14), on which he worked during the first six months of 1919, was related to war: 'It was possible even in the War', he asserts in his reminiscences, 'to establish . . . a peaceful atmosphere and of hope, and some sort of constructive life was sustained in this way. I was impressed with the calm way the wounded men spoke to each other—about some cabbages they had been trying to grow for instance. . . . A homely atmosphere was being preserved in spite of what was happening. . . . [It, the picture was] not a scene of horror but a scene of redemption from it and I was as right in making it a happy picture, as the early painters were right in making the Crucifixion a happy painting.'

He recalled, later, how the idea came to him, in a letter to Hilda Carline (summer 1923): 'I was standing a little away from an old Greek Church, which was used as a dressing station, and coming [there] were these rows of travoys with wounded and limbers crammed full of wounded men. One would have thought that the scene was a sordid one, a terrible scene . . . but I felt there was a grandeur about it . . . All these wounded men were calm and at peace with everything, so that pain seemed a small thing with them. I felt there was a spiritual ascendancy over everything.' (Plates 15 and 16.)

Like his *Swan Upping*, the *Travoys* was finished in June 1919, shortly before a further attack of malaria. Yockney saw it on a visit to Cookham in July, when he also asked him to paint two smaller pictures for the Museum, at a fee of £33. 6. 8. each, the fee being based on time spent. Although tempted at first, and Stanley did make two sketches for them,[7] he declined on further reflection. As he explained in a letter to Henry (20 July): 'I set to work, but before many days elapsed, I began to feel too much as if I was cooking, and so I wrote at once to Yockney to knock me off the job.'

The *Travoys* was an immediate success, when it was shown later

14. *Travoys with Wounded Soldiers Arriving at a Dressing Station at Smol, Macedonia*, oil, 1919. Imperial War Museum.

15 & 16. Sketches for *Travoys*, 1919.
17. Sketch for *Travoys*, 1919. Imperial War Museum.

that year at the War Paintings Exhibition at Burlington House in London (December 1919). There was an evening preview for artists to meet members of the organising committee and others. Stanley was, of course, invited, and I recall my brother Sydney and I escorting him there—all three of us being exhibitors. Being, myself, the first to ascend the stairs, I was taken aback and somewhat flattered by the effusive greeting from Charles Aitken (Director of the Tate), D. S. McColl (Keeper of the Wallace Collection) and Robert Witt, who had all obviously mistaken me for Stanley, whom they had not met.

For some months following his return home, Stanley's joy continued unabated. He tried to slip back into the routine of his life in Cookham before the War. In Macedonia, he had liked to contemplate how he would spend an ideal day in Cookham, and he repeated this to Henry (17 March 1919): 'Get up at about quarter to seven. Go down Odney bathing pool; have a . . . swim just where the sun reflects in the water; then home; then one or two preludes and fugues; then breakfast (a little porridge and one rasher and perhaps one egg); then one more prelude; then to my big picture till dinner, doing about one square foot of painting. Then, if I have to wait for dinner a few minutes, hang about in the street and watch the people living. Then have dinner (boiled bacon and parsnips please); then another good solid chunk of painting till 4 o'clock, and then tea—bread and butter and a little marmalade.

'Then do a delightful assortment of odd things; you know the things one sees during the day that you would like to do. After that, at about 7 o'clock, carry on with a composition until supper. Our summer supper times are rather great, to gossip with mother and eat cherries and custard. Then a bit of a walk; then more to composition; then to bed and then I open several books at the pages I have got to and lay them face downwards on the bed in a row.'

Before writing this idyllic account, Stanley had begun to feel restive. His long absence in the War could not fail to break the rhythm of old habits. But chiefly, post-war restrictions during the winter months, made Fernlea seem very cold; throughout his life, warmth meant more to Stanley than food or drink. His mother, to whom he was devoted, was often unwell. 'Her coughing is very bad', he had told Chute in January 1919. It was from his mother rather than his taller father, that Stanley inherited his small frame. 'I am afraid to breathe too hard', he wrote to Henry (4 January 1919), 'lest I blow her away.'

Stanley's relationship with his father was not always so harmonious. The few letters he received from his father would sometimes question the amount of money he sent home from army pay. Such financial considerations irritated Stanley, and on one occasion he complained to Florence about his father in resentful tones. But his grievances went much further. After recovering from his bout of malaria, he aired them to Henry (20 July 1919): 'I am very bothered about the way we have to carry on our work. You see, we have no rooms to work in except our bedrooms. It is bad for these reasons:

1. Not healthy.
2. Distracting to be conscious of household and domestic affairs. For instance, laundry arrives; nobody to answer door; have to answer it. Pupils arriving. Pa loses his collar-stud. Somebody coming upstairs, passes thud, thud, by your door; good egg, does not come in. Bang goes the door—silence. Pa blows his nose.
3. Not nice to go to bed in the room in which you have had such varied experiences during the day.

'The only alternative is for each of us to have a place built. . . . I cannot tolerate the idea of having a tin-shanty army hut affair. I want bricks and mortar. . . . I expect this would cost about £1,000, and I have not that. . . . There does not seem to be a system of thieving which does not entail the inconvenience of being caught.'

Nevertheless, Stanley continued to live at Fernlea throughout 1919. A search for places in which to paint met with no success, and on 28 November, he again ventilated his complaints to Henry: 'We are both determined that no work will be done by us until we have proper conditions to work under. . . . I wrote to the biggest landowner in Cookham, who has several large disused buildings, and he wrote to say that "he was sorry etc." I am equally determined not to leave Cookham. I know of several places hereabouts that would suit us admirably, yet not one of these disused places can we have. Isn't it a "knock-out"? And there are no reasons put forward why we should not have them.'

Stanley's attitude in this was surprising, since he was usually content to paint anywhere, attic or bedroom, however cramped.

Apart from the Burghclere Chapel, the only studio he ever had was in the garden at Lindworth, in Cookham, used by him only for a short while in the early 1930s. His main concern was to be alone and undisturbed.

An opportunity to leave Fernlea came in November 1919, when the Behrends took him and Gil to tea with the Slessers[8] at Cornerways, Bourne End, on the opposite bank of the Thames. Stanley gladly accepted their invitation to stay there, but he did not make the move until April 1920. He never lived at Fernlea again, until the last year of his life.

Notes to Chapter 7

1. Married to a Cambridge don, she was now Mrs J. M. Image.
2. He was not finally demobilised until 12 April 1919.
3. There are, in fact, seven of his sketches in The Imperial War Museum.
4. Subsequently exhibited at the New English Art Club in 1920, when he was elected a member. It was bought by Mr and Mrs Behrend for £100.
5. The Staffordshire Priory of the Dominican Brotherhood.
6. He wrote to Hilda (20 February 1929): 'I was given to understand that Eric Gill wanted to discuss some building scheme, and those interested in it were going to meet at the monastery. I was got there more or less under false pretences, so that you are quite wrong in thinking I went there to try the experiment of becoming a Catholic.'
7. Two small oil panels of *Laying out the Red Cross* and *Soldiers Washing in a Stream* were bought by Gwen Raverat.
8. Subsequently Sir Henry Slesser, Solicitor-General in the Labour Government of the 1920s.

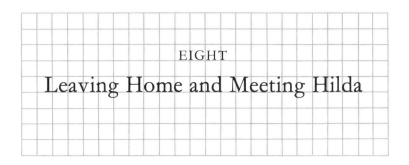

EIGHT

Leaving Home and Meeting Hilda

Music was the special bond of interest which Stanley and Henry Lamb had in common. Henry's playing of the piano drew Stanley like a magnet. 'The effect on me', he wrote to Henry, 17 March 1919, 'is something of the same sort as the sun and a planet. The planet gets its impetus from the sun and I get mine from your playing.' Henry had returned from war service to his studio on the top floor of the Vale Hotel on Hampstead Heath, and Stanley wanted us—myself and family—to meet him. But this had to await our demobilisation, my brother Sydney and I being officers in the Royal Air Force, and not due back from the Middle East until autumn, 1919.[1] It was only then that I could write to Stanley, receiving his prompt reply (25 November, 1919): 'I look forward to seeing you and your work; . . . I have only seen a little but "multum in parvo" (if you will excuse my using this little bit of Latin; it's the only bit I know and it comes in alright just here. I understand it to mean "much in little").

'I am often accused of not taking any interest in or showing any curiosity towards modern work. This is the "modern one's" fault and not mine. I am not incapable of feeling curious or interested to see a "modern" work, and I know this, that I am at this moment so wanting to see some work of yours that I do not like to think of one second of time coming between the time when I shall see it.

'I go to a local Technical and Art School here, as I can get models, on Tuesday evening, Wednesday afternoon and evening and Saturday all day. Any other day I could come to London and see you. I should love to see those precious old sketch-books of yours again.' He made these journeys to Maidenhead by bus, but walked the three miles home, telling Henry (28 November): 'I have felt my pace instinctively quickening as I have neared the gates of the building.'

47 Downshire Hill, Hampstead, was now our family home, our parents having moved from Oxford to join Sydney, our sister Hilda and myself; Sydney and I also acquired studios across the road. Stanley paid his promised visit for dinner in December 1919. He referred subsequently to this first encounter with Hilda: 'As she came round to me and Jas [Wood] and the rest of us with the soup, I thought how extraordinary she looked. . . . I could feel my real self in that extraordinary person. . . . I felt a longing for her, as at once I saw a life with her.' He was inhibited from expanding these feelings, however, because his brother, Gilbert, had already indicated more than a little interest in her. Hilda had been at the Slade School since the autumn term 1918, awarded, incidentally, a first prize in painting. There she met Gil, who was continuing his studies interrupted by the War. Meanwhile, Stanley's visit to us in Hampstead was soon followed by further visits.

Being particularly sociable by nature, Stanley may have enjoyed meeting the various artists who visited us at that time, who included Robert Bevan, the painter, and his artist wife, S. de Karlowska, Selwyn Image, Slade Professor at Oxford, A. S. Hartrick, who had been my father's fellow student at Julian's Academy in Paris in the 1880s, and Sydney's contemporaries from the Slade, before the War, such as Nevinson, Allinson and Gertler.[2]

Meanwhile, Stanley wrote to Sydney and me on 8 December 1919, thanking us for his visit: 'I long to see Miss Carline's picture of the sheep painted;[3] I mean a larger one of it.' He wanted it, together with a little sea painting by me,[4] taken to the Slade School by Hilda, so that Gilbert could bring them to Cookham, where they could see them in daylight. 'I like more and more', he added, 'as I think of it, the later portrait of your sister.[5] I think that, probably, doing the earlier one put you on the scent. . . . Your visit to Lamb seemed to do him a lot of good; he seemed radiant and happy. . . . My love to the cat (even though he bit me).'

A further letter reached us a few days later (12 December): 'Would three guineas be enough for the "Sheep" picture and five guineas for the "Sea" one?[6] . . . When I saw how much Gil liked the pictures, I felt more confident in my powers for finding out good things. . . . He could not say enough in praise of the "Sea" picture. I think there is something heavenly in your sister's picture. . . .

'Now that I have seen those paintings of yours at the Royal Academy,[7] Sydney, could you show me some more . . . "un-war" pictures of yours, when I come to see you next? . . . Gil and I and Gilbert Solomon[8] (you remember him at the Slade) admired tremendously your small painting of the Troops moving up along the road. We were all three of us liking it before we knew who it was by. . . .

'On Private View day, I was having an amusing time. You see Gilbert had brought with him to the show a Miss Harvie from the Slade, and I had come with him to help him show her round, in case he was not up to it, and I had engaged our invaluable friend Edmunds (of the Slade) to render us assistance in carrying out this little affair successfully. Well, the affair was carried out, and so was I very nearly. I don't know what Miss Harvie must have thought of Gil and I. But it was hopeless. I decided it was hopeless, when I came bang up against Tonks. I have to keep my head well tilted back when I am talking to him. I shall call on the off-chance of seeing you, when I am next in London.'

Stanley wrote again on 28 December, addressing it 'Dear Miss Carline': 'Gilbert and I had both been behaving in a way anything but the way good little boys behave on a bright and happy Christmas morning. In olden days, when we used to drag our Christmas presents . . . down the passage in a huge clothes basket, in those days we had something to shout about; but present-day Christmasses are no sorts at all. . . .

'About your picture, the more I look at it, the more I love it. This is expressing what I feel rather bluntly. Konody,[9] no doubt, would disapprove of it as not being "criticism", but I am not Konody. But I must say something, as the painting is so moving. I thought what you said about my picture [*Travoys*] was very true; it is "different" and somehow strange. I did not feel quite happy in that picture, only in parts. . . . How curious that you liked the recollection of my picture more than you liked looking at it, because that is exactly how I liked it. I feel like that about a lot of pictures.

'Gil and I both thoroughly enjoyed our visits, and we shall probably come whenever we are in London; if that will not be too often for you, it won't be often enough for us. Please call me "Stanley"; I should like you to, or "Cookham" if you like. I am *THE* Cookham, you know. Gil is only A Cookham. . . .

'I should like to know what you thought of Gil's, Roberts', Wyndham Lewis', the Nashes' and Meninsky's works at the R.A. Oh and Colin Gill's and Darsie Japp's. I want to know what you thought of Japp's and Bernard Meninsky's in particular. . . . Perhaps Meninsky's are a little bit coarse, but they seem to me to be rather fine. . . . Perhaps they are influenced by Peter van Brughel or whatever is his name, but I think not. . . .

'We both had a jolly Christmas. We sang carols all the evening, like two young skylarks. Gilbert sang more like a nightingale "with full-throated ease". Of course, we are now both very hoarse and have to keep clearing our throats.'

Two days later, came a letter to me: 'There is a certain amount of pleasure to be got from expressing one's appreciation of a picture by buying it. . . . I felt rather dubious at first about asking for your sister's painting, as I felt it might be depriving her of a part of the joy of her life, a slice out of it that she might miss, though it was quite a thin slice. . . . When we have both erected a large studio, one each, we intend to embellish the walls with them. That is when we have large studios and when we have walls to embellish (too many ells in this word). But just now, we are like Mr Micawber fiddling his watch-chain—but we have no watch-chain to fiddle— and waiting for something to turn up. We have been in this "just now" state for many weary months. However, something is going to turn up in a very little while, and we shall both then begin to be REAL artists. . . .

'I have nothing to show at home now. . . . People write to ask to see some of my work, and I have to keep saying: "I'm very sorry, but I have nothing to show you", "I regret to say I haven't any drawings", "I'm deeply grieved to say" etc. But Gil has some things you ought to see.'

Before finally leaving Fernlea to stay at Cornerways in Bourne End with the Slessers, Stanley was overjoyed to learn that he was one of several young artists chosen by Sir Michael Sadler to carry out decorations in Leeds Town Hall, subject to their designs receiving William Rothenstein's approval. Such an opportunity was something that Stanley had dreamt about, and he visited Leeds in March 1920. Unluckily, Rothenstein found his preliminary design unsuitable (Plate 18).

Having, meanwhile, joined our family at Seaford[10]—his first prolonged stay by the sea in England and the first in our company, he replied to Rothenstein from Seaford, 23 April:[11] 'Do not distress yourself over this misunderstanding [the Leeds project]. I make mistakes, especially ones like these, every day of my life. Of course, I felt very vicious at the time . . . but this was the result of disappointment and that makes me vicious always. . . .

'I am staying at Seaford with the Carlines and I did not want to break such a delightful holiday with another visit to Leeds. Your brother [Albert Rutherston] thinks I have seen all that is necessary.

'Yesterday, we all went out on to the Downs and did paintings. The "artists" were: Mr Carline (the father of the flock), Hilda, Sydney and Richard Carline and Gilbert and Stanley Spencer. We did the paintings first and set them in a row in a dear old barn and admired them for all we were worth, because you see there was no one else to do so.'

Sadler was reluctant to omit Stanley from his project, and invited him to Leeds for a more extended visit, on 21 June. This gave Stanley his first real impression of the industrial north, and his letter to Florence (25 June) reveals the impact of this new environment, which produced a lasting effect, comparable only with that of Macedonia: 'It would be impossible to describe the place. . . . Just to give you an idea of what Leeds is like, I poked my head out of my bedroom window the other day, and I heard people singing in another building; they were singing Christmas carols! . . . I was in the worst slums most of the time. The smells were vile, but it was very sad and wonderful. I am particularly keen on the washing day in the slum. I have a magnificent idea for the Leeds picture. They hang the washing on a line which hangs from the windows and swings forward on to some railing in front of the house.'

Some weeks later, he outlined his idea for the mural in a letter to Henry (22 July): 'My Leeds idea is, I think, going to be a great success. . . . I walked about the slums. I noticed that there would be one long road and several little blind alleys leading out of the road. It was these blind alleys that gave me the idea, at least part of it. Everything that happens in these slum homes, happens on the pavement, so that you can see the difference between each "happening", as you can see all the different "lives" of the families going on all at the same time. And then the washing is wonderful; each alley is chunk full of washing, all blowing upwards. The wind is very blustery in Leeds.' Alas, this promising project never materialised.

Stanley's threat to refrain from painting while without a studio, proved an empty gesture. He felt compelled to implement the ideas fermenting in his imagination. At Cornerways, he had a bedroom overlooking a backwater of the Thames, and painted there his *Last Supper*, for which he had made a composition as far back as 3 September 1919 (mentioned in a letter to Henry). He told Hilda (17 June 1920) that he had just painted St John's hair. Completed by mid-July, Harry Slesser promptly bought it for £150. Stanley had also finished his *People on Cookham Bridge*, which he considered unsuccessful and did not wish to offer for sale.[12] He was changing his range of colours, and his paintings were generally paler in colour or tone than his earlier ones.

No longer having the Leeds project to consider, and with the Slessers going away in July, Stanley was glad to accept Henry's invitation to join him and Gilbert at Durweston in Dorset. Stanley now had the opportunity to try landscape, as Gilbert did, working direct from nature, something he had scarcely attempted hitherto. On his return to Bourne End in September, he brought back with him several landscapes, some of which he completed later, and he did others of Quarry Woods[13] and of the river[14] during that autumn and the spring.

Subsequently, he repudiated his painting of landscapes, claiming that compositions were his only valid creations, and told Hilda (July 1923) that he 'hated doing landscapes'. Still later (1937), he wrote to her: 'Every landscape I have painted I did purely and solely for money and for nothing else.' He was manifestly exaggerating, referring only to those he was then painting and overlooking his earlier landscapes, which were not commissions and only parted with many years later. He must have forgotten the one sold to Eddie Marsh in 1914, which he described to Henry in 1923 as 'marvellous—the first I ever did'.

The 'place' element in his painting was paramount, but derived from memory rather than from sight, and incorporated in his

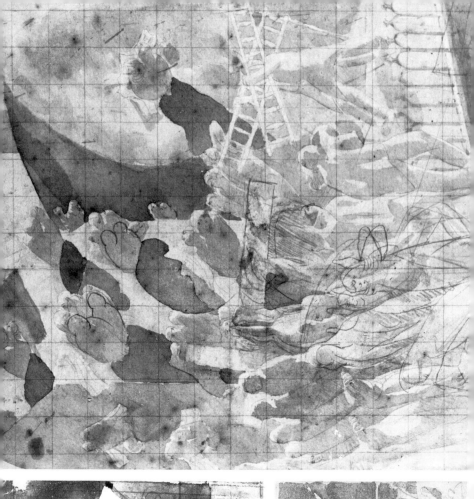

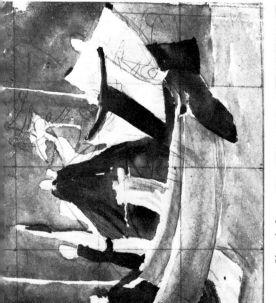

18. Sketch for a composition, possibly for the proposed Leeds mural, 1920.

19. School concert, sketch for a mural for Bedales School, not carried out.

20. Sketch for *Christ Carrying the Cross*, in front of Fernlea, Cookham, 1920.

compositions. He revealed this feeling for nature, when writing in 1944 about his picture *The Last Day*: 'The eastern aspect of Cookham had a look of great promise. Hearing the crowing in the early morning, my thoughts would veer to the sky above Cliveden Woods. Whatever the sky happened to be, it always had that special meaning when seeing it over the woods. . . .

'Opposite us was a farm . . . and the cows would come up from Widbrook to be milked. Somewhere on this great Common there was a cottage, about which I imagined the early morning life going on round about it. To actually locate the spot and place one has formed in one's mind, from these early morning sounds coming through the window, is not easy. It is like trying to find the source of the rainbow. A great life is going on and yet, when I go out to see, all is early morning mist and everything deserted. I might hear a blackbird singing away in the Widbrook direction. I go that way and the singing gets nearer, but no sign of any bird. I at last see its beady eye in the darkness of the hedge by me; it was in its nest; wasn't up.'

He visualised the coming of Christ over Cliveden, and he drew a composition of a mother holding her child on the back of a cart-horse, the child's arms spread open towards the eastern sky.[15] 'It was', he wrote in his reminiscences, 'an effort to express what I love in this place . . . Vision gives birth to itself . . . and the joy one feels . . . causes other joys to join in. . . . But vision may work both ways; it bloweth where it listeth.'

Stanley was pleased to be back with the Slessers in Bourne End, and wrote to Henry, who was still in Dorset, on 19 September 1920: 'If I do not really love the people I live with, I become selfishly indifferent to them. I cannot live with people I "just like". There is a time when the rub will come. This is why I feel that living here with the Slessers is the best thing for me. The "atmosphere" of Harry and Margaret Slesser inspires me in the impersonal way as the tree does outside my window. . . . The danger, here, is that of seeing too many people, which I find very distracting.'

He began work on his *Christ Carrying the Cross*, for which he made several pencil studies[16] and a final sketch, squared for enlargement, in pencil with sepia wash (which he gave me a few years later), being his first departure from pen and ink (Plate 20). In his reminiscences of the 1940s, he described how he had visualised the scene in front of Fernlea: 'When I was thinking of the picture and wishing for it to come into the light of day, so to speak, I saw Fairchild, the builder's, men go past "The Nest" [next door] carrying ladders. . . . The picture went through several changes. The movement of the "Way to Calvary" passes from right to left — rather the movement of a breaker approaching a shore.

'As youths, we stood with other village youths in a gate opposite our home and watched the people go by on Sundays and in evenings. The three men in the . . . bottom of the picture form this "onlooker" part of the scene. To the left of these is a wide street coming towards the spectator through the iron palings, at the side of which other men peer down at the sitting and stooping figure of the Virgin. Other onlookers in the left bottom corner shade their eyes and one is clearing his eyes. . . . Up above, the windows being open, the draught blows the curtains out.' He adds: 'The shape I liked was *one* shape with smaller shapes projecting from it here and there . . . the form of a potato with little ones forming on it.' It is surprising to find Stanley thinking thus of form in the abstract.

He had several other ideas, on which he worked early in 1921, describing them to Hilda on 21 March: 'Today, having a thick head, I began a painting of Christ tipping the tables over in the Temple (Plate 21). The table which Christ is turning over is warm deep red and the other table which the man is climbing over is white. Christ is white. The man on the white table is the same colour as the other table. The two end men leaning over the red table—they are grabbing the cloth to save the money from falling off—are yellow; the bags are white. The man who only just shows above the red table is red also. And here [a second sketch], you have another on the same idea. I like it.'[17]

Another idea was *Christ Coming down the Street*, which he was painting in May and June 1921, describing it in a letter to Henry (7 June), while still working on it, as 'another dud', adding: 'All that lovely light which I got on the people running down the garden is not in the painting. But I am going to do another a bit smaller.'[18]

But by this time, June 1921, the 'distractions' he had complained of at Cornerways were beginning to prove overwhelming, as he told Lamb in the same letter. There were 'arrangements, visits, meetings, committees, telephone bell, and you know: "Oh, is that

21. *Christ Tipping over the Tables*, a sketch in a letter to Hilda, 21 March 1921.
22. *Stanley and Hilda Reading Letters*, sketch in a letter to Hilda, 22 May 1930.

you? How are you? What? Oh yes do, what, frightfully." My head buzzes.' His long stay at Cornerways, so fruitful in work, was coming to an end. After painting his small *Sword of the Lord and of Gideon* (oil on paper), his restless state of mind set him on the move once more. He left Bourne End at the end of June 1921, and, indeed the environment of Cookham, from which he was absent for nearly a decade; for several years ahead he was to live without any settled home of his own.

Notes to Chapter 8

1. Sydney, some years my senior, and I had been commissioned under the War Artists Scheme in 1918 to paint pictures of the War as seen from the air, for which we made sketches while flying, and in January 1919, we were posted to the Middle East to make studies for a further series of paintings, which we completed in 1920.
2. Harold Gilman had been a visitor until his death in the influenza epidemic in 1919.
3. Painted at Wangford, Suffolk, where she worked as a land girl in 1918. The painting is now lost.
4. *Off the Coast of Greece* painted by myself in 1919, also lost.
5. Painted by myself in 1918 (now in the Tate Gallery). The earlier portrait mentioned is now lost.
6. The first paintings that Stanley bought.
7. At the War Paintings Exhibition, Burlington House, December 1919, and now in the Imperial War Museum.
8. Son of Solomon J. Solomon, R.A., he served in the R.A.F. and painted for the Imperial War Museum.
9. Art critic for the *Observer*, and one of the most influential of critics at that time.
10. The visit to Seaford is wrongly dated by M. Collis (op. cit.) as taking place 'in the Summer of 1920'.
11. Quoted from William Rothenstein, *Men and Memories 1900–1922*, Faber and Faber.
12. Although dated in the Spencer Gallery catalogue, Cookham, as '1919', Stanley himself has recorded its date as '1920', which is probably correct.
13. One of these, acquired by the late G. C. Shiels, is at Cookham.
14. Was in his possession when he died; now in mine.
15. Whether still in existence or where has not been recorded.
16. Preliminary drawings in pencil (one in the Spencer Gallery, Cookham) show that he first considered having Fernlea seen from in front of 'The Nest', instead of from the other angle as in the painting.
17. Now in the Stanley Spencer Gallery, Cookham.
18. Although Stanley has given 1920 as its date in a notebook, this is evidently a mistake in view of his letter to Henry, which states that 'Gil has nearly finished his "Sermon on the Mount"'.

NINE

At Petersfield and a Visit to the Balkans

STANLEY DID NOT SEEK to capture Hilda for himself, feeling that Gilbert had the prior claim, and he did not wish to act as his brother's rival: 'I feel sure', he wrote to Henry Lamb in 1920, 'that Gil's affair with Hilda will all come right in a little time.' Two years later, he still thought all might go well if Hilda would write him, Gilbert, 'a few dozen marriage proposals' (a letter to Henry in July 1922). Only then did he begin to recognise that Hilda's affections were unattached and that he, himself, might contemplate asking her in marriage.

Hilda had spent the summer of 1920 in the Italian Alps with Sydney and myself, and we were journeying south with our parents, when my father's sudden death in the street at Assisi in November compelled us to return home unexpectedly; thus contact with Stanley could be renewed. He was still at Bourne End when Hilda and I visited him on 23 February 1921. 'I cannot say for certain if my picture', he wrote to me, presumably meaning his *Christ Carrying the Cross*, 'will be here, but . . . I have some other sorts of ideas which you can see.

'I liked Sydney's big picture at the New English . . . the women carrying the long bundles of "bambooy" stuff.[1] I thought it was inspired. . . . Look out for me at Bourne End station.' He was carrying two little paintings (oil on paper) of a piebald pony beside a beehive, when he met us, giving one to each of us.[2]

Stanley would often claim that his involvement with Hilda was prompted by his interest in her as an artist, and he would ask her to send sketches of her ideas with her letters. Henry had bought a small oil painting by her, and Stanley wrote to her (21 March 1921): 'The more I look at that little

129

painting of yours up in Henry's room, the more I love it.'

We, as a family, were invited by Muirhead Bone to stay in his house Byways, Steep, near Petersfield, while he and his family were abroad. I had enrolled, part-time, at the Slade and could only join the others at weekends. When the Bones returned at mid-summer, and we returned to Hampstead, Muirhead, a great admirer of Stanley's work, invited him to Byways[3] to paint a mural for the club-room in Steep. This was opportune, as Stanley wanted to quit Bourne End, and he left for Steep in July 1921.

Months passed without Stanley deciding what to paint for the club-room (Plate 8). He was preoccupied with other ideas. He wrote to Henry on 1 December 1921: 'I have just finished a large painting, oil on paper, of the *Crucifixion*'; and he was at work on his composition *Unveiling the Cookham War Memorial*, which he described, later, as 'what I call my Ascot fashions, my sweet-pea colours'.[4]

Circumstances changed dramatically when Muirhead, in some exasperation, on 1 December asked him to leave Byways, as Mrs Bone found his long stay disturbing. Stanley was dismayed. Doubtless, his excitable temperament combined with his unending flow of conversation, monopolising attention, fascinating though it might be, may have wearied Mrs Bone, and created this embarrassing situation.

Now homeless, Stanley promptly moved to lodgings in near-by Steep. He liked being near Bedales School with its social atmosphere and even formed ideas for a mural there, as he told Henry on 26 May 1922[5] (Plate 19.) For the first time, he had to consider a reliable source of income, and he sought Henry's advice (2 February 1922), as usual in emergencies: 'Do you think it would be wise, if I have time, to take two or three pupils? Some people want me to teach their children. What shall I ask if I do?' He had never hitherto contemplated teaching, and nothing came of this plan.

Henry, some years older than Stanley and more sophisticated, welcomed having his advice sought. He admired Stanley immensely, and could also be helpful to other artists whom he liked. Stanley would confide his ideas to him whenever possible. 'I have done a rather nice big study in oil', he told Henry in July 1922, 'of my servant-girl flirtation at the back garden gate.' It was, he explained: 'half in and half out of the drawing-room back window, at which one of the servants is looking.'

Early in 1922, Stanley moved to Petersfield, where he lodged with Mrs Lewis at 25 The Square, while finishing his *Cookham War Memorial* picture.[6] His obsession with gravestones re-emerged, when describing his room to Henry (2 February 1922) as 'overlooking Petersfield Churchyard, so that I am in immediate communication with the dead. They are buried in the side of a bank, so that they only have to push the gravestones a little bit forward and lo! they are in my room, like extinct gentlemen—a very Cookhamesque place, as you can see [pencil sketch]. But Cookhamesque or not, its a grand place, Henry.' He described other ideas for compositions to Henry (26 May), as belonging to 'my hosiery department', adding: 'They each came out of their shell so nicely, without breaking the yolk.... They are all belonging to the Christ table-turning category. It is a special branch line of mine. I know it isn't the "broad gage".'

Feeling somewhat isolated at Petersfield, Stanley's visits to Hampstead increased in frequency. Islamic culture now had a special appeal for him, perhaps prompted by nostalgic memories of Macedonia, its mosques and bazaars, combined with reading Lane's translation of *The Arabian Nights Entertainments*. On one of his Hampstead visits, we looked at the *National Geographic Magazine* with photographs of Bosnia and Herzgovina, where relics of Ottoman rule still flourished, and were inspired by a wish to go there. The possibility of spending some weeks with Hilda doubtless contributed to Stanley's determination to join us.

Back in Petersfield, Stanley poured out his feelings in letters to Hilda. He wrote to her on 15 June 1922: 'It's lovely to say things to you and I long to see you again; it's lovelier to hear *you* say things. When I met you for the first time (when my collar-stud broke) I remember the . . . thing that must have been filling me with delight was thinking . . . "I wonder what the things she says are like." I have an "over the wall-ish" feeling about what you say. . . . If you would kindly lift me up and let me look over, it would be almost as marvellous to me to hear you speaking, now at this moment, as it would be if St Peter suddenly began to speak in Masaccio's picture of Peter casting his shadow. Would the "magic" disappear, if you were here speaking?

'In the case of looking at a place somewhere distant . . . one feels how wonderful it would be to be just there. When one is there, however, lo! the feeling's gone; it was a mirage. "Here" is always such a dull uninspiring place to be in, but the joyful part of this statement is that it is not true. It is the weakness of our imagination. There is hardly any "here" in my pictures, for instance; though, on the other hand, they are not quite *all* "there". There is a little bit of "here" represented by a tuft of grass, utterly unexplained and only there through an unhappy unforeseen circumstance.

'I begin my pictures by letting them grow out of the sky on to the roofs, then slide down the roofs on to the ground. Then I run out of the bottom of the picture as soon as I can, so as not to allow any "foreground" to appear. Giotto and Masaccio were marvellous at getting things to *happen* in the foreground, "here" as I call it. You would not cease to happen in a foreground, I mean if you came here, though I have nothing to show you that I like and a lot that I don't. But I have my old "pic" of the resurrection that I did years ago; do you remember it? I think in a way it's the best thing I ever did.

'*June 22nd.* I don't know what it is, but down here everything seems so inauspicious to me, . . . I hate this filmy something that I get down here across my eyes. When I get up, I don't feel as if I was getting up. This non-existence feeling is suffocating me just at present, though it will pass off. When I am with people down here, I can feel myself trying to come to life. You see, it's a sort of betwixt and between—no quickening east or tranquil, melancholy west; it's just a whole lot of nothing at all. . . . But the feelings I have about you and Mrs Carline and Sydney and Dick are auspicious. . . . It's the feeling of being a real human being talking, that I get when I speak to you, that I want. When I am talking to some people down here, I can hear the monotonous sound of my voice, and do not feel what I am saying; and I stop dead in the middle of a sentence. . . .

'About Austria, I have decided to come, mainly because I want to see more of you, and having you, all three, working round me would be inspiring. It was so, when I was at Seaford. I have written and asked Gil to come . . . and Henry I have asked.'

The final collapse of the club-house project clinched his decision to join our party. 'Bone has given me the sack', he wrote to Henry

(23 July): '. . . Of course, it was a great blow to me, because I loved having the idea of doing that place at the back of my mind and I wanted to cogitate about it for years.' 'I *am* going to Yougo-Bosnia [sic],' he added a few days later, 'but if I get fed up I shall come straight back. . . . I want to leave Petersfield now that I am not doing the Club.' He did not finally vacate his lodgings, in case he should want to return, but being inexperienced as a traveller and nervous of being left alone in a strange environment, he could not have 'come straight back' on his own.

A few weeks later, at the end of July, we set off abroad with Sarajevo, capital of Bosnia, as our destination.[7] (Plate 23.) We travelled across Germany to Vienna, where we stayed some days, and our visits to the national art gallery (Kunsthistorisches Museum) gave Stanley his first sight of masterpieces outside the British Isles. Travelling was congested, and we suffered from heat, bugs and flies. Stanley was never very fastidious by nature and scarcely conscious of hygiene, and he horrified my mother by laying our sandwiches on the grimy, third-class railway carriage seat. Any chance remark might provoke an irate rejoinder, as when I thoughtlessly remarked, as we looked out of the carriage window at the swiftly passing scene: 'The landscape seems to be getting much better now.' Stanley could not let this pass without the sharp retort: 'Of course, it is not better; the country is neither better nor worse.'

But these small sources of friction were soon forgotten in his entertaining observations and his keen appreciation of whatever came our way, such as the gypsy bands playing Turkish music, the Muezzin's call to prayer from the minarets, and, indeed, whatever reminded him of Salonika. The War was too recent to be forgotten, as when two German ex-soldiers, arrogantly describing themselves as 'warriors' joined us uninvited, and Stanley enjoyed discussions with Kusmic, a Serbian, who had participated in the revolt against Austrian rule, which precipitated the War in 1914.

Stanley painted from sight, as we all did, often working beside Hilda, and he joined me in painting the curious headstones in the Mohammedan graveyard. After a month, we went on to Mostar and then to Ragusa (Dubrovnik), Montenegro and Lake Scutari, finally returning by sea to Trieste in October, stopping a few days in Munich and Cologne to visit their art galleries. These were the last collections of masterpieces that Stanley ever saw abroad. Back in England, he moved to new lodgings at 19 High Street, Petersfield.

While painting with Hilda in Sarajevo, Stanley had proposed marriage, and after our return, he wrote to her regularly, beginning in October: 'Rain has been pouring practically all day, every drop of it containing within its crystal sphere the sad news of our cancelled trip to the source of the Buna. But personally I enjoyed the day; I liked the cosiness of it, and when everything becomes very unfriendly out of doors, everybody becomes very friendly inside.

'My conscience, not having done any painting today, has been feeling rather ill at ease and no wonder! "He" has been standing under the bridge that looks towards old Mostar bridge, wondering if "he" ought not to be painting that view. Of course, "he" did one and very bad it was. "He" pulled himself together this afternoon, and did two 2 ft × 16 in. paintings, one of the view from my window and one from Dick's; both were masterpieces. "He" becomes very busy on rainy days.

'Oh! I must fill my mind with something. What can it be? When I am happy, I feel I want to chronicle every cubic inch of it. I want to measure it and store it and add to it. There, that is a bit better; here is another delicious line to fill. What can we put in it? Just this empty space of paper below may unravel something beautiful. It is just the fact that it is possible that is so exciting; makes letter writing a great adventure. I often get the most unexpectedly lovely thoughts, when I am in the sort of empty-headed mood that I am in now. About five minutes have elapsed, during which time my head has remained sturdily empty. I want to celebrate.'

Stanley hoped after marriage to move into Henry's studio, but Henry wanted to use it himself. This set-back made Stanley hesitate. He wrote Hilda that he had 'thought things over' and wanted 'everything to remain as it was' explaining: 'not that I don't think there was a reason for my sudden change of mind, but that I find that that . . . did not affect the foundation of our relationship. . . . But the sad thing is that he [Henry] wants to do portraits, . . . which means we must find some other place somehow'.

Hilda could only regard this letter as breaking off their

23. Stanley Spencer with the Carlines at Sarajevo, 1922.
Left to right: Stanley Spencer, Hilda, Mrs Carline, Sydney (in front), George, Richard, May Piggott (cousin, in front).

24. In front of the Spencers' motorcar in Maidenhead, 1929.
Left to right: Jas Wood, Stanley Spencer, Hilda, Shirin, Mrs Carline.

engagement, and there was a tacit agreement that they would not meet or even write. But Stanley soon found himself unable to refrain from writing: 'I am sick of having lovely thoughts about you and not saying them to you. Day after day they come alive [from] their hot-house existence and die. It may be wrong to write to you, but let it be wrong. . . . Saying all these sweet nothings to you is more wonderful than uttering the profoundest thoughts to anyone else. I know that it is only Dukes of York that can be given in marriage and that "da Cookhams" can't, but it seems so unnatural to go on as though it's cheating really, because I am continually talking to you and taking you for walks, and admiring your appearance at breakfast-table.'

He wrote to her again, a little later, that he was going to Garsington: 'While I am in this hateful undecided state, it will be impossible for me to be here, so I have "gopecked" all my things, which was nearly as big an undertaking as for Mr F. Gray's gigantic flying roundabouts. . . . I have been among the Lost in Lamb's *Book of Life* this last fortnight. The Fair on the Heath seemed to be in keeping with my sentiments, which were mainly "hellish"; so also were the dragons' heads on the roundabouts, with great red fiery tongues. I began to "tinken" that this must be "ell" itself.' After the Balkan visit, Stanley would sprinkle his letters with German-sounding words.

He wrote to her from The Manor House, Garsington (home of Lady Ottoline Morrell) that he presumed she did not wish him to return to Downshire Hill: 'I do hope . . . that you can feel your true self as if nothing had happened. . . . To carry on as we were doing at 47 would have been fatal to us both. I know I am almost entirely to blame.' He returned to his lodgings in Petersfield.

Stanley was now giving lectures and criticisms to the students of the Ruskin Drawing School in Oxford. His role was that of 'Visitor' under my brother Sydney, who had just been appointed Ruskin Master. Gilbert Spencer, John Nash and I were invited to assist in the teaching. Stanley made two or three visits each term, usually staying overnight. It was the first and only teaching assignment that he ever undertook. After his first attendance at the school in October 1922, he wrote to Hilda that he was 'rather enjoying the job'. After his second visit, he wrote on 2 November, about the lecture he had given the students the previous afternoon:

'I was very nervous at Oxford, and in the lecture I kept pausing, oh, Lord, for ages; I should think there must have been more pause than lecture. It was a kind of mesmerism and somehow I felt a kind of melancholy depression. I felt as if I was depressing everybody. Still, I hope it blew over.' It is unlikely that his audience of twenty or thirty students were depressed. They were invariably fascinated by his manner of talking with expressive gestures, as if convinced that they understood everything he said, and the expectation of his usual visit had an electrifying effect.

Later he became much in demand for lectures at schools or societies, generally writing out his lecture in advance. Ultimately, he acquired a facility in speaking impromptu. One of his first Oxford lectures began as follows: 'It is very strange that the idea among people, not artists, that art is a tame sort of job, should be so prevalent. All artists are filled with the love of adventure. Some people, not artists, go to the ends of the earth in search of adventure and come back with nothing in their heads and nothing in their pockets. But when these travellers meet, on their return, the artist who is still walking up and down the same old ash-path in the back garden, and has probably been doing so ever since they left, they find he has, in spite of this, had most wonderful adventures. There are not many of us who have not experienced the fascination of Stevenson's *Treasure Island*. . . . Well to me, a person gives me the same feelings of adventure as a place. When I contemplate what the time of one whole day may reveal to me, I am filled with the romance of adventure. I am *Treasure Island*. . . . The most unexpected thing I ever came across was myself.'

To lessen the emotional trend in their correspondence he would exchange views on art with Hilda, as in his letter of 2 November: 'What you said about light was very clearly explained, though I think you made the discovery in the painting of the nude at the Slade, . . . about which I remember saying to someone that it was a spiritual portrait of light.' Nevertheless, he invariably gravitated back to himself. On 10 November, he wrote her: 'What I have discovered about Henry is that he and I see clearly one thing which is essential to both of us. As soon as his wits begin to dance, mine unconsciously do the same. . . . Of course, I love myself more than anybody . . . I collect "Stanley Spencers" just as George[8] collects stamps. . . . I don't like to feel that I stop, and that there is no more me beyond that 25 inches—army regulations space—of earth that I occupy. . . . There are times when I feel "Good Lord, I could o'er stride the world like a colossus". I love myself in much the same way as a baby loves a tin soldier. . . . It is this that shows me what something else is like.'

He had begun his *Betrayal* earlier in the summer of 1922, visualising the scene at the back of Fernlea, a gap separating the schoolroom, with its corrugated-iron roof, from the orchard wall, where there was the rubbish heap. This provided the 'place feeling' so essential to his compositions. The idea was inspired by a sentence in the Bible: 'They went away backward and fell to the ground.'

Emulating the Florentine Masters, he planned to paint 'predellas' to hang below the main picture, explaining his concept to the Ruskin students in November 1922: 'It is rather interesting to think of pictures in the way musicians think of music. The early Italians would sometimes do a series of pictures related one to the other. . . . You have people . . . who are interested in having pictures that go together, but that is not quite what I mean. I mean the dramatic integral relation, such as one has in a sonata in music, between the first, second and third movements, in relation to painting each movement being a picture. . . . A Predella is rather like a Prelude to a fugue in music, or a prelude and codetta with a fugue in between. I feel there is a fine architectural element in this.'

His indecisive state of mind in respect of Hilda hampered progress and in December 1922, he resolved to return to Hampstead again, bringing his unfinished *Betrayal* with him, her attraction for him proving irresistible. He hoped to use Henry's studio for painting. As he explained to him (20 December), writing from 47 Downshire Hill: 'I have done no solid work since my return from "foreign parts", having been so busy "Oh, Hildering" and "Ah, Hildering", and shifting my lodging and giving lectures at Sydney's school. Your studio inspires me to great efforts, and I want to have a good long spell with the picture I am doing [the *Betrayal*].' He had declined Henry's invitation to join him for Christmas in Poole. 'I must get on with my *Betrayal*', he told him and on 7 January 1923, he reported: 'I am going on very slowly with the picture, . . . but instead of looking like night, as I hoped it would, it looks like a picture painted very low in tone.'

Soon after arrival in Downshire Hill, he explained to Henry his delight at being there; 'I am at Mrs Carline's now, and it is as good as a resurrection. I know they could do things perfectly in Petersfield, lavish with good taste, huge copious knowledge of folk-lore, knew all the *real* names of wild flowers (names I had never heard of and never wanted to) and with a "hey derry dum do" and to bloody hell with them all.

'I could stick it all but the "hey derry" and that did for me. What I noticed was that in spite of the tastefully arranged vase—a simple old pot, a beer pot that had some good old rollicking British legend all round it—standing on the good old oak table—real carved oak, none of your shams—in spite of the fact that it might have been sprigs of may or lilac, in spite of all this, it would give me not the least degree of pleasure. It was "pseudo" everything.

'But here! I can't explain what it is, but just to look at those tall long windowed red buildings at the bottom of the garden or to make honourable mention of Mr Carline's three pictures⁹ in the dining-room, gives me just the very kind of "grace" of this life, that is so hard to find.' He wrote to Henry again in the New Year, 1923: 'I am just beginning to enjoy my big picture, after much sore travail and labour among the walnut leaves and the corrugated iron, and now I am just doing the stinging nettles against the falling into them of the High Priests.' By 10 March, he was able to tell him that it was finished:¹⁰ 'I am not displeased with it, but it is not one of my best.'

In January 1923, Stanley had joined me in attending the Slade School for the Easter term, drawing during two days a week. Tonks welcomed him. 'I am having a grand time at the Slade', he told Henry (letter from 47 Downshire Hill undated). 'It's like being sat on a cloud and floated through the sky twice a week. I love the journey down on top of a bus and the journey back better, as you can see into the upstairs rooms. I like having these feelings of curiosity again.'

Stanley's relationship with Hilda remained unsettled. Their engagement was sometimes on and sometimes off. He had told Henry earlier (20 December): 'Hilda and I are not affianced, . . . but every fortnight we *nearly* are.' But on 7 January 1923, he asked Henry whether he might live in the studio, instead of merely painting there while living in Downshire Hill: 'I have at last definitely finished the affair with Hilda', he told Henry. 'I have allowed it to drag on too long as it is. I hate the idea of leaving her and the Carlines as I am very happy there. . . . Hilda quite agrees and the others, though they regret it, realise it is the only way. Oh dear! I do feel miserable. I shall be so lonely and unhappy without Hilda.' Nevertheless, he was writing to Henry again a few days later (undated): 'I have not left 47 after all, as there seems to me no immediate necessity. I hate doing drastic things, and everything seems to be cooling off nicely.'

Stanley and Hilda respected one another's sincerity, but both could be stubborn. A mere statement of opinion did not suffice; each demanded complete agreement. Sometimes, his mood softened, as when he wrote to her from Poole in August 1923: 'There might be lots of things I don't agree with you about, but it matters not what you say; there is always that living quality in it and so it always does me good.' Sometimes, he realised that he had pushed her too hard as when she had told him that she was trying to see things with his eyes: 'I just wonder whether you ought to try to be like me. I don't want you to be.' He modified this in another letter: 'I feel a little bit of me in your work would improve you, just as a bit of you in my work would greatly improve mine.' Her style in painting did change nearer his without her realising it nor he wishing it.

Their views on art differed fundamentally, being derived from quite different sources. She was instinctively sympathetic to the new ideas from Paris, which he could only oppose, finding: 'A rebellious aggressiveness, an absence of peace and an utter lack of spiritual grace. . . . I do not like the Renoir atmosphere.'[11]

It was religious views that mainly divided them. Hilda was hostile to orthodox doctrine, She believed that Christian Science expounded the truth. From the wealth of correspondence, one can only pick out a few characteristic assertions to reveal Stanley's ever-changing attitude, as in one of his many letters from Poole in 1923: 'Deep down, I don't trust your religious convictions one bit, but I am so eager to make my thoughts harmonise with yours that I prostitute them, . . . so that a deep and terrible feeling of guilt comes over me . . . I hope I am not Judas, but it looks very much as if I am.' In another letter Stanley accused her of 'ringing up God' to ask whether his (Stanley's) views were acceptable: 'Your telling me to throw myself over this spiritual precipice is very nearly like Satan telling Christ to throw himself off the pinnacle of the Temple.'

Stanley was for a while persuaded by her views, writing her in 1924, when she was at Wangford: 'It is quite uncanny the light that you ... and Christian Science throw on everything I think and look at ... which is what I have often longed for.' He even accompanied her to Christian Science services, sometimes attending them on his own, but neither of them ever sought membership of this or any religious sect. Having been lent a book on Catholicism, however, and feeling in antagonistic mood, he retracted, telling her (12 December 1924) that if he had to choose one or the other, it would be Catholicism, and he knew he would wound her in writing (2 December 1924): 'I doubt very much if God is as vital to me as Shakespeare or Beethoven.' And in a very acid frame of mind, he was prepared to contradict what he had always professed in telling her that he doubted whether God even existed.

Despite all these disagreements, Hilda exercised a spell over him, which persisted all his life, even surviving the bitterness of divorce, typified by the confession in his letter to her from Poole of 18 July 1923: 'No one, no matter how much better they may understand me, can provide me with the atmosphere you provide or give me the power to live.'

Stanley usually fetched Hilda for long walks on Hampstead Heath, but in the evenings at Downshire Hill, she was only one of many. Stanley was at the centre of discussion at the dinner-table or round the fire in drawing-room or studio. Jas Wood, his taxi waiting an hour or more, was Stanley's rival in discussion, the gathering usually including Hartley, David John, sometimes his brother Edwin,[12] Mark Gertler and others, with Henry Lamb and Gilbert when in Hampstead.

Stanley was to the fore when we had charades and even attended the fancy-dress dances in the studio, though he did not dance. He seemed able to detach his painting from social activities, though these must have distracted him from his work.

Kate Foster, a fellow student of mine at the Slade and frequent visitor, has given in her diary a revealing impression of our life in Hampstead at this time. Her entry for 1 July 1922 recorded her first meeting the Spencers: 'They are perfectly gorgeous kind of hatless "farmers' boys", with red cheeks, blue eyes and thick long black hair, . . . who suddenly come out with clever remarks about Bach . . . Stanley Spencer ought to be on the "movies"; he has such an expressive face.

'We go back to the Carlines for dinner. Professor Gardner comes in with his two daughters—two learned "Grecian" ladies.[13] The combination of incongruous characters is almost too much. The Spencers do a very Biblical charade with Hilda as the angel.' For 20 December 1922, her diary reads: 'To Hampstead at 11 a.m. to pose for Dick, the studio rather cold . . . A large party for lunch [at 47], including both Spencers . . . At tea in the studio, Stanley cuts three slices of "lady-like" bread and butter for me. Jas Wood insists on taking us all to Gaudin's [Soho] for dinner . . .—quails, wine etc., then a taxi to the Philharmonic Hall where we see a film of the Tibetan devil-dance.'

For 6 January 1923, her diary runs: 'Stanley reads Spenser's *Faerie Queene* at lunch—the end of the slaying of the dragon: "So down he fell", with its three repetitions. A dissertation upon the diabolical nature of cats with Stanley quoting King Lear: "Purr, the cat is grey." ' And on 2 January: 'Tea in the studio and then to supper. A friend of Stanley and the Carlines, Sturge-Moore, comes in, bearded and apostolic[14] . . .—we are looking at a Raphael portfolio. Stanley had quoted earlier Max Beerbohm's description of Moore as a "sheep in sheep's clothing" and had given an imitation of his reading the *Forsaken Merman*.' Again on 17 February: 'A huge party in the evening. Besides the family and Stanley, there were Hartley, Jas Wood, together with Ethelbert White[15] and wife—he in corduroys and she in black velvet with red neckercher and straight bobbed hair . . . Charles Ginner[16] there—a dear old man, something between a tabby-cat and a retired stock-broker. He talks hardly at all, but if he catches you looking at him, he smiles as if he understood everything.'

Henry Lamb had brought Macnamara, and a diary entry by Kate in July records him and 'Bobby' (Kathleen) Hale[17] 'talking about Nietzsche over supper in the garden, and David John there'. Visitors also included Dorothy Brett, Mark Gertler's friend, when we had drawing from a model, and Slade friends included Marjorie Hodgkinson, who met Mark Gertler there, subsequently marrying him, Mary Adshead, later marrying Stephen Bone, Catharine Alexander and Noel Carrington. Stanley got to know them all intimately. At the fancy-dress parties, Ethelbert White would play the guitar while Betty, his wife, danced with castanets, and guests whom Stanley knew or met included the Rushburys,[18] Randolph Schwabe, who later succeeded Tonks at the Slade, Ivon Hitchens, Leon Underwood, the sculptor, Julia, Dick and John Strachey and Bobby Bevan. Others whom he met, a little later, included Rodney and Dorothy Burn, Tom Monnington[19], Robert Medley and Helen Taylor (later Mrs Moggeridge), all of whom had been leading students at the Slade in the 1920s. With this social life, Stanley acquired a large circle of friends.

Stanley renewed his intention of leaving both Hampstead and Hilda in April 1923, when Henry repeated his invitation to stay with him at Poole. Henry had acquired his house at 10 Hill Street in February of the previous year, while retaining his Hampstead studio. I was staying with Henry for a few days in April 1923, when Stanley wrote him: 'I came to the conclusion that I must clear out of 47 and I told Mrs Carline so, and she agreed. So I packed up everything and now I am wondering where I can live.' He went to Poole after Easter, his engagement to Hilda again broken off.

He could not, however, detach himself from her so easily, writing soon after arriving in Poole: 'I am happier when I am angry with you than I am pleased with someone else.' And a little later, he ended: 'As soon as I finish this letter to you, I am going to begin another. I would love to go on doing this forever.' This was a true forecast, since he continued writing her despite the breaking of their engagement, without intermission, often devoting an entire morning to these letters. Nevertheless, they did not meet again for six months.

Notes to Chapter 9

1. *Italian Peasant Women Carrying Canoper*, painted at Lake Orta in 1920.
2. Perhaps painted at the same time as his *Two Girls and a Beehive*, 1910.
3. Wrongly dated by Maurice Collis (op. cit.) as taking place 'early in 1921'.
4. Recorded by Kate Foster in her diary.
5. The headmaster of Bedales School, J. H. Badley, recorded in *Memories and Reflections* that Bone proposed Stanley painting a twenty foot square mural for the end wall of the school dining hall, to make Bedales 'a Mecca of artistic

pilgrimage'. Badley adds that he did not 'admire' Spencer's 'large figure pieces', and had little wish to live, or to compel others to live, in the perpetual presence of one of these on a still larger scale', and therefore made the condition 'that it should be on canvas that would be removable if we found it too overpowering'. The project was not proceeded with.

6. A letter to Henry of 26 May 1922 records that he had just sent it to be framed before showing it at the New English Art Club. The date '1921' given by Wilensky (op. cit.) and Newton (op. cit.) and by Elizabeth Rothenstein (op. cit.) was when the picture was begun. 1922 is the date when it was finished. Stanley, himself, in a list of his pictures, made in Glasgow in 1941, dated it in 1922.

7. The party included, besides Stanley and myself, our mother, brothers George and Sydney, Hilda, a cousin, May Piggott, and an Oxford friend, Dr Hume-Rothery.

8. George R. Carline, our eldest brother, anthropologist and Keeper of Bankfield Museum, Halifax, died in December 1932.

9. My father, George F. Carline, R.B.A., painter and illustrator. The three oils referred to, *The Swing at Hampton Court, The Summer Cloud, The Red Parasol*, (now in the Tate Gallery) had been exhibited at the Royal Academy in the 1890s.

10. The year '1922' given by Wilensky (op. cit.), Newton (op. cit.) and by Elizabeth Rothenstein (op. cit.) is correct only for the commencement of the painting, not its completion. Stanley himself, in a list of his pictures made in Glasgow in 1941, dated it in 1923.

11. The interesting suggestion has recently been made that Gauguin had some influence on Stanley's early work. Nevertheless, Gauguin is never mentioned in Stanley's correspondence; nor did he possess any reproductions of Gauguin's paintings.

12. A characteristic letter to me from Henry reads: 'I ask if Edwin John may be admitted to the "Cercle Pan-Artistique" of Downshire Hill. He is working at the R.A. Schools and seems in need of the corrective stimulants he is likely to get in the above mentioned society.'

13. Ernest Gardner, Professor of Greek Archaeology and Vice-Chancellor, London University; his elder daughter, Phyllis, had studied at the Slade with Sydney and Stanley. Our two families were close friends.

14. Sturge-Moore, poet and wood-engraver lived in Hampstead, where we, with Stanley, often enjoyed his poetry readings. Stanley in his entertaining commentaries was 'sometimes savagely waspish', as Kate described him.

15. Ethelbert White, member of the New English Art Club and London Group, lived in the Grove, Hampstead.

16. Charles Ginner, painter, founder-member of the Camden Town Group (subsequently London Group) lived in High Street, Hampstead.

17. Kathleen Hale, painter as well as author and illustrator of *Orlando the Marmalade Cat* series of picture books.

18. Sir Henry Rushbury became Keeper of the Royal Academy.

19. As Sir Thomas Monnington, he became President of the Royal Academy.

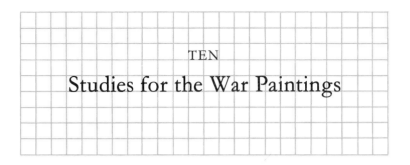

TEN
Studies for the War Paintings

S INCE COMPLETING his *Travoys* in 1919, Stanley had not painted any of the scenes that had moved him so deeply during the War, though he had drawn some sketches for future use. Other ideas had taken precedence. But his intention to paint an epic of his war experiences lay at the back of his mind, and the opportunity to develop this came his way in Poole.

I received a letter from Henry Lamb dated 10 June 1923, telling me that 'Stanley sits at a table all day evolving acres of Salonica and Bristol war compositions.'[1] Henry's house was in a terrace, having a long room with windows at front and back. The rear half contained a large circular table,[2] on which Stanley drew, while the front half contained the all-important piano.

Stanley conveyed his preliminary concept of the scheme in a letter to Hilda on 31 May 1923, though most of the subjects envisaged were never painted: 'Since I have been here, I have hardly been out at all; I have been so much moved by a scheme of war pictures that I have been making compositions for, that all my time here has been on this. I have drawn a whole architectural scheme of the pictures (Plates 25 and 26).

'The end wall is to be a tall circular topped picture of that idea I told you about—the resurrection of soldiers in Salonica. This idea, as far as what it appears like, is at present the vaguest, and yet it will, I know, be the best. The frame round this picture is broad and is composed of, on either side, four pictures, quite small, of incidents occurring outside tent doors . . . [a sketch], a man lacing up a tent door for the night, a man pinning his handkerchief on the tent to dry. There will be one of men having their rations brought to the tent door, which happened on a rainy day; all the men in the

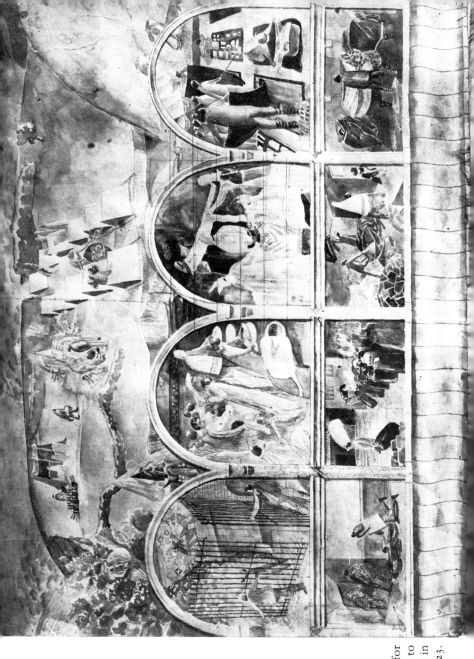

25. Working drawing for
the left-hand side wall to
be carried out in
Burghclere Chapel, 1923.

26. Working drawing for
the right-hand side wall
to be carried out in
Burghclere Chapel, 1923.

tent are handing out their mess-tins to the "orderly buff", who is outside with the "dixy". It will be just a tent door with a lot of arms thrust out of it, holding mess-tins, and a man crouched down on the ground outside.

'Another will be "lights out"—a man tapping the tent with a stick. Another will be two men with long poles, and brushes on the end of them, daubing brown mud over the tent; this tent will be piebald. The three remaining ones are rather vague; one is with the "brailing" of the tent up and the door wide open, and a row of men sitting outside on their blankets and kits. Another will be men walking round the tent and hammering the pegs in. And another will be a closed-up tent with no figures at all.

'The circular frame-work of the top part of the picture is a series of "fire bays" in trenches. It is just one long line of trench, rather like this [a sketch] with men coming to life in them. This also is only a vague notion. But the idea, to me, is full of possibilities, and it has an architectural meaning also. . . .

'There are the two ideas that I actually thought of in Salonika. One is rather nice; there was a sergeant of the Berks named Challenger, who always reclined on the top of the parapet, when heavy shelling was going on (in the night of course), while we stood trembling in the trench. When the shell burst, the light of the shell lit him up in a ghostly way, and made him appear like a kind of angel, . . . [a sketch]. But the most complete of this scheme are the two side walls of this "Castle in Spain". I will tell you about these another time. I would like to, if you would care to hear, as it always helps me to make them clear.'

In a lecture given later to the Ruskin Drawing School students, autumn 1923,[3] he outlined some of the motives that underlay this project: 'The thing which interests me and has always done is the way that ordinary experiences or happenings in life are continually developing and bringing to light all sorts of artistic discoveries. There seems to me nothing that ever happens to me where I would have to say to myself: "This has got nothing to do with art."

'In a few months time, I hope to embark on painting a scheme of pictures where I did all sorts of things. In this scheme there is a picture of myself scrubbing a floor in a bathroom in a hospital (Plate 34). First of all, I was satisfied that these things had to be done and that it was right I should do them. . . . Therefore there must be some sort of meaning in all this kind of thing . . . I began to feel there was a great deal of order in domestic doings. . . . When I scrubbed floors, I would have all sorts of marvellous thoughts, so much so that at last, when I was fully equipped for scrubbing — bucket, apron and "prayer" mat in hand — I used to feel much the same as if I was going to church. . . . My life in that place became infinitely less boring. I could feel that the order or work for the day was very much like the order in which a sonata is arranged; it had only to be looked at imaginatively.

'In this scheme there are many pictures of very ordinary moments in the kind of life I was living at the time. It gives me a feeling of delight when I think of doing a painting just of "arriving" (a convoy . . .), and another of ablutions, and another of scrubbing, and another of sorting . . . (Plate 33) All these activities will reveal in each of these pictures a kind of spiritual meaning.'

Stanley's preoccupation with this project did not prevent his enjoyment of social activities that came his way. He described such events to Hilda in June 1923: 'Since last Friday, I have been up at John's [Augustus and Dorelia], doing nothing, but just wandering about aimlessly. On Saturday we went down to the sea and bathed; it was very cold. . . . I rather like Bournemouth, but I hate Poole. I sent three paintings to a Bournemouth Municipal Art School exhibition (I was requested to send), and Mrs John bought one of them — the painting (oil on paper) of men carrying punt cushions, the one of Slessers going on the river at Bourne End and all the punt slats on the grass.

'I slept in the garden at John's. . . . It made me feel I would like to live the life of a cat. It is rather wonderful one night to sleep near an ilex tree and the next night near a stream, and the next near a dustbin and so on. You choose a new architecture and wall-paper for your bedroom each night, so to speak.

'Just now, that mysterious Colonel Lawrence, the uncrowned "king" of the Hejaz, arrived on his motor-bike. He came this time to see what I was doing; Henry is away, painting duchesses. . . . He [Lawrence] has joined the Tank Corps as a private soldier, simply because he does not know what to do with himself. He looks just like what he now is — a private in the Tank Corps. He seems to be very worried and puzzled about life in general . . . As Henry was away, he and I were able to have a heart to heart talk about God and all the things I like to talk about. He is rather miserable and gets bullied by the N.C.O.s. Of course, they do not know who he is and he wants it kept secret. It was very pathetic the way he said: "I have been like this a year now, and simply don't know what to do with myself, and there doesn't seem to be any sign of my finding anything I would specially like to do. All I do is to dash along country roads at sixty miles an hour, and for no earthly reason." He can't rest, and it was so exactly what I feel myself sometimes.

'He seemed to be appealing to me to think of something for him to do. He liked very much my scheme of war pictures and thought a job of that kind was certain to turn up for me. This aimlessness in Lawrence is not a pose. I think it is the loneliness of being unable to love, through absence of religion. He hates the thought of women.'⁴

Another letter to Hilda of 8 July followed: 'It is stifling hot just now. Henry and I have just been out again in a boat and had a bathe like we did when Sydney [Carline] was here. I liked seeing him again. He has a great capacity for enjoying life, so long as he is given a chance to do it in the way he likes to, and is not interfered with. . . .

'When we were out with Sydney, we saw some cows in the sea, just like they stand about in the river. You see I was able to feel something that I was familiar with . . . They made me feel on homely and friendly terms. . . . I always think the most thrilling and vivid moment of a long sea voyage is just the getting on the boat. I had this feeling when I left England for Salonika, not knowing where I was going.'

In July 1923, we decided to travel to the Pyrenees and Andorra, the party consisting of our family together with Kate Foster, Stanley was reluctant to break off his work on the war studies and wrote to Hilda on 19 July: 'I shall miss not coming this time with you. I feel sure that without me, Mrs Carline will lose her little leather bag and then find she has got it in her hand all the time.' Having completed his preliminary designs for the murals by midsummer (Plates 25 and 26), his letter to Hilda continued: 'I have pinned them on the wall; Sydney saw them when he came and liked them, I think. Henry likes them; so does John [Augustus] . . . . Behrends have just been and they greatly admired the war designs. Louie Behrend (Plate 28) thought it was the best thing I had ever done.'⁵

28. *Louis Behrend*, Burghclere, *c.* 1928.

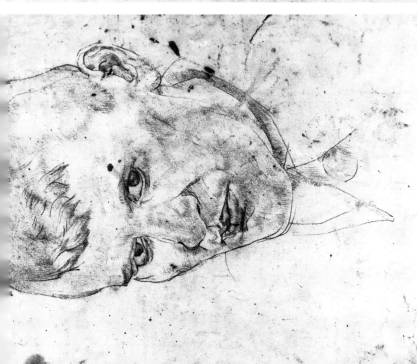

27. *The Orderly* drawn at Tweseldown Camp, 1916.

He had drawn a design of the complete scheme showing how he wanted the pictures to appear on the walls, but leaving the arched area of the end wall blank, not having devised a composition that satisfied him. Many of the pictures would be changed or abandoned ultimately, but ten or so were to be retained in the final painting. He discussed the launching of the project with Henry, who made the suggestion, as Stanley reported to Hilda in July, 'to get up a subscription for the purpose of having a place built for them. . . . The people I have thought of asking to subscribe are Louie Behrend, Harry Slesser, Mrs Harrison,[6] Sadler, Bone, Leverton Harris, [Augustus] John (he was very keen on their being done), Raverat, Rothenstein, Eddie Marsh, Hutchinson,[7] Lord Henry Bentinck, Lady Ottoline. . . . The idea is that Kennedy[8] should erect the building—by far the most expensive item—to fit my pictures. . . . I am in no hurry over this scheme, although all the ideas are complete (there are thirty pictures) except the biggest one.' These suggested subscribers were, in fact, his principal patrons or friends.

With the fate of the war compositions undecided, Stanley was, unusually for him, without definite plans: 'I feel rather flat', he wrote to Hilda in the same letter, 'as I generally do feel in midsummer. . . . I wish I was doing a big 'pic' [picture], but I seem to have nothing I consider good enough, and so I am doing a self-portrait, which will not be any good, I am afraid, as I have my head in such a position as hardly to be able to see what I am painting.'

He returned to Henry's studio in Hampstead in August for a short stay, and was overjoyed to receive news from him (16 September 1923) that the Behrends were so impressed by his war studies that they wanted them carried out and had sent a builder's plan. Stanley replied to Henry promptly: 'I did not expect quite such glorious news. . . . The general proportion of the building seems perfect; the window seems a bit "artist's studio-fied" but it is most sensibly placed. I would like the door to be carved eventually. . . . I must say this news you have sent has put a bit of ginger into me.' He proposed a meeting with Mrs Behrend with Henry present to discuss 'judicious alterations' etc., adding: 'I have decided they must be done in fresco.'

He had to share this good news with Hilda (undated but posted in September): 'Even supposing they did not give me the job, I should still hope to do this idea, as it becomes more and more a definite thing to me, living by itself.

'I would like to explain what was at the back of my mind when I began to want to do these pictures. Well, when I first enlisted, . . . after about three weeks, I began to feel . . . I was dying of starvation, spiritual starvation, and this feeling intensified my desire for spiritual life. "I must find it. Where is it? I used to find it in painting pictures. Where is it now?"

'And then suddenly I began to see and catch hold of little particles of this life in the scrubbing of a floor or the making of a bed and so, gradually, everything began to reveal to me. Everything I did meant a spiritual revelation to me. Everything I had to do became a key to my conception of spiritual life. Just cutting up bread and butter in the kitchen in the ward revealed to me as much of the spiritual life I longed to attain to, as if I had sat down and had half an hour's talk with God.

'I felt with everything I did an inspiration to do it. Of course, I was often depressed. . . . And so it came about, at last, that tea-urns, bathrooms, beds etc. all became sort of symbols of my spiritual thoughts until at last I felt I could reveal the whole progress of my soul by stating clearly these impressions of my surroundings. . . . So at last things became sacred to me by association, . . . had a relation of difference just as the movements in a sonata have to each other and I began to be observant . . . of these differences. . . .

'During the War I lived not as an artist but as a quickening spirit. My great moments so to speak were not when I had an idea for a picture but just any moment. . . . I remember one night arriving on the Doiran sector. . . . It was near Christmas time and everything felt "Christmassy", and all was muffled in the silence of snow. It was not snowing, but the snow covered the ground and the mountains in the dark northern recesses of Macedonia. On these mountains, . . . the snow which capped them had the appearance of huge white ferns hanging upside down.

'It was while I was plodding along behind a mule in the dark towards our transport lines which were at the foot of one of these mountains—I had a loaf of bread tucked under my arm—that I suddenly had a feeling of the completeness and fitness and ultimate perfection and redemption of everything, that everything was really becoming more and more perfect. And this realisation . . . so inspired me that I felt that having seen this, I could "depart in peace" as Zacharias did. And for one brief moment in my life, I felt what a beautiful thing it was to feel unselfish. Oh, how I wish I could have retained that moment. I felt then that I could see so clearly that nothing I might have to do could destroy or take away from me that spiritual vision. This is the selfishness that I guard against, the selfishness that is the result of fear—fear that unless you are careful, you will lose that vision. But the beauty is that if this vision is clear, you never care whether you or anyone else lose it or find it; the mere fact of its existence is sufficient. If I could only live in that state and keep my mind continually on that perfection, which I can see but which I sometimes turn away from, I could do anything, because I should be free from the chains of selfishness. . . .

'As I walked along towards this place in the snow, I felt I was a walking altar of praise. And that night I slept with a blanket over me in a shelter, which was open in front so that my feet touched the snow, and in front of me the snow stretched right down to the reedy bank of Lake Ardzan. I believe you really feel with me over these thoughts, . . . because pure imagination can only be attained by unselfishness, as it is the clear understanding and most perfect love of beauty.'

A further letter to Hilda followed immediately: 'Hilda, just think! A plan of the building, sent from the builder they are going to employ, and he is going to make specially damp-proof floors and walls.

'Nothing is certain yet, and I am going tomorrow or Saturday to see them and to "inspect" the land that the place is going to be built on. It is not going to be big. The measurements are 24 ft × 14 ft, height of walls 15 ft. I can have it a bit bigger if I like. . . .

'What makes me feel happy about this job is that now that I have this to do, I shall now be quite happy to paint landscapes and portraits and everything. It makes me feel so jolly when I think that just a few spiritual thoughts I had recently are now going to give employment to some brick-layers. I love to feel that they are taking part in the making of a beautiful thing.

'Of course, they will be done in fresco. When I have done this job, I shall feel more at peace. . . . I would love to do several portraits of you—about six in your different moods and about the same number of you in different dresses. Of course, I think Dick's portrait of you in the *Family Group* is perfect;[9] it is so good that it makes me want the picture, and the portrait of Mrs Carline in that picture is extraordinarily good; he seems to have improved it somehow.

'Why don't you try another "selbst-bildnis" and spend less time over it than you did over your other one.[10] I feel you did that one too easily, too "lacadaysically". It all went to sleep, except the necklace of amber beads, which was lively and crisply painted. One feels you enjoyed doing that. All the planes of those amber stones were so clearly understood, and so definitely and decidedly put down, that it made me wish you could have retained that vigorous and lively vision, when you came to painting the face. . . .

'Of course, I am nearly as great a criminal as you are in this respect. I think this last big picture of mine [the *Betrayal*] rather went to sleep, especially among the stinging nettles; and that was because I went to sleep when I was painting them, and painting in one's sleep is about as dangerous as walking in one's sleep.'

On returning to Poole at the end of September, he wrote to Florence: 'I have been here since last Easter, but I prefer Hampstead. When I am up there, I have a feeling of wanting to climb all the lamp-posts. . . .' Referring to his 'recent scheme of war pictures', which the Behrends had seen, he continues:—'These pictures were a sort of Odyssey. . . . They don't look like war pictures; they rather look like Heaven, a place I am becoming very familiar with. There are to be two pictures about 28 feet long and 10 feet high [the side walls]; then there is one about 14 feet square [end wall], and eight pictures with arched tops, each of these will be about 7 feet high [side walls]; then there are eight "predella" pictures below the arched pictures, and eight little pictures of incidents happening outside the door of a tent, these last to go on either side of steps leading to altar. . . . The whole thing will take, I expect, from two to three years to do. . . . Possibly, if the money is forthcoming, Boris von Anrep[11] will do a faint-coloured stained-glass window and a few mosaic "medallions" in the floor. I would like to design an altar myself and I believe in time I should be able to get what I wanted. I would like it to be bas-reliefed.

'I have decided the proportions of everything, length of building, height of roof, kind of roof, kind of tiles, height of dado and cornice, projection of moulding of arches, size and place of window and door, so that the architect only has to make a builder's drawing from my measurements. The other day I went and inspected the site and I was by myself. It is in a little plot of ground near Highclere Station, near Newbury, and I loved measuring the ground. I felt this is life, this is, and I have fallen into a habit of measuring everything, and every building I enter I want to know the height of the ceiling.'

As the scheme became clearer, problems multiplied, such as whether the building would 'allow one to get far enough away from the big picture on the end wall', he told Hilda (29 September): 'And there are scores of other things, and all the time Mrs Behrend is saying: "You see, Stanley, we want to start building before the frost comes." ' More money might be needed, he felt, and perhaps Sydney could ask his pupil, Mrs Harrison, to solicit the support of her friend Asquith, the former Prime Minister.

The chief obstacle, however, was Stanley's determination to work in fresco, as the Italian Masters had done. He had experimented with this medium in Petersfield, using Vitruvius' recipe, but he needed more information, which Mrs Sargent-Florence, alone, could give. Back in Hampstead, early in October, he had a frame made, so that he could try painting on lime plaster, and wrote to Henry (undated): 'I shall do a bit of fresco painting on the quiet in Sydney's outhouse at the back of his studio [14a Downshire Hill]. I shall tell the Behrends nothing of my fresco studies . . . as it would only bother and worry them.'

We all discussed these plans after our return from abroad in October 1923, causing, incidentally, more delay. He wrote to Henry later that month: 'The Carlines are unanimous in thinking that the building ought to be in Cookham, or Cookham Dean or Hedsor. . . . This would be grand from my point of view, and there are thousands of visitors to Cookham. . . . It would inspire me if the building were in or about Cookham.' A discussion one day with Kennedy produced the proposal that Henry should direct with Kennedy and Stanley, leaving the Behrends to provide the finance with possible contributions from others. As regards

29. *Richard Carline*, oil, Hampstead, 1923. Rugby Art Gallery. 30. *Stanley Spencer*, oil by Richard Carline, Hampstead, 1924.

design, Kennedy had suggested a 'narthex' like the outer porch in Byzantine churches. 'There have been many conflicting opinions going on in my mind,' he wrote to Henry at the end of October, 'owing largely to some things called "Dick's contentions", which are that my own ideas about the building are the best; that it ought to be plain outside, just like a box, and that there ought to be no . . . . architectural ornament or features outside whatever. He said that the Padua [Arena] Chapel was just a plain block sticking straight out of the ground. . . . I think there is a lot in "Dick's contention" that I should stick to my original idea, excepting that a sympathetic architect, such as Kennedy, helps one to realise one's own ideas, as I feel he has in the 'narthex' idea. First, I always like seeing one building peering over the top of another, which I felt when I did the "Cowl" picture. It makes the main part of the building somehow a little removed from its immediate surroundings.' If adopted, he proceeds, this would change the lighting: 'I love clerestorys so much that I want Kennedy to architect the whole of that end of the building before I consider frescoing it, though I have the things I want to do there ready. Then again, inside, you get a feeling of being more detached from the outer world, which is exactly what I want.' Kennedy's idea of little windows 'coming through the arched frescoes' appealed to Stanley, though fearing lest the arches might be reduced in importance, and he continues: 'Whereas, . . . these arched pictures are really the important things and the long ones [above them] just a vague surrounding.' He hoped the walls might be thick 'as it is always more restful to look out of a window through a thick wall'. He would like the entrance to be at one side 'a secret unobtrusive door'. Finally, he hoped, that 'Kennedy and David [John] could do it half in half', as architects. In the end, none of these proposals were adopted, nor his wish, as he explained, to paint a series of 'domestic incidents occurring between myself and Louie' while working on the scheme. His letter to Henry proceeds: 'I thought of a subject last night when I was telling Kennedy how delighted they (the Behrends) seemed. He said: "Did Mary clap her hands?" A picture of the "clapping hands incident" could be made into something tremendous.'

Meanwhile, a further problem occurred to him: 'The first question . . .', he told Henry in the same letter, 'is: "What is it for?

What purpose will it serve, and where is it to be built?" Well, I have come to the conclusion that it is obviously intended for a memorial hall or chapel to be attached to some hospital; it need not necessarily be a military one. . . . It would help to ennoble and reveal the sublimity of medical services.'

Meanwhile, as he told Hilda (29 September), he was making 'drawings from life for the war compositions' and 'full-sized cartoons in pencil and sepia'. (Plate 36.)

Stanley felt some apprehension, very naturally, as to whether the Behrends would react favourably to these new ideas, and he sought support from Muirhead Bone and Eddie Marsh. Mrs Harrison brought Asquith who 'seemed very struck with the "war decorations" '. All these reconsiderations delayed the immediate commencement of building, and no final decisions regarding the design were reached by the end of 1923, as Mary Behrend had hoped.

Notes to Chapter 10

1. The date '1922' is given for the war studies in the pamphlet published by the National Trust, who now own Burghclere Chapel. This date is based, I understand, on a statement made by Louis Behrend (Plate 28), shortly before he died. It is, very naturally, repeated by his son George in *Stanley Spencer at Burghclere*, 1965, and by Gilbert Spencer in *Stanley Spencer*, 1961. On the other hand, Wilensky (op. cit.), whose book was published very soon after the event, i.e. in 1924, and under Stanley Spencer's scrutiny, includes a reproduction (Plate 35), of the preliminary sketch for the chapel compositions as they were to appear on the walls, with the date 1923. One cannot wholly rely on anyone's accuracy of memory after forty years had elapsed. The confusion is added to, however, by Stanley himself, writing notes (10 October 1959) from his sick-bed, a few weeks before he died. In one paragraph, he states: 'At this time (about 1923–24) I was doing the Burghclere drawings', but in a later paragraph he writes of 'a pencil and wash drawing which I did for this Chapel in 1922'. This probably refers to the one planned for Steep Village Hall (Plate 8). Here again, after forty years and being very ill might account for any confusion.

The written evidence at the time, which is quoted here, shows that he was living at Petersfield and working on major compositions throughout 1922, apart from frequent visits to us in Hampstead, during the spring and early summer, with three months then spent in the Balkans. There was no opportunity for him to make any stay in Poole, sufficiently prolonged to carry out these drawings and there is no evidence of his having visited Poole in

1922. Moreover Henry was in Ireland for much of the summer. But chiefly, the making of these war studies is not mentioned in any of his letters until 1923, when he writes of them as an entirely new project which was occupying his mind and time. Later, in the thirties he wrote in red ink in a notebook: '1923, the Chapel compositions.' Altogether the evidence for 1923 as the year when he began the project of a series of war compositions seems overwhelming.

2. Henry Lamb's oil painting of the breakfast party seated round this table, includes Stanley and himself with Leverton Harris, M.P., whom we had met when he was studying at the Slade School from 1922.

3. He sent me the draft in 1929.

4. Stanley describes in this letter seeing two swans fighting, which he tried to separate while other people just looked on. A decade later, he painted a composition called *Fighting Swans*.

5. The above statement indicates that the Behrends were seeing them for the first time.

6. Mrs Harrison, a student of the Ruskin Drawing School.

7. Geoffrey Hutchinson, K.C., M.P. (subsequently Lord Ilford) lived in Keats Grove, Hampstead. Janet, his wife, was a frequent visitor at Downshire Hill.

8. George Kennedy, architect, and close friend of Henry Lamb, was the subject of Lamb's picture *The Kennedy Family*.

9. This large *Family Group* round the dinner-table at 47 Downshire Hill, painted by myself in 1923 was exhibited at the Whitechapel Art Gallery, bought by Eddie Marsh for the Contemporary Art Society, then housed at the Tate and lost in the flood there in 1924.

10. Now in the Tate Gallery.

11. Anrep, close friend of Henry Lamb, well known for his mosaics.

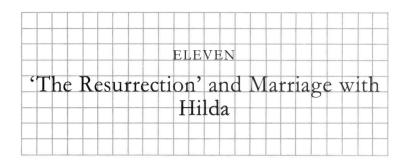

ELEVEN

'The Resurrection' and Marriage with Hilda

STANLEY HAD ALWAYS at the back of his mind his varying concepts of *The Resurrection* (Plate 32). Visualising it in Cookham Churchyard, it became uppermost in his thoughts, now that his war compositions had to remain temporarily in abeyance. Back in Poole in September 1923, he made a sepia wash drawing for *The Resurrection*, feeling that he must tackle a large painting while waiting for the war project to reach a solution. He wrote to Hilda about this new idea on 1 October 1923: 'I am puzzled as to how to paint this big picture in oils, which will take me years to do and at the same time be studying fresco . . . and doing cartoons and, Heaven knows, how many studies for the War pictures. The actual frescos ought not to take very long. They are quite different to my big pictures; they are very simple and the painting of them will have to be very systematic and ordered, whereas in the Resurrection picture, oh, I just want to browse on this thing until my last day. I want specially to do *The Resurrection* in oils as the painting is to be thick and solid like my Apple Picture and it is to be all sort of gold and full of sunlight. Oh, I dream about this. Do you remember my telling you about it one day in Sydney's studio? It is really a completion of that ancient resurrection idea I showed you in Henry's studio. . . . If I get the colour in this picture cold, as is usually my fault, . . . it will be fatal as the whole point of this picture will be the warm sunshine, an effect I have never yet attempted to paint. I shall make some studies in oil just of the sunlit limestone wall of Cookham Church and of the old grave-stones with the lichen growing on them.'

He expanded this concept of light in a letter to Hilda (undated) in the autumn of 1924: 'My way of thinking of light would be so integral with the whole concept of an idea (the same with form and everything else) that it would be arbitrary to separate it out . . . As one cannot see a planet when it is very near the sun, so the light idea can't be readily seen because it is so near the main idea and inspiration. I think of light as being the holy presence, the substance of God, so that everything is in and part of that substance. . . . I think all shapes and forms so love the fact of light that . . . in this way light influences and suggests to form what shape it should be. . . . I think my big "pic" is full of it. . . . All the varying forms in my "pic" make a most comfortable chair for light. . . . I think perhaps I am benefiting from these ideas you have expressed to me about light.'

The painting was to be much larger than any he had as yet attempted. Size and proportion were important to him, explaining to Hilda in 1923 (undated): 'With me, proportion is a spiritual thing, so also size, shape and form.' He greatly resented Hilda's suggestion that size might be merely a convenience, since 'a little unimportant thing can do as much for one as a big picture'. She had liked his little painting of hyacinths; to which he retorted angrily: 'I did it just to kill time, because I had no big picture to work on. It has nothing the least characteristic of me.'

In contrast to this irate tone, he wrote to her in early autumn 1923, of ideas which he would paint of her 'living perfectly', as he put it: 'Thinking about you and all you mean to me has gradually led me to this desire, which at last is a *real* one, but what has made me so happy that I want to do nothing but shout for joy is this: Right up until only a few days back I was feeling that all my ideas for pictures were dead, as they had no centre. . . . They were no real part of my life, . . . and then I suddenly felt that if I did a picture about you, it would not be just an incident; it would be an actual living part of my life put in the picture.' He embodied these ideas, to some extent, in his *Resurrection* rather than making a separate picture. He never completely relinquished any visual idea, and he revived this conception many years later.

That autumn saw a renewal of Stanley's and Hilda's engagement, and he asked Henry if they could now take over his studio in the Vale of Health, which Stanley had been using: 'I have a sort of "against his parent's consent" feeling about writing to you about this. . . . You know, Henry, I feel very happy.' Hilda and my mother made preparations for the wedding. I recall Hilda standing on the table in the basement to be measured for her wedding dress, a procedure that dismayed Stanley. His doubts revived, and he told my mother that he was morally unfit for marriage, though he would hate to be separated from Hilda. The engagement was broken off for the third time, and he wrote to Henry at the end of November: 'At first I felt, well, I can't be so cruel as to break this off, ... but nevertheless the thing was done. What was most terrible was the fact that I realised in a moment that I had practically destroyed something in her, that by my dithering about, I had muddied and blurred her vision. ... When I decided *not* to marry her, I was immediately tortured with longings to marry her, and that when I had decided to marry her, I began wondering whether I loved her. Well, of these two tortures, the "wondering" was the greater.'

Stanley, however, continued to reside with us in Downshire Hill, as if no change had occurred, and painted in Henry's studio. A typical evening is described in Kate Foster's diary for 11 October 1923, immediately after our return from abroad: 'To supper at Downshire Hill where are assembled all the Carlines, Stanley, Hartley, Fiske Warren[1] (staying for a day or two) and no end of rabbits and blancmanges besides. Stanley is in an aggressive mood, talking of Ibsen and malthouses, frescoes, religion and morality; Hilda half asleep but looking attractive in striped silk, dull yellow and black.'

Stanley did not begin painting *The Resurrection* until February 1924,[2] when it became clear that the project for his war pictures would not be completed for some time to come. Meanwhile, he made preparatory studies for the new picture. I recall posing for him nude for a figure on a tomb and he similarly drew himself. He also made a sketch of me for a stone apostle with hand over my head—he thought this a characteristic gesture—as well as lying on a tombstone back view (Plate 32).

Being nine feet high and eighteen feet long, the canvas stretched nearly the entire length of the studio, facing the window, leaving only a narrow space by which visitors could squeeze their way in. To reach the upper sections, he had to stand on a box placed on his work-table. As with all his compositions, he relied on his final sketch with its grid of lines, which he repeated on the canvas. The

…it as as it more or less is in the picture:—
& this is really all the
time what I had in my
mind:—

But not even this, because this is all I saw

When you look at this last it is quite ob

31. The river-steamer, sketch in ink for top left corner of *The Resurrection*, in a letter to Hilda, December 1924.

32. *The Resurrection*, a detail, oil, 1924–6. Tate Gallery.

composition was drawn on it in detail before painting, which he began at the top-left, gradually working downwards. Kate Foster described him in her diary as 'teetering on a box, while painting white roses in a corner, just a patch at a time, and holding forth 'from his elevation on Tonks and the Slade.'

Hilda was in Essex, painting, when Stanley paid a brief visit to Cookham, writing her (20 April 1924) that Jas Wood had asked him to point out the 'round tombstones' in the churchyard. This caused him to think that he ought to be painting his picture there if he was to capture the authentic 'Cookham' feeling, but removal of the canvas at this stage would be impractical. His claim to proprietary rights over Cookham were renewed. I recall how he resented anyone expressing a liking for Cookham, as I did one evening.

Meanwhile, with Hilda away, he would wander on Hampstead Heath at fair-time, watching the roundabouts, and describing them to Hilda in the above letter as 'the same green and red glass eyes in the dragons, same people riding them as last year'. In the evening, he met the Gardners.[3] 'They are all "Blake-ites"; I was against Blake's pictures and engravings.' Most evenings, he joined us in our Downshire Hill studio. Kate Foster's diary for the 21 May 1924, records that 'Jas Wood, wearing new and painful brown boots, took us by taxi to Jack Straw's Castle for an old-fashioned dinner, and Dick has to fetch Stanley, who comes looking sad but talks with enthusiasm of Donne's Sermons', and in a later entry in July, when Hilda had returned, we read: 'Stanley there at Downshire Hill with a sore throat, but holding forth in a hoarse whisper and showing Hilda *Paradise Lost*.' Stanley was always ready to expound his thoughts to anyone, confident of their understanding him, as when he explained something about Mantegna to our gardener, who replied, 'He must be a good artist that man Taylor.'

Stanley had posed for my large painting of tea-time on our terrace (Plate 10);[4] he then joined Hilda at Wangford, where he painted a landscape, and wrote her on his return, in November, after going to 47: 'But all was dark and it was dark in the studios, so I went up to my place and looked at my picture and at my Wangford landscape and was more intrigued with my landscape than with the big "pic". The studio looked very spectral and the picture looked like a ghost. Why do things change when you go away. . . . Next morning I took my landscapes down to 47 and Mrs Carline and Dick were there. Dick liked the way I had painted the row of willows. They both looked at it in "Da's" room.'

In his next letter to her, he recalls those *Cautionary Tales* (quoting 'Mathilda told such dreadful lies' etc.), which always appealed to his 'sense of humour', something he felt was 'quite false': 'When I have said things that have made Jas slap his knees with delight, I have known in my true consciousness that I had said something quite worthless and untrue.'

He took his Wangford landscape to the Goupil Gallery in Lower Regent Street to show Marchant, the first art dealer with whom he established contact. He wrote Hilda (24 November 1924): 'He gave me a big lunch and I drank one pint and a half of beer. . . . I ate a chop and brussels-sprouts and potatoes and fruit salad and cream and ginger. It is extraordinary how beer makes one able to eat such a lot. Then I went back up to Hampstead and fetched my long Wangford landscape . . . and asked him to ask £65 for it. . . .

'As I was talking to Marchant, in walked Dick and Hartley and so we looked at one or two of the pictures, they intelligently and I unintelligently.'

They went back to the studio in Downshire Hill and Stanley's letter continues: 'The argument for this evening was between me (Hartley with me) v. Dick (with him Jas). Golden text: Is Art teachable? If so, in what way? The scene was rather this—Jas far back in the chair looking up at the ceiling with a sort of "Oh, Lord, how long, how long will the Stanley Spencers and Henry Tonks's continue to suffocate me with their denseness." Dick with an exasperated smile, "Yes, but that's what I keep telling you"; Jas, "Only you won't listen." . . . Then Guy Poolman's[5] subdued voice to Mrs Carline in reply to the news of Aunt Minnie, . . . "Yes, I think I did, her father was a don at St John's." This Jas takes up as a kind of refrain.'

He wrote to Hilda of a visit to the Hampstead Cinema: 'I was moved by Lilian Gish. . . . It was quite as usual—close-ups, wistful looks, . . . lying back on the pillow with eyes cast upwards and hands folded across her bosom, having gone into a kind of trance.' Another letter (undated)[6] tells Hilda: 'I am writing this in bed. . . .

There is always something about early mornings that I love, and I don't see why that fresh, new, untouched, untarnished quality should not last all day. The place outside my window in the early morning seems a mystery place, a place where all sorts of happenings, real happenings are taking place, and everything you hear is reminding you of a confident and harmonious life going on—the life of the cock, the life of the moorhen and the life of the duck . . . and makes one realise that one is oneself a part of nature, a part of that sunrise affair. I must get up now.'

He usually painted *The Resurrection* until dusk, when he would report his progress to Hilda. Another undated letter tells her how he envisaged the picture: 'I was thinking how to paint God's face. . . . I am very vague about it, but I think, perhaps, it's a face that has that same unanalysable expression that a flower has. His face should be a new and never-before-seen thing like a new and never-before-seen flower that is more convincing of its flower-likeness than a rose and with a more sweet associationess than there is in the scent of a rose. . . .

'It would be nice if I could write a kind of miniature *Divine Comedy* of my picture. . . . It would be a picture of the joys of the new real life. . . . There is the joy of the *reality* of the resurrected life, expressed by the fact of the people who are reading their own memorial notices on the tombstones, the joy of helping each other and tending to each other's needs, expressed by the husbands and wives in front of the tower. Then there is the joy of contemplation expressed by the people leaning and reclining on the tombs. The joy of solitude is the person in the big ivy tomb. The joy again of reality and of smelling, I have in the girl seeing if a sunflower has any smell. The joy of being is the man (me) lying on the two great slabs, and the joy of giving is the two girls discovering, the one to the other, that it was she who put certain wreaths on the other's grave.

'I think the row of saints really represent the joy of becoming holy through study and understanding. Oh dear! I begin to feel like Adam must have felt, when God kept bringing animals to him to name.

'Then there is the joy of being beautiful in the nude figures and in the richly attired man by the cypress tree. Then the grave where the flowers are bending over one side and the other is the joy of resurrection, the new birth, and the grave here is like the opening womb.

'I don't know yet what the three rows of figures mean. They may be black people; they may be the joy of intercourse and communion of people generally, like the talks after the testimony [Christian Science] meetings. Or it may be the joy of touching and feeling. Then there is the joy of the earth giving birth to joy, sometimes, through hard sunburnt cracks and, sometimes, through soft grassy or flowery openings just according to how they would prefer.

'Then there would be the joy of individual inclination bringing about variety, expressed in the way ivy likes to collect itself up into great clumps and virginia creeper likes to fall like soft green icicles and the cypress tree likes to stand stiff and upright and grasses like to rank themselves in little armies and cow parsley likes to range itself alongside of a hedge and so on.' Two days passed while writing this letter and before he continued: 'Where I did not realise the importance of retaining one's vision is in the top left-hand corner of my picture—the way I have painted the boat and the people in it. . . . I lost sight of my true idea. . . . There is a black mass with a white elipse with a black spot on it in the middle. But I got muddling about with the piano on the boat and goodness knows what not and thus by losing sight of what I had originally meant to convey, I made a mess of it. It is a white boat with all the people dressed in white and the sort of captain of the boat in dark navy blue (Plate 31).

'When I got back last night, I was too tired to write and went to bed, but I did not sleep until six this morning. I was thinking of all sorts of interesting things really, and I could, I believe, have written you a real letter, a thing I feel I have never done. . . . Then I come to the bit in your letter about the all-powerfulness of God, which is beautifully clear; it shows your grasp of the true way to go about composition. . . .

'It is really very cosy in here. . . . I have the stage up against the picture and near to the anthracite fire. . . . It has always been a matter of importance to me as to the exact place in a room of the light. . . . I had the same feeling about where the light was placed when I worked in the kitchen of Wisteria Cottage.'[7]

By November 1924, Stanley had begun painting the central

feature of the composition—the ivy-covered tomb. He wrote to Hilda of his friend Hartley's visit: 'Hartley's appreciation is very stimulating; he is so quick to recognise. I love to feel this longing to paint certain parts of my pictures [as Hartley had suggested] and it's marvellous how that longing never gets tired or one never gets past the point of "hunger" or that one never "improves" in one's vision so that one longs for something "better", which shows that the thing that one is longing for, if it is true, is all the time revealing beauty and truth and is not subject to time and improvement.' Stanley never believed in the need for improvement or progress. His latest work was not to be "better" than previous ones. But he had problems to resolve, and explained one of these to Hilda (6 December): 'I have been continuing the ivy-covered tomb and I came to the point where I was to decide the exact shape of the (as I hoped) two people in it. There has always been something wrong about it and I have managed, not to get the two people but only a bit of one person, but somehow that one person is so grand, although you can only see a little bit—just an arm and bit of the face—that I really prefer it to the original notion. . . . Then I tried to draw this and couldn't because I was still suffering from disappointment at being reduced to head and arm.' He then tried a 'bare arm' but could not get it 'associated with the ivy', and thought it should have some 'intimate personal feeling'. His letter continues: 'So I tried to draw your arm when you wear the grey woollen jumper with green "dado". It was the sleeve and the shape of it that . . . I liked. It used to get bell-shaped round the wrist when it wanted washing and it is the bell-shape I like. As I drew it, I got a fresh notion. [a sketch] . . . One sees the hand a little way up the sleeve in a little world all on its own. . . . I shall get my hunger for bare arms satisfied when I come to paint those rows of people with arms out over the ground just above the tomb.'

Soon afterwards came another letter to Hilda (undated): 'Dick and Sydney have just been up here and Sydney was very encouraging about my person in the ivy tomb. He seemed to get the idea straight away. . . . I discussed my difficulty about the black people in my picture. . . . As I talked with Sydney, I began to realise much more the idea about touching. I realised that the touching of each other must be done in the same way as leaves are touched or pieces of rock. After they had gone, I did a fairly elaborate drawing of the touching idea. On the "tables" of earth, so to speak, in between each slit, there are different objects. The three people in the left-hand slit are each feeling or touching these objects. The first is touching a biggish round stone; the second a small portion of a trunk of some rock plant and also an arm of person in slit opposite. The next person is feeling something soft and feathery; it may be a bird or animal. In the middle slit the nearest person is pressing his hand into a piece of clay and his other hand on the next table is running sand on to a conical pile of sandy earth that another person in the right-hand slit had made for the purpose of making and enjoying a hole in the earth; he has his hand in the hole. The second man in middle slit is on one side feeling the surface of the earth and on the right the surface of a nugget of some kind of rock which has several different planes and surfaces. The third man in this row is also on that side feeling the same piece of nugget rock, and on the other side is feeling some leaves on the trunk aforesaid. The man behind him is feeling on one side only two differently-sized things; I have not decided yet. The man in the right-hand slit, behind the "hole" man is on one side with his hand in a little pool of water and in the other he is touching the hem of Christ's robe. In haste for post.'

Hilda was back at home in December, and Stanley spent Christmas in Downshire Hill as usual. Soon afterwards, he and Hilda were once more engaged. This time, there was to be no special dressmaking for the wedding in Wangford Parish Church, March 1925. Both painted during their honeymoon there, being joined by Gilbert, whom Hilda had invited, and they drew one another. Stanley was soon back to work on his *Resurrection*. He had told her how Jas had suggested: 'You'll have to be careful not to overdo the flowers', to which Stanley retorted: 'If I emptied the whole of Sutton's illustrated catalogue of flowers into the painting, there would not be a petal too many. It's like the inside of a railway carriage, whatever you do in it only makes it become more and more what it is.'

Stanley wrote to Henry on 3 March 1926, that he had 'practically finished it'. It became the central feature in his exhibition at the Goupil Gallery the next year (February 1927), creating much sensation. During the remainder of the year (1926), he was able to carry out a commission from Chatto and Windus for twenty-five pen and ink drawings for an almanac,[8] in which he used some of the ideas he had incorporated in *The Resurrection*.

Nearly twenty years later, he summarised the ideas he had when painting it: 'No one is in any hurry in this painting. Here and there things slowly move off but in the main they resurrect to such a state of joy that they are content and happy to remain where they have resurrected. In this life we experience a kind of resurrection when we arrive at a state of awareness, a state of being in love, and at such times we like to do again what we have done many times in the past, because now we do it anew in Heaven. And so in the resurrection there are the same beloved human ways and habits. Hilda mooches along and slowly goes over the stile. She wears a favourite dress of hers. The people read their own headstones. By the ivy-covered church tower, a wife brushes the earth and grass off her husband. . . .[9] Another woman buttons a man's coat up and another straightens a man's collar. Further down you see Hilda smelling a flower. . . . She wonders about its scent and with curiosity pushes it against her face. She here wears a jumper I liked, one that had been pulled into being very floppy from much washing of it.

'There is a wish in me, as I remember the composing of this, to draw near to and to love those things which in this life may have seemed awesome. . . . Like Bunyan looking back at all the fearsome objects after he had passed through the Valley of the Shadow of Death. And so love casts out fear and stakes its claims on things previously dreaded. The men lie on or lean against their tombs in no hurry to get away from them. . . .

'All the time you will notice a wish to emphasise the meaning in the resurrected life by giving it some link with this life, showing some sort of familiarity. For instance, what about the stone recumbent figure forming part of the table tomb by the porch? That figure was always there . . . and now in the resurrection he comes into his own and joins in with the other men reclining on table tombs. (Plate 32.)

'The light on the wall of the Church is rather in feeling like the light I could see when swimming under water; it was the only thing I could see and that I felt drawn towards. But as I thought of this sunlit wall, its wonder seemed to increase as I saw there was some large dark object practically eclipsing the light or merging into it, and this was the dark ivy-clad tomb-stone. This ivy, bunched up, made a kind of nest-shaped top to the tomb, and I wanted this bird-in-the-nest feel. . . . The next shape, suggesting a house, made me want both husband and wife and it would not work, and I felt very put off as one person seemed lonely—nasty single bed feeling. . . . At last I became so unloving, I asked myself if I loved anything at all in the world . . . just anything—any port in a storm, and Hilda was wearing her old jumper and I saw her hand over-lapped by it, her hand in its nest made by the sleeve. And I felt yes. I love that. I came to rest there and so in it went. (Plate 32.)

'In each part of this picture . . . the meaning of the resurrection is conveyed by bringing people into contact with their customary surroundings and show how they feel about them in their resurrected state, and here to emphasise this there is a group of negroes resurrecting just by the Church porch. And as I feel that these African people have a wonderful sense of the beauty of this life, especially in regard to the simple objects in nature, I have shown them in the act of appreciating various things. . . .

'I do not know about the porch. I know that "The rose round the door made me love the resurrection more." I think it clinched the matter. I wanted the roses to be those little white roses with a curious scent such as grew on the porch. I think they are called "seven sisters". Under the roses and sitting in the porch is Christ with babies in His arms. God is behind the seat and affectionately holds His hand in Christ's hair. I feel the nude babe in Christ's arm will be content to lie there for ever.

'Ranged along the wall . . . are sort of prophets, each one wrapt in thought. In fact, these express, so to speak, the resurrection of thought and their gestures indicate some state of contemplation. I wanted this peaceful thinking to be one of the most active and positive parts of this picture and . . . the thinking prophets crest the whole right section . . . carried on by the hanging virginia creeper. . . . The others below so love the atmosphere that they lay about, basking in the place.

'I and my brother-in-law, Dick Carline, both seen nude, stilled by the wonder of it all, are inactively thrilled. I am very fond of the girls taking it easy, seen just below the prophets. Especially I love the girl in the black velvet dress with a black velvet rose gathered in at the knees. Hilda had a dress like this. I love the unawesome way she uses the very shape of the headstone to loll against, the casual gesture of the girl with arms flung back over the other stone. The entire race are destined to peace and joy. There are those who are resurrecting without quite such flowery ease, but these are only self-inflicted mild penances.

'Below the girl in black velvet there is a girl rising from her grave and the profusion of wild flowers and long grass in her grave flop over as the ground opens. Because she liked flower-patterned dresses, she is resurrecting in a dress, where the pattern is not very dissimilar from the wild flowers round her.[10]

'Here about are some "untenanted" headstones, the occupants having moved off. Below this are two of the men who rise under hoods of earth and to their left at the bottom of the picture is a grand sort of mayor in robes (more or less a portrait of Sir Henry Slesser) rising out of a much-wreathed grave. I loved the wreaths of garden and hot-house flowers—arum lilies etc., resting gently among the wild meadowland growth of clover, marguerites, plantains etc. Two items more. Below the virginia creeper, one girl shows the other girl the ticket on the wreath, which the other girl has put on her grave. She thanks her for it. And finally a portrait of myself, lying back in the fold of two stones, passionately doing nothing. To emphasise the place and the bare fact of myself, I have thought of an open book. Being satisfied where they are and in no hurry to shift indicates their state of sureness as to the good that has come. And when you read a book you settle down to it, and it may be that the open book and getting to a state of rest and contentment are associated, and this me, settling down between the two lids of that tomb is my signature to this painting.'

He wrote to me in 1929: 'I had in the box-shaped tombs some wicked people being prevented from getting out of the graves. Apart from the fact that I did not think there were any "wicked" people at all, I found that the idea disturbed the genuine tranquility of the main outlook. . . . But the deed was done.' He adds that he would have liked to 'expunge or alter this detail', but 'the compositional balance would be upset'.

His description above, written in Glasgow or in Cliveden View, continues: 'John Donne describes the churchyard as being "the holy suburb of Heaven". When it comes to why and how I came to concentrate so much on the subject of the Resurrection, I think I can explain. My wish is to reveal the meaning of things. I am aware that there is a special meaning in what I experience, that I love and wish to express clearly. And I begin to search for the means of doing this. And . . . this search brings me to the contemplation of the resurrection. . . . And then I, full of hope, think: "And what might that life be like?" Then I say: "There are many things in this life that I love and that I feel are for ever loved, and these things are a key to the Resurrection." . . . A sort of reciprocity begins. This life being a key to the next, tells me something of the next life and causes the resurrected life to tell me more of what the resurrection in this life is like. This intercourse brings out the meaning I see in this world.

'The resurrection [in the picture] has, so to speak, partially taken place, through the already perfectness of some things (I hope I find grass and rabbits in Heaven). . . . The contemplation of the Resurrection throws back into this life a light which picks on this life's perfection and its special meanings that I so much love and seek.'

Notes to Chapter 11

1. Fiske Warren of Boston, a pioneer of Single-Tax, had met us in Andorra, where we stayed in his villa. An ardent admirer of Hilda, he soon became friendly with Stanley, and joined us in 1929 at Cookham.
2. Although 1923 has been variously given for the beginning of this painting, Stanley, in his notebook, has stated: '1924, began the Resurrection', which he also repeated elsewhere.
3. Professor Ernest Gardner and family.
4. The life-size figures included my mother, Sydney, Hilda, Henry Lamb, Hartley, Jas Wood, Kate Foster, as well as Stanley.
5. We had met Guy Poolman, a frequent visitor, when we lived in Oxford and he was an undergraduate.
6. Stanley re-read these letters many years later, dating them in pencil when possible, this letter being dated 8 December 1924.
7. He was painting in Wisteria Cottage on and off from 1912 to 1915.
8. In subsequent years, he made oil paintings of some of these compositions, such as *Christmas Stockings*, now in the Museum of Modern Art, New York.
9. 'Suggested as a result,' he wrote me later, 'of seeing people getting up off the grass, when they had been lying on it.'
10. He explained to me in 1929 that 'with one or two exceptions', the figures were in 'positions I had noticed people in when in a happy, interested, studious or inspired state'.

TWELVE

The War Paintings at Burghclere

THE DECISION to build the chapel for Stanley's war paintings was finally reached early in 1924. Louis and Mary Behrend had asked Lionel Pearson, their architect friend, to design it with two almshouses either side on a site by the railway line.[1]

Stanley had made a sketch for floor mosaics, in squares and hexagonals enclosing such scenes as a woman with a child, an event in hospital, a soldier sleeping in the open, as well as making a design for the window and spandrels on either side, but it was felt that the extra expense of all these must preclude their realisation. His wish to work in fresco also had to be relinquished. The paintings were to be in oil on canvas, stretched on to wooden frames, except the largest ones, for which the canvas would be glued to the wall. The end wall was also changed; the two doors flanking the altar required a rectangular shape instead of the arched one, originally planned.

Stanley was impatient to begin work while in Hampstead, his exhibition being over early in 1927, without waiting for the completion of the building. For his first canvas, in the series, which he called 'predellas', being below the arched panels, he chose an idea derived from Beaufort Hospital. It was of scrubbing the floor, showing an orderly, who threw himself down full length with arms stretched forward, while other orderlies approach with trays (Plate 33).[2] He broke off to paint *Soap-suds* on the studio floor as a study.[3] In a letter to me in 1929, he described this scene: 'The corridor leads to the main kitchen and stores. . . . The men are fetching bread etc., from the kitchen and store; the man leaning against the wall is re-adjusting the loaves of bread on his tray, before he continues his journey with it to the ward.'

176

Sorting and Moving Kit-bags (Plate 33) was the next to be painted in Hampstead, described in the same letter as follows: 'Immediately on arrival at the hospital, the kit-bags of the soldiers just arrived would be stacked all together in the courtyard. . . . The patients who happened to be not "bed cases" would point out to the orderlies which ever happened to be their respective bags. The orderlies would then carry them to wherever the patient wanted them, or open them if so required. They were all padlocked.'

Seeing these two paintings just after he had painted them, I felt disappointed with the colour, limited to a range of browns and greys, in contrast to the rich variety of colour in his earlier work. Later, with all the war paintings completed, one could appreciate that he had kept the colour subdued to secure a unity throughout. That first picture of *Scrubbing* established the character of the scheme and is, perhaps, the most original, fresh and exploratory of all.

The building being finished by May 1927, Stanley could work on the site.[4] He and Hilda, with their daughter, Shirin, born in Hampstead the previous November, took lodgings at Palmer's Hill Farm, Burghclere, whence he could cycle across the railway bridge to work in the chapel. First to be painted there was *The Arrival of a Convoy at the Hospital Gates* (Plate 33), for the first arched space on the left. The gate-keeper pulls open the iron gates at the approach of the red bus, crowded with wounded men. Stanley told me that he liked the white triangular slings on the men's arms, and that they exchanged souvenirs or examined holes in their helmets to escape boredom.

He concentrated, first, on these hospital scenes, ranging the pictures round the walls as he finished them. The next to be painted, for the lower register, was *Sorting Laundry* (Plate 33), of which he explained: 'As each orderly called out the name of each article, the laundress would write it down in the respective orderly's "check-book".' This was followed by *Filling Tea-Urns* (Plate 33); these were handled by the mental patients who had remained in the hospital since the time when it was an asylum. These four 'predellas' and the arched picture were thus completed during 1927, and were secured to the wall, *Tea-Urns* being the only one to be in a different position from that indicated in the sketch. Stanley had, originally, envisaged eight 'predellas' and three

33. Burghclere Chapel, left-hand side wall: (above) *Camp at Karasuli, Macedonia*; (arched panels, left to right) *Convoy of Wounded Soldiers Arriving at Beaufort Hospital Gates*; *Ablutions at Beaufort*;

Kit Inspection at Tweseldown; *Stand-to, Macedonia*; (predellas below, left to right) *Scrubbing the Floor*; *Kit-bags*; *Laundry*; *Tea-urns*, all at Beaufort Hospital.

34. Burghclere Chapel, right-hand side wall: (above) *River-bed at Todorova, Macedonia*; (arched panels, left to right) *Reveille*; *Filling Water-bottles*; *Map-reading*; *Making a Fire-belt*, all of Macedonia;

(predellas below, left to right) *Frost-bite*; *Tea in the Ward*; *Bed-making*; *Scrubbing Lockers*, all at Beaufort Hospital.

arched panels of hospital scenes, but one of them, his favourite, the *Surgical Operation* was withdrawn as being too traumatic, and although the idea had been almost the first to inspire him, he never painted it.

The 'predella' that had a particularly poignant meaning for him, though left till the last of the hospital scenes, was *Washing Lockers* (Plate 34), placed first on the right-hand wall, showing an orderly, namely himself, half concealed between two baths as he scrubs the floor. When painting it in November 1929, Stanley explained to me: 'The baths were deep sort of magenta colour and shiny, and when you had a row of them end-view on, they looked marvellous.' In a preliminary sketch, before designing the scheme as a whole, he drew the figure seen lying towards us instead of away from us, as finally painted, and he wrote on the back: 'Me scrubbing: I say "me", because I have only mentally to place myself between the baths to feel at once inspired.' He told his friend, Peggy Andrews, similarly, in an undated letter, 'All my figures are simply "me", putting myself in places and circumstances in which I want to be, [but not] literally portraits of myself.' The 'predella' spaces were appropriate for the hospital scenes, being on a lower level, not only because the scenes were close up and intimate, but they often involved looking down on the floor. A unity in the size of the figures had to be maintained throughout, despite one or two exceptions, such as *Ablutions* in 1928 (Plate 33).[5] with the men's heads in their wash-basins, much larger in scale.

Three remaining hospital scenes for the lower register included *Patient Suffering from Frost-bite* (Plate 34), 'wrapped', as Stanley explained, 'in an elaborate red counterpane', and *Bed-making* (Plate 34),[6] given a different position from that in the original plan. Neither were painted, however, until 1932, when he had left Burghclere to live at Lindworth, Cookham.

The sketch for *Bed-making* shows the wall bare of ornamentation, but the painting has a striped wallpaper, with 'pin-up' photographs and postcards, such as Stanley himself liked around him. There is an early photograph of Hilda in the garden at Downshire Hill, as Stanley remembered her when they first met,[7] also one of his father in the porch of Hedsor Church, where he was organist, and of their younger daughter, Unity, still a baby.

The remaining 'predella' of *Tea in the Hospital Ward* (Plate 34), painted also in 1932, was not in the original plan, slices of white bread, which the patients are eating, being Stanley's favourite diet. If hospital subjects are more numerous, the Macedonian ones have been given the more prominent places, and if the series is regarded as autobiographical as it should, Macedonia is presented as the climax of his war experiences. In depicting the everyday life of soldiers at war, he managed to convey an element of mystery, even remoteness, in contrast to the mundane happenings in a hospital.

For *The Convoy of Wounded Men Filling Water-bottles at a Stream* (Plate 34), he described the sketch in a letter to me (1928): 'There is a great crowd of men round a Greek fountain or drinking-water trough (usually two slabs of marble, one set vertically into the side of a hill, having a slit-shaped hole in it which the other smaller slab fits . . .). What rather amused me was that often above the fountain, you could see the water trickling down the little groove made by it in the rock.

'In this picture, the groove of the water-course is indicated on the face of the rocky hill-side. . . . The bottom part of the picture shows men and mules drinking. Above them . . . are men who have climbed up the hill-side and are lying on little ledges in the hill-side in order to be able to get at the fountain that way, there being too great a crowd below. The peculiar wing-like looking things coming from their shoulders are army mackintoshes, which being only attached to the back of the collar, naturally slide off the backs of the men . . . and droop downwards.' The final painting, one of the last to be produced in 1932, was substantially like the sketch.

He had decided to omit *Kit Inspection* (Plate 33), when he wrote to me in 1928, feeling that the composition in the original sketch, with its series of rectangles—the blankets or ground-sheets on which each soldier had to lay out his equipment—was unsatisfactory and the figure of a soldier in the foreground was too large compared with figures in the adjoining panels. However, in 1930, he revised the composition as in the painting, making the soldier smaller, and the sheets on the ground curved instead of rectangular. Stanley confirmed, in his reminiscences of 1944, that it was a recollection of Tweseldown, thus being the only scene in the series associated with that camp.

He had already in 1929, begun painting the scene called *Reveille* (the end panel on the right-hand wall, Plate 34), showing men awakened inside their mosquito-nets, while others look through the tent opening. This, again, was different from his original sketch, which showed men emerging from white tents to place weights on their mosquito-nets. He later included the tents in another scene, called *Making a Fire-belt* (Plate 34). Stanley explained to me some proposed changes in his letter of 1928: 'Both of these pictures [the "Camouflaged Tent" and "Kit Inspection"] I hope to paint some day, but they cannot go into the scheme unless a rehash of the *Kit Inspection* turned out better than the *Reveille* picture that has taken its place. In the pictures called *Stand-to* and *Reveille*, there is something confusing in these titles. Both are things I thought of as being parts of the big central *Resurrection* picture, and in the general weeding or rather thinning out they both had to go.' Ultimately, they were both included.

The scene called *Stand-to* (Plates 33, 35) was painted in 1928 replacing *The Surgical Operation*. Given an entirely different composition, he changed the name *Stand-to* to *Dug-out*. It proved to be one of the most poignant and dramatic of his Macedonian ideas. He described it to me in his 1928 letter: 'The idea, apart from the way the shapes of the dug-outs interested me, occurred to me in thinking how marvellous it would be if one morning, when we came out of our dug-outs, we found that somehow everything was peace and that war was no more. That was one thing—the thought of how we would behave. Another thing I noticed at that time was the quiet way the sergeant would stroll out of his dug-out and tell the men to get ready.

'This picture really depicts the scene I had imagined, supposing that at the moment of "stand-to", it had been suddenly realised that the War had ceased. And so the men are about to put on their equipment but have paused as they become conscious of the change. It is a sort of cross between an "Armistice" picture and a "Resurrection".

Stanley continued his description elsewhere in his letter: 'At "stand-to", the man has to come out of his dug-out and be ready for action at a moment's notice. To facilitate this and to ensure things being done in an expeditious manner, the equipments of the men were arranged in such an order on the sides of the dug-outs that when the order was given, they could come straight out into the open where there was room for them to put equipments on quickly.

'Coming out of the nearest dug-out, a sergeant is in the act of camouflaging his hat (Plate 35). In the next dug-out the men are about to put on their equipments. It was always at this moment that I used to feel what a marvellous thing peace was. . . . It is not a picture of "stand-to". That is merely the framework or the circumstances in which the resurrection finds these men. This picture is really an introduction from the side-wall, ordinary army life pictures, to the end wall *Resurrection* picture. It is a mixture of an ordinary circumstance with a spiritual happening.'

In his first concept of this subject ('Stand to'), the upper part was to include figures, which he subsequently decided to omit. It was this earlier concept that he had in mind in continuing his description: 'In the top of this picture is an outpost in which two men are on guard; the reclining figure above symbolises peace.' After mentioning the sergeant lit by bursting shells as he reclines on the parapet, already described, Stanley proceeds: 'Then all would be blackness again. . . . Outside the outpost, the very tufts of grass against which one rested the rifle partook of the supernatural atmosphere, which came into existence as soon as an attack commenced. . . . As one was lying flat on the bottom of the outpost, one had a feeling that this sergeant reclining on the parapet was like a kind of angel, a supernatural being. One did not see him; one daren't look up. One knew and felt he was there.'

Stanley then describes his *Reveille* subject: 'Each man, as we always did, dresses under his own mosquito-net. I shall try, but may not succeed so well, to express the fact that though this is a "Reveille" scene, yet the idea is, again, really the resurrection. The men looking in the door of the tent are clearly doing nothing and are free from any hurry. . . . This picture is, as in the other, a mixture of real and spiritual fact, as the underlying intention is a great feeling of peace and happiness.'

Of the remaining two arched pictures (on the right-hand wall), he mentions *Map-reading* (Plate 34), which is the only one of the series to depict an officer: 'The map nearly fills the picture, with men, down below, resting on either side of the road. I loved this scene for the obvious reason of resting and contemplating.'

In painting this picture in 1932 at Lindworth, he reduced the officer and map in size to conform with the general scale of figures, and he included in the upper part an idyllic scene of men picking bilberries, which gave him the rare opportunity in the series to depict leaves and vegetation. The *Fire-belt*, with soldiers pitching camp, was also one of the last to be painted in 1932, replacing an earlier idea of soldiers playing cards in front of a camouflaged tent. In writing to me in 1928, he mentioned: 'We were allowed to carry our equipment in wheelbarrows — most unregimental and free.'

These arched pictures, like the 'predellas' could be painted on his easel, each taking five to six weeks. For the two long paintings above them and for the end wall, the canvas being glued to the wall, scaffolding had to be erected by Mr Head, the builder, during the summer 1928. Stanley began work on his *Resurrection of Soldiers* (Plates 36 and 37) on the end wall that autumn.

Visitors would find him high up on his platform, his small figure seeming part of the painting. He used the same small wooden palette, as for his smaller pictures. He never used a tray or marble slab as many artists do for work on a large scale. Nor did he wear an overall and his every-day tweed suit soon told of the colours he was using.

His first idea, formed in 1927, for this all-important *Resurrection* had been an arrangement of crosses and mules, surrounded by a bank of vegetation. By 1928, he could describe to me how this idea was developing: 'The trouble . . . was that I would start with some general idea and then I would find myself getting a more satisfactory general idea from some incidental idea appearing in it, so that the incidental would gradually become general, and the original general idea would be reduced to "acting lance-corporal without pay".' This was how the soldiers conceived the lowest rank above private. He continues: 'For instance, my first notion . . . was that as every other picture in the building was very much cut and defined and clear, it would be rather a relief if this [end] wall was composed of something that would give a feeling of a different texture, that if the side walls gave a feeling of hard edges, then this wall should be soft, with just as much substance and more; but it should be all soft, though clearly defined. This desire led me to the notion of filling the whole end wall with barbed wire. Inside the wire and influencing the shape of the wire were men in

35. Sketch for *Stand-to*, Burghclere Chapel, *c.* 1928. Tate Gallery.

36. Working cartoon for *The Resurrection of Soldiers*, end wall, Burghclere Chapel, *c.* 1927.

37. *Resurrection of Soldiers*, end wall, Burghclere Chapel, 1928–9.

different attitudes, but all praying to a figure supposed to be Christ, who is disentangling them.

'Far fetched as it is, I liked the idea and still like it, but every composition I did of it turned out wrong. I still wonder if I could not carry out this idea in the form of a mosaic to cover the floor of the chapel, it would have lent itself very well as a stained-glass window. In fact, the figure on the left, standing with bits of wire sticking to his clothes, I thought of as the result of thinking of a stained-glass window. When this wire idea was reduced to being a secondary idea, it lost all meaning. The herd of mules then threatened to inundate the whole picture and at that juncture, I left the end wall alone for some time, excepting that I had by then thought of making the men coming out of dug-outs (the *Stand-to* picture) the main central motif of it. I felt then very much, and do still, though nothing like so much, that the picture was too much a lot of unrelated incidents patched together, that I ought to leave it alone and get once again to some general idea that would comprehend this wall in one "lump".'

Having abandoned the 'barbed-wire' idea, Stanley made several large cartoons, drawn to scale (Plate 36), in which crosses held by the soldiers predominate, and retaining the figure of Christ, in the centre, receiving the crosses. He also introduced the two white mules, who turn their heads to gaze at Christ behind them. In the cartoon, however, the foreground was occupied by two soldiers lying on the ground and much foreshortened. When, in 1928, he was about to begin the painting, he felt again doubtful about the composition, especially these two large figures just over the altar, and decided to make a fresh cartoon of soldiers with crosses. He explained how he arrived at these revisions in his letter to me later that year: 'When I painted the "Tate" [i.e. Cookham] *Resurrection*, . . . I liked "squaring up" this picture, and also I had a habit of taking a mount and placing it here and there on the picture to see what sort of little pictures it made. No doubt you, in your secret moments, have indulged in this game. . . . I felt that the picture, as it was, was all falling to pieces and that there was nothing to hold it up. I also felt that if I could get this picture "squared up", if I could get a mass of "frames" over the whole picture, so that one could look at details independent of the other parts, . . . would be grand.

'The part . . . where Christ is and where the men are handing their crosses in, (symbolic of the way that on being demobilised one handed in one's equipment) is perhaps the main subject notion, . . . meaning that in the resurrection they have even finished with that last piece of worldly impedimenta.

'All this part of the "cross" idea was thought of as a result of the "squaring-up" of pictures. In this particular case, I feel that the notion of the men round Christ with their crosses was very much governed . . . and dictated by the behaviour of the men.

'The lower part . . . is also a cross idea, which I have only just done and which does not come in the photo you have. I wish, if you had time, you could come down here and see this big drawing. I think I showed you a small sketch for it. . . .

'Once I had thought of the crosses, I began to think of different subjects in which the crosses could come. I thought of how a man might stand between two crosses so as to give the appearance of a man standing in the door of his cottage in the evening, looking out on to the street and the things he sees there. I have tried to convey this by making him have his arms on the two uprights of the crosses. I have deliberately composed this so as to convey the feeling of he being in a home. On the other side is a similarly arranged system of crosses, only this "home" is in the form of a Greek temple. (I liked the way it took away the Latin cross look and dissociated the cross from Gothic associations.) I also, in these homes, wanted to convey the feeling of home and domestic life that Macedonia gave me in places where there was no sign of it.

'The whole of the bottom of the picture is a sort of portrait gallery formed by soldiers coming out of the ground and the crosses arranged so as to look like frames. There used to be a sort of frame made, which usually had texts in them, and I have had those frames in my mind, as some of the "frames" in my picture look just like it [a sketch].

'As this idea comes just above the altar, the cross on the altar itself will be a similar design to those in the picture . . . down a little way behind the altar. I have all this drawn on the wall and it has a suggestive look of being a Last Supper. As these portraits are nearly life-size, and as they are so near the sacred precincts of the altar, I have given a slight look in the faces of their being aware of the altar. I have tried to "holy" them up a bit.

'The way the men are holding the crosses has been completely dictated by how each individual is feeling in his attitude to what the cross means. The man lying on the cross and leaning on his elbow finds it an absorbing study and is, as many others in the picture, contemplating the truth it reveals. The truth that the cross is supposed to symbolise in this picture is that nothing is lost where a sacrifice has been the result of a perfect understanding. This is rather important as I thought of this at the time when I did the drawing and it very much influenced me in deciding on the behaviour of the men. They are all, for instance, meant to be happy.'

Stanley followed his cartoon in painting the upper part of the end wall, described at length in his 1928 letter to me: 'It is not necessarily a resurrection from the dead. All the pictures . . . are meant to lead up to it in a mental way. It is a more positive and final declaration of a feeling that has been going on in all the other part of the scheme. There were times during the War, when I felt more spiritually conscious than at others, and I instinctively associated whatever I was doing with what I was feeling. So that after the War, when I thought of different incidents, I remembered the state of my mind I was in, especially where I felt spiritually conscious. This scheme does not entirely represent . . . incidents where and when I felt spiritually conscious and therefore happy but they do to such a surprising degree that it is fair to regard it as the main spring of the general idea. . . . Five minutes of being by oneself was during the War a great spiritual experience. It was an oasis in which, for a moment, one came to life.

'The place where the Resurrection takes place . . . is called Kalinova, where I spent the happiest time I had during the whole War. We were just outside this deserted village or town; it had a wall round it, which gave it a feeling of being a big place. In the picture, the only thing that is like the place is the bit of wall of the town in the top right-hand corner. . . . There are bits of places that belonged to other parts of Macedonia. For instance, the series of switch-back roads seen at the top is something I vaguely remembered when I was on my way in the dark to join the infantry, . . . behind which Kalinova was situated. Immediately below . . . them are a number of men lying in all sorts of directions under blankets on top of a hill. In the picture, they are just waking up. I remember the first night I slept up the line, I was with about twenty

R.A.M.C. men, and we slept under blankets on the open hill-side. Beautiful starlit night; far below us there was Lake Ardzan and, above it, a hill with some old Greek fort on it; a grass fire was burning the whole length of the lake. . . . Everything was muffled, quiet and peaceful. . . . These men under the blankets is as clear a memory drawing as I could do.

'Below this, are a lot of mules in a great herd and most of them lying down. I got this notion in two separate ways; one was the fact that mules gave me a feeling of Macedonia and the other was the description of the herds of whales in *Moby Dick*. Do you remember the description of . . . how they swam in the form of a horseshoe and that the extreme outside edge was composed of the fighting whales, then the next inner layer would be the father whales and the next . . . the mother whales? Then, if one were able to enter the narrow strait into the little bay or lake which the inner edge formed, one would see the baby whales still attached to the mothers. It was rather cruel this getting into this mass of whales by this narrow strait and attacking them on their weakest front, that appeared to be the Nantucketers' method. I thought this sort of land and bank formed solely of whales sounded grand.

'In among my mass of mules, I have, here and there, just conveniently growing under some of the mules' very noses, some green stuff specially to their taste. . . . These two mules [to the left], at the time when the resurrection takes place, have been carrying packs. The one on the left, it being the Resurrection, has been relieved of his burden of army biscuits which, perhaps you remember, came up the line in tins rather similar to Shell petrol tins, only they were squarer. We always knew when we were going to have two days of bread or two days of biscuits. When it was bread, . . . you would hear no sound, so that if the first you knew of the mules' arrival was suddenly seeing them being unloaded in your camp, you then knew it was bread. . . . But if you heard in the distance a hard, jangling, tinny sound and turned your eyes to the hills and saw a column of mules coming and realised this rattling sound of tins came from thence, you knew you were in for goodness knows how many days of army biscuits. The right-hand mule of these two is being relieved of a burden of bread on one side and a truss of straw on the other.

'The central motif of this picture is also mules. They are lying on the ground in the same order as when they were harnessed to the limber wagon, . . . the wheels and the mules and the men, who were the riders of them waking up, it being the Resurrection, and contemplating the surroundings. This that I want to tell you . . . is gruesome. . . . It is that I once saw a scene very similar . . . of riders fallen down between the mules. . . . It helps to show that this idea is very logical. . . . You remember I was telling you about this mule idea when we were looking at those Chaldean things in the British Museum. How I thought of those two mules turning their heads round in opposite directions was one day up in the Vale of Health studio. Looking out of the window as usual, I saw the oil-cart, which was always drawn by two sleek-looking horses, and they were both looking round in this manner. . . .

'The man rolling up his puttee [centre right] and the man on the ground with his puttee streaming behind him, was suggested to me when I remembered, after having carried several wounded men through a barbed-wire entanglement, noticing my puttee not undone but neatly cut clean through and trailing along the ground. And so I have imagined that when a man is wounded or killed that his puttee might get cut as mine did.'

With the painting of the end wall progressing, Mary Behrend proposed having it described in a 'brochure', which she would have printed,[8] and Stanley informed Hilda accordingly in 1929: 'She would like Dick to do it, as what he had done in *The Studio* was, she thought, so very good.[9] . . . She asked me to make a list of what each incident represents and then to let Dick have it.' Delighted with this proposal, Stanley added to the descriptions he had already sent me, as follows: 'In every picture in the scheme there is a feeling of joy and hopeful expectancy, as though what they were doing was all a part of a graduated course, leading distinctly and logically to the resurrection. But it is as well to know the framework of this *Resurrection*. . . . Half is plain circumstances and half is the effect of the resurrection on the circumstances. . . . Then comes a very predominating feature in the picture—the mules. There were nearly as many mules in Macedonia as there were men. I became mixed up with them even though I was only an ambulance man. And the mules always seemed to reflect the feeling the country gave me, just as certain men did. The mules on the "switch-back" road are in the same order as when carrying goods or conveying "sitting-up" patients. The mass of mules are as they usually are allowed to remain when only stopping on the way to some place. The mule with the boxes is a pack mule, . . . lying down, the burden having broken and the tins lying about. . . . A pack saddle is lying on ground a little above these mules. . . .

'Some dead Bulgars I once saw gave me some idea of the circumstances under which they had been killed. They were lying as though asleep on the side of the road. . . . When I saw these things I had already notions of doing a picture of the Resurrection. So much for the mules. . . . Some of the men have pieces of barbed wire still in their clothes. The men on the right and left in the foreground are coming out of graves. Tortoises and an animal supposed to be a jackal can be seen in the foreground.

'Crosses were not often procurable in Macedonia, but some graves had them. I used to think of the idea I had in mind of the Resurrection when digging graves. The picture is revealing a particular aspect of the resurrection, namely the transition from several states of imperfection—ordinary physical happenings such as being killed on a road or buried or caught in barbed wire, . . . to the one state of perfection.

'In a sermon by Donne, in which he speaks of the journey of his soul from "this life to the next", . . . he goes on to show how that his soul not only will not die but will not so much as even suffer an "interruption". Nothing is so tremendous as happiness which results from perfect truth. . . .

'The men looking at the crosses are meant to be expressing happiness, . . . which is the result of certainty; the certainty in this case being clearly understanding . . . the meaning of "He that loses his life for my sake shall save it." . . . They are thinking of ideas arising from the words quoted, . . . that it is actually impossible for anything good to be lost. . . . So that where one is satisfied that sacrifice is absolutely right, one need not fear to lose anything.

'The love which comes as the result of realising and understanding some spiritual truth . . . is being expressed by the figures round Christ in this picture. There is something akin in these grave crosses to the feeling of being at home and in the heart of domestic happiness—the one thing that one longed for in Macedonia. . . . The longing for home which Macedonia gave me was . . . [due] to a peculiar domestic suggestiveness that seemed to pervade the country.'

Stanley and Hilda had moved, in February 1928, into the red-brick cottage the Behrends had built within sight of the chapel on the other side of the railway line. Being within a short walking distance, Stanley could discard his bicycle. He took a break for Christmas, spent as usual at Downshire Hill, but Hilda remained on in Hampstead in January, while Stanley returned to Burghclere, as she wished to attend her brother Sydney's exhibition at the Goupil Gallery. Meanwhile, Stanley reported his progress to her in January 1929: 'I have just this morning painted something that I have been waiting and looking forward to for three years. It was one of the mules.'. In another letter, he added: 'I have painted in the last three days, the left-hand big white mule, quite successfully, as far as my opinion goes', and elsewhere he writes: 'It is really wonderful to see its look of understanding, of knowing the truth; it is confident and content.'

Stanley was able to have the scaffolding removed from the end wall by February 1929, in order to paint the lower section, and he could then see his work as a whole. By the end of March, he had nearly completed it. He had spent barely nine months on this huge painting.

In the summer that year, Stanley decided to break off work in the chapel to spend some months in Cookham, proposing to paint landscapes there. He and Hilda took lodgings in the High Street, joined by my mother and myself. It was then that he painted the *Tarry Stone*.[10] Stanley having acquired a motorcar, which he or Hilda drove, we were more than usually mobile. On the return to Burghclere in October, he painted landscapes and portraits,[11] working from sight, before beginning work once more in the chapel.

Stanley had to give up much time, when working in the chapel, to receiving and talking to visitors. He was not resentful over these unannounced disturbances and readily discussed what he was doing. In many cases, the visitors were known to him and were welcome, such as Arthur Waley, the poet, and Robert Gathorne-Hardy, the young friend of Lady Ottoline, who came in 1929; and the following year, he was visited by Duncan Grant with Vanessa Bell, a pleasurable surprise, since Stanley was not very acceptable in 'Bloomsbury' circles. Noel and Catherine Carrington brought his sister, Dora—they lived near-by. Other visitors that year and in 1930 included Stephen Tomlin, the sculptor, with his wife Julia Strachey, Stephen and Mary Bone, and, of course, Henry Lamb with his wife, Pansy, and many others.

To Charles Aitken, who had just retired as Director of the Tate Gallery, Stanley described what he was then painting as: 'A symphony in rashers of bacon' with a 'tea-making obligato'. There were also tiresome visitors, like the elderly lady, who asked if he would be exhibiting at the Royal Academy one day. This was not accepted as a compliment, and Stanley replied with some irritation: 'No, not me, not much hope of that', her answer being, to make matters worse: 'Well, don't despair'. He recalled another visitor, a clergyman, as always shutting his eyes when preaching, 'and he always looked at my pictures in the same way'.

Early next year, he began work on the two long side walls, above the arched panels, after fresh scaffolding had been erected. They were ready for him to begin painting in March 1930. He had chosen the left-hand wall first (Plate 33), the scene being the camp at Karasuli with its rows of white tents and soldiers cooking breakfast, distributing bread, carrying a cauldron of tea and removing litter. The scene included himself, as he told Henry on 23 June 1930: 'I am just about to paint the portrait of "me", striding past a bivouac and delivering the "coup de grace" with an old rusty bayonet to bits of the *Balkan News* lying about (see jacket).' Stanley liked painting litter for the interesting forms it could provide, just as he liked painting piles of laundry, as in the soldier washing his shirt in a stream.

A compositional challenge was posed by the spaces formed between each arch. He met this, in one case, by surmounting it with the steeple-like white tent, and in another, he has a dog descending into the ravine to ferret among discarded tins. In a letter to Hilda in Hampstead, he described what he was painting (22 May 1930): 'I am once again waiting for the kettle to boil for tea. . . . I have had tea now, and have just painted the cauldron in the chapel. I am still in the Chapel, but it is too dark to paint any more. Yesterday and today, I have done a lot. As far as "looks" are concerned, what I have just done seems more stimulating than anything else in the Chapel. The little person [in the centre of the picture] is meant to be me that is holding up, between two flat pieces of wood, a big bunch of rashers of bacon. And it was very amusing trying to get the difference between the unfried rashers in the box and the friend rashers in the dixie. But the incident was not big enough to display my talent to its fullest. The tea in the cauldron, due to the movement of the men carrying it, is lurching up the side.' A few weeks later (15 June), he told her: 'All day I have been working at the "avenue" of men (the men having the tea dished out to them). They really are turning out well. The chap with a fork and spoon sticking up out of his puttee, [in front], is very jolly. He is the one that is tipping up the mess-tin lid to see he has his fair share of bacon.' By July, only the right-hand section with the group of stone-cutters remained to be painted and by August 1930, he had finished the wall.

During that autumn and on into 1931, Stanley tackled the right-hand wall (Plate 34) depicting the river-bed at Todorova, with men washing clothes on the rocks,[12] soldiers playing bingo while others make a mosaic in coloured stones of the red-cross and regimental badges. With its completion during 1931, Stanley was able to turn to the few remaining panels yet to be painted.

They—Stanley and Hilda with Unity, born in May the previous year—spent that summer of 1931 at Burghclere, joined by my mother. Stanley did portrait drawings of them and of my eldest brother George, when he visited them.

Stanley had no intention, at that time, of leaving Chapel View. In fact, he wrote to Henry (23 June 1930), who wanted to paint his portrait:[13] ' I expect you will make a "Velasquez Dwarf"[14] portrait of me; . . . that would at least distinguish it from Strachey's. I am in no mood to leave this here abode at present and if I have my way I never will; so that if you seriously came to the point of wanting to paint it, it might have to be done here.' As it would have meant Henry having to stay at Burghclere, the portrait was not painted.

In the late summer of 1931, however, Stanley with Hilda and Unity went again to Cookham, and despite Stanley's previous determination never to leave Chapel View, they looked at prospective houses and bought Lindworth, using the thousand pounds he had received by the sale of *Resurrection* for the Tate Gallery. They finally left Burghclere to live at Cookham in December. Having several of his war subjects still to be painted for the chapel, Stanley had a ready-built studio erected in the garden at Lindworth.[15] By midsummer 1932, Stanley had completed them, the entire work for the chapel having taken him just five years.

Notes to Chapter 12

1. It was dedicated in 1927 as the Oratory of All Souls to the memory of Mary Behrend's brother, Lieutenant H. W. Sandham, who died in Macedonia in 1919 from illness contracted during war service (recorded by George Behrend, op. cit.).

2. He recorded in a notebook in the 1950s that he made two small studies for this and soldiers' ablutions (Plate 8) and for the *Laundry* scene in 1921 at Steep for the proposed decoration of the village hall, which he did not carry out.

3. An oil in my possession.

4. Not in 1926, as stated by Elizabeth Rothenstein (op. cit.).

5. See footnote 2 above.

6. George Behrend (op. cit.) locates the scene in 'a requisitioned house in Salonika', but does not state on what authority. Stanley may have had more than one place in mind. In any case it has to be classed with the hospital subjects.

7. He always had this photograph of her on his mantelpiece, and it was there, at Fernley (previously Fernlea), when he died.

8. It was never printed as Stanley disapproved of my first draft, and I decided to abandon it.

9. Richard Carline, 'New Mural Paintings by Stanley Spencer', *Studio Magazine*, November 1928.

10. These included a painting of the Tarry Stone, usually called *High Street, Cookham*, in Canon Westropp's collection, hitherto dated 1936, as in the Spencer Gallery catalogue. My photograph of him painting this picture with Shirin and Hilda in the background confirms the date as 1929.

11. Besides portrait drawings, he and Hilda painted their maid, Elsie, life-size. Stanley greatly admired hers, which was hanging in Fernlea when he died.

12. Of a soldier washing clothes (lower centre), he observed ('Reminiscences', 1945), that enlarging the figure had spoilt the rhythm: 'I should have left it the original size it was in the composition.'

13. Stanley had paid a visit to Henry and Pansy Lamb at Coombe Bissett in Wiltshire, when Henry's proposal was discussed. He had, however, made a small portrait of Stanley in oils, as well as one in pencil, much earlier.

14. Stanley refers to Lamb's well-known full-length portrait of Lytton Strachey, with the view of Hampstead Heath as background, painted in his Vale of Health studio in 1912. Bought by Mary Behrend, it is now in the National Portrait Gallery.

15. His studio was removed about a decade later, after his second wife had disposed of the house.

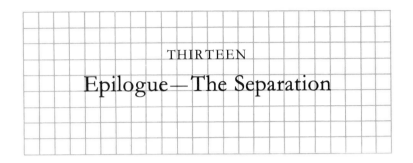

THIRTEEN
Epilogue — The Separation

STANLEY'S MARRIAGE with Hilda had its periods of rapture. He found in her personality much that was essential to him, which no other women whom he met could provide. They were devoted to one another, despite all their differences, and this mutual feeling persisted long after their separation. In a curious way, Stanley did not accept that they were separated, even when she died, and he had pressed her to re-marry him, but she declined.

When Hilda was absent, Stanley would at once begin writing her letters, often spreading them over days, even weeks. One, which he designated his 'hundred page letter' begun in May 1930, was not finished and posted until the end of June. He described an evening walk (15 June) at Burghclere, watching night-jars (or goat-suckers) gathering in an oak tree: 'I like to think of their having a cosy time, like we have, that they might love to see their wife's head against an oak leaf, just as I might see your head against the towel-horse (as in my drawing). Animals and birds have such absolute "'belongness" to places.' He would write such letters in the evening after tea, with the day's work in the chapel finished, sometimes interspersed with 'compositioning' as he called his drawing of new ideas. Hilda would respond with equally long letters.

Seeds of future discord were, nevertheless, evident from the beginning of their marriage, and these chiefly revolved around household management. Hilda was not entirely impractical nor indisposed towards housework or attention to her family, as long as she was allowed to do things in her own way, unconventional as her methods might seem. She had suffered since youth from severe pains in her back, which sapped her physical energy and left an

38. Stanley Spencer,
Hilda and Shirin,
Cookham, 1929.

39. Stanley Spencer
with Unity,
Cookham, 1932.

40. Hilda with
Shirin, 1926.

41. *Hilda with her Hair Down*, Burghclere, 1931.

inertia, which grew with passing years. Being reluctant to perform tasks that bored her, she readily abandoned efforts when they were constantly criticised. Stanley always prided himself on being practical, and fancied his own method of looking after children or carrying out housework. He would assert that Hilda did things the wrong way, and eventually would complain that he had to do everything, sometimes airing his complaints to their friends.

Stanley's work in the chapel was often hindered by bouts of illness. He had quinsey in 1929 and 1930, and an operation for gallstones in March 1932. These attacks would add to his irritability; when opposed, his temper could be short-lived. On many occasions, time and energy would be wasted in quarrelsome debate. Stanley possessed exceptional vitality, which he could maintain even with a short night's sleep—he usually woke early— and he would take a nap in the afternoons. Their arguments, as I recall, could be heard far into the night, with 'what I mean to say is' constantly repeated. Her passive even languid state of mind would prevent her keeping pace with him in argument, and this, combined with her stubborn disposition and reluctance to give way or concede a point, would increase his irritation.

Daily life with Stanley, though never without its absorbing interest, would not have been easy for anyone, even if more robust than Hilda. Though they shared ideas and feelings and were both equally afraid of boredom, they were unlike in upbringing and behaviour, and periodically she felt compelled to leave him in order to recuperate, if she was to avoid a breakdown.

She had, however, other reasons. When her brother Sydney fell ill and died in February 1929, soon after the opening of his Goupil Gallery exhibition, the overwhelming tragedy made her feel she should stay to console her mother. Then, in 1930, she was in Hampstead for the birth of their second daughter, Unity, in May. Stanley acquiesced wholeheartedly in the need for such absences from him.

But he grew impatient over the various tasks which she wanted performed, and which she explained at length in her letters. In angry mood, he wrote her in May 1930: 'The difference between me and my wants and you and yours is that my wants are nil, apart from bed and food. . . . All your ideas in order to be carried out must involve a ghastly amount of inconvenience and loss of money. . . . I am not going to budge one particle of an inch in a matter that does not in the least interest me.' Hilda countered this by complaining that her desires were trifling compared with what he had spent on buying a motorcar and laying out a tennis court, which, she affirmed, they did not need.

Chapel View, their home since 1928, was built in an open field, and Hilda found an outlet for her creative interests in planning the garden and designing the interior of the cottage. She also wanted an extra room built as a studio for her painting. Stanley was frankly not interested in gardening, and it was a constant source of annoyance to him, returning from the chapel for lunch or tea, to find Hilda immersed among shrubs she was planting or half concealed in a trench she was digging. Her labours, however, did produce in course of time vegetables and fruit. There was an incident, which always amused them and Stanley liked to retell. They had pressed a reluctant visitor to receive a cauliflower as a gift, after wrapping it in brown paper, which happened to bear their address. A few days later, the postman delivered it to them, saying that the porter had picked it up beside the railway line, thinking it might be valuable. The visitor had apparently thrown it out of the window as soon as the train had started.

Stanley's frankness, and confiding disposition, which endeared him to many, would prompt him to discuss Hilda's faults as well as her virtues with any sympathetic listener. On one occasion, when he was visiting the Behrends alone, 'Louis said to me before I had said anything about you: "You know, Stan, I don't believe I have ever met such an extraordinary and mysterious person as your wife; she is the best critic of pictures I know, . . . if anything over-intellectualised", and this, he thought, accounted for the difficulty you have in feeling comfortable with just anybody.' Stanley, overjoyed, promptly retailed this tribute to Hilda (6 May 1930).

Whereas before the birth of their baby, Stanley's letters to Hilda were often sharp and caustic, their tone changed after the baby was born. The day after this event, Stanley wrote her thirty pages spread over five days: 'I love you because you have an infinite capacity in *all* directions . . . and I feel it. I love you because you find out things I know I should never find out that I need. I love you because I feel that you are all-powerful and can go with me everywhere and anywhere. I love you because I feel that the moment you feel exactly what I feel, that you will feel it as strongly as I feel it. I love you because all your thoughts and feelings have the same infinite capacity of conveying meaning as the different parts of your body. It was really those feelings that made you physically attractive to me. . . . Seeing you at the table at 47, just the front part of your jumper and the edge of the table gave me not just a thrill and feeling of joy . . . but all that with something else that made that thrill all the more irresistible . . . that I could feel all my creative spiritual desires being given an extra meaning. . . . I felt if I could go with you and wander through your thoughts what a marvellous thing that would be. . . . I feel the pleasure that one feels when one finds an English daisy growing in Egypt or somewhere quite different.

'I have been reading bits of old letters of yours just now. . . . Friday; what I mean by you being like your chest of drawers is that your mind is full of drawers, some . . . brim full of . . . pictures you one day will paint.

'I am getting much greater feelings of excitement from your thoughts now, because in those days I was too worried to enjoy the food, so to speak, whereas now I, feeling more confident and peaceful, can more clearly see what every nook and corner of you contains.'

After receiving such letters, Hilda was overjoyed to return to Burghclere. She never wished them to be parted indefinitely, and he would equally welcome her return. By the end of the year 1931, they had left Chapel View and moved to Lindworth in Cookham.

Hilda was back in Hampstead in August 1932, in order to help her mother look after our eldest brother George, who was very ill. She told Stanley how much she missed him and wished to return. Stanley replied: 'Coming back to each other is marvellous, but I can never understand why the feeling does not last'. This was the first hint of change in his feelings towards her. In a further letter, he announced: 'I dislike meetings of any kind, catholic, protestant, political, social. . . . There is only one thing that I feel vital about and that is art.'

Hilda had planned to return to Lindworth, but the inexplicable absence of letters from Stanley later that autumn, something so unusual, caused her to suspect a change in his relationship towards her. After George's death in December, she felt crushed by the receipt of a letter from Stanley (January 1933), which discouraged her from returning. He had frankly admitted a new attachment. This was Patricia Preece, who used to join our picnic parties on Odney Common in 1929, but a close friendship between her and Stanley had developed only recently. He did not wish Hilda to absent herself, quite on the contrary, but expected her to accept his new attachment. She presumed, however, that more than this was involved, though Stanley strongly denied it.

Stanley returned to Burghclere for a while in February 1933, to finish work in the Chapel, and Hilda decided to return then to Lindworth. Although she considered her marriage sacred and indissoluble, she decided not to remain in Cookham, feeling that the new circumstances made separation, even if only temporary, inevitable. Subsequently, however, she insisted on a divorce, feeling that her principles should be sacrificed so that he could re-marry. But Stanley continued to oppose the divorce.

Having no wish to lose Hilda, although he had only just remarried, he asked her (24 July, 1937) to stay with him at Mrs Lambert's in Wangford, where they had spent their honeymoon: 'To me everything depended on getting this very same room,' he added. Hilda declined, regarding it as adultery.

Stanley and Hilda had been together throughout the most fruitful period of his painting, the Cookham *Resurrection* and his war pictures. Thenceforward, when he was living alone, despite having re-married, and was within a few years deprived of his home, Lindworth—and so exiled from Cookham—his work acquired a fundamentally different character: in my opinion less inspired. Although after the Second World War, he was able to reside in Cookham Rise, he was not again to live amidst his early surroundings in Cookham village until the last year of his life, spent once more at Fernlea.

Notes on the Plates

Frontispiece. Stanley Spencer photographed as a private soldier in the R.A.M.C. at Cookham during leave, summer 1916.

1. *The Mayor of Maidenhead Visits the Technical School*, drawn with pencil in a notebook, *c.* 1932, 9 × 7in (23 × 18cm); a recollection of student days, 1907/8. Tate Gallery Archives, No. 733.3.22. The Mayor lays his hat on the cast of the Roman Gladiator, with other casts on walls and shelves. Spencer likened the scene to a postcard showing two tramps observing a cow grazing in a field: 'Just think, everywhere it looks is something to eat.' The scene was subsequently re-drawn in his 'Scrap-book' series. (p. 22)

2. *Paradise*, pen and ink, 13½ × 15¾in (34 × 40cm); submitted for the Slade Sketch Club, 1911. Slade School of Fine Art, University College, London. (p. 24)

3. *Grape hyacinth*, watercolour 3 × 2¾in (7.5 × 5.5cm) painted in Macedonia, probably 1918 and enclosed in a letter to Florence. Inscribed on the back in pencil: 'I had no white so that rather upset the thing.' (p. 35)

4. *The Centurion's Servant*, oil on paper, part of a letter, 7 × 4½in (18 × 11.5cm), to Henry Lamb, 1 October 1914. Lady Pansy Lamb. (p. 35)

5. Sketch for a composition, pencil and sepia wash, 6 × 6in (15 × 15cm), probably at Cookham *c.* 1912 to 1914; perhaps related to either the *Nativity* or *Zacharias and Elizabeth*. (p. 35)

6. *Richard Hartley*, pencil, 14 × 10in (35.5 × 25.5cm), probably at Burghclere signed and dated September 1927. The sitter was one of the artist's earliest friends among artists and a frequent visitor to Cookham, Hampstead and Burghclere. (p. 42)

7. *Henry Lamb*, pencil, 16 × 12in (40.5 × 30.5cm), drawn by
   Gilbert Spencer, R.A., *c.* 1921.   (p. 42)
8. *Scrubbing the Floor and Soldiers Washing at Beaufort Hospital,*
   Bristol in 1916, pencil and grey wash, $9\frac{15}{16}$ × $14\frac{3}{8}$in (25 ×
   36.5cm), previously entitled *Recollection of Bristol Hospital,*
   1924, but more probably one of the two sketches made when
   in Steep, 1921 or not later than January 1922, described by
   him subsequently: 'for a decoration that Sir Muirhead Bone
   wanted me to do for a village hall there ... never done but
   later done in the Burghclere series', i.e. in two predella
   paintings (Tate Gallery Archives, notebook, 733.3.86).
   Fitzwilliam Museum, Cambridge.   (p. 73)
9. *Troops out for a Rest*, pencil and sepia wash, $8\frac{1}{2}$ × $8\frac{1}{2}$in (21.5 ×
   21.5cm), 1919; a recollection of bivouacs at Corsica Camp,
   Macedonia in 1917. The sketch has the title inscribed. (p. 73)
10. *Travoys along Sedemli Ravine on the Way to Le Naze, Macedonia*,
    pencil and sepia wash, $8\frac{1}{2}$ × 10in (21.5 × 25.5cm), 1919; a
    recollection of the R.A.M.C. at Corsica Camp, 1916. Imperial
    War Museum.   (p. 75)
11. *Soldiers at a Well with Mules and Mountains in the Distance,*
    Macedonia, pencil and grey wash (with some patches of oil
    discolouration), $9\frac{1}{4}$ × 11in (24 × 28cm) 1919. The Imperial
    War Museum possesses a somewhat similar sketch.   (p. 75)
    Spencer wrote in Glasgow: 'Just after the 1914 War, I did a
    small composition of some mule lines on a plain with these
    mountains in the background; I felt not satisfied.' Though
    perhaps not referring to this drawing, one mountain impressed
    him especially: 'It seemed so remote, so long since gathered to
    its mountainous forefathers. It was covered nearly to its base
    with snow, a sort of grave-shaped thing. At intervals slices
    seemed to have been taken out of it; three long gashes there
    were. . . . They looked like slices taken out of the side of a
    Christmas pudding. . . . Every sound was muffled . . . only the
    faint jingle and squeaking of the mules' harness. But
    somehow, though some of my worst experiences were ahead
    of me, I felt hopeful. . . . I thought what sort of goings-on
    could take place on this mountain side . . . ravines fingering
    their way upwards clearing its side and making huge dock-leaf
    shapes.' It was the setting for his *Crucifixion* (Aberdeen).

12. *The Commandant Emerging from a Dug-out on the Hill-side, Macedonia*, pencil and sepia wash, 6¼ × 8¾in (16 × 22.5cm), 1919; a recollection of his infantry service, June 1918. Imperial War Museum. (p. 89)

13. *Drinking Water, near Mirova, Macedonia*, pencil and sepia wash, 8 × 6¼in (20.5 × 16cm), 1919; a recollection of the R.A.M.C. at Mirova Camp, May 1917. Imperial War Museum. (p. 89)

14. *Travoys with Wounded Soldiers Arriving at a Dressing Station at Smol, Macedonia*, oil, 72 × 86in (183 × 218.5cm), 1919; a recollection of the R.A.M.C., at Corsica Camp, September 1916. Commissioned by the Ministry of Information for the Imperial War Museum. (p. 113)

15. *Wounded Soldier on a Stretcher*, pencil and sepia wash, 8½ × 6¾in (21.5 × 17cm); a sketch of the second stretcher from the left in *Travoys*, 1919. (p. 114)

16. *Wounded Soldier on a Stretcher*, pencil and sepia wash, 8½ × 6¾in (21.5 × 17cm); a sketch of the right-hand stretcher in *Travoys*, 1919. (p. 114)

17. *Travoys with Wounded Soldiers*, pencil and sepia wash, 7 × 9in (18 × 23cm); sketch for the oil painting, re-drawn 1919 after losing the original sketch made in Macedonia. Imperial War Museum. (p. 114)

18. Sketch for a composition, pencil and sepia wash, 3½ × 4⅛in (9 × 10.5cm); on the reverse in pencil (barely legible) '. . . with Leeds idea.' If this is correctly read, it may be the first of several preliminary sketches for the Leeds mural in 1920, rejected as unsuitable. Alternatively, it seems related in style to his series of *Christ Tipping over the Tables*. (p. 124)

19. School concert in progress with opened-up grand piano: preliminary sketch, pencil and sepia wash, 1921 4½ × 3¾in (11.5 × 9.5cm) for a mural in Bedales school, not carried out.

20. Sketch for *Christ Carrying the Cross*, pencil and sepia wash, 14¼ × 13in (36 × 33cm), 1920; included in the Goupil Gallery exhibition, 1927, and then given to the author. The scene is in front of Fernlea, Cookham. (p. 124)

21. *Christ Tipping over the Tables in the Temple*, two sketches in pen and ink, part of a letter, 7 × 4½in (18 × 11.5cm), to Hilda from Bourne End, 21 March 1921. The letter explains his idea for these compositions. (p. 127)

22. *Stanley and Hilda Reading Letters*, part of a letter, 10 × 7¾in (25.5 × 19.5cm), pen and ink, to Hilda from Chapel View, Burghclere, 22 May 1930. (p. 127)

23. Stanley Spencer with the Carlines, photographed in the hills above Sarajevo, Jugoslavia, August 1922. Left to right: Stanley Spencer, Hilda, Mrs Carline, Sydney (in front), George, Richard, with May Piggott (cousin in front). (p. 135)

24. In front of the Spencers' motorcar in Maidenhead, 1929: Jas Wood, Stanley Spencer, Hilda, Shirin, Mrs Carline. (p. 135)

25. Working drawing for the proposed arrangement of paintings for the left-hand side wall, to be carried out in Burghclere Chapel; pencil and sepia wash, 22 × 28½in (56 × 72.5cm), Poole, 1923. Stanley Spencer Gallery. (p. 146)

26. Working drawing for the right-hand side wall to be carried out in Burghclere Chapel; pencil and sepia wash, 22 × 28½in (56 × 72.5cm), Poole, 1923. Stanley Spencer Gallery. (p. 147)

     Plates 25 and 26 are from photographs taken shortly after the drawings were made, and given to the author in 1928. After long use by the artist, both drawings are now much faded and discoloured by oil. These photographs provide, therefore, the only true record of the scheme as originally devised.

27. *Theatre Orderly from Beaufort Hospital*, pencil, 11½ × 9in (29 × 23cm), drawn at Tweseldown Camp, signed and dated 1916. The artist recorded in Glasgow, 1944, that the sitter had accompanied him from Bristol, and he drew him in their hut, this and another portrait drawing (whereabouts not recorded) being the only ones to survive the War. (p. 151)

28. *Louis Behrend*, pencil, 11½ × 9in (29 × 23cm), drawn at Burghclere *c.* 1928. The sitter was one of the artist's earliest patrons, who, with his wife, commissioned the Burghclere paintings. (p. 151)

29. *Richard Carline*, oil, 21½ × 15½in (54.5 × 39.5cm), painted in the Vale of Health studio, Hampstead, 1923; bought by Sir Edward Marsh and bequeathed to Rugby Art Gallery. (p. 157)

30. *Stanley Spencer*, oil, 24 × 14½in (61 × 37cm), painted by Richard Carline in the garden at 47 Downshire Hill, Hampstead, in 1924, as a study for *Gathering on the Terrace*, showing the Carlines, Lamb, Hartley, Wood and Kate Foster. (p. 157)

31. Sketch for the river-steamer, top left corner of the *Resurrection*, pen and ink, part of a letter, 10 × 7¾in (25.5 × 19.5cm), to Hilda from Hampstead, undated but probably December 1924. The letter explains his revised idea for this part of the picture. (p. 164)

32. *The Resurrection in Cookham Churchyard*, detail, oil, 108 × 216in (274 × 548cm), painted in Hampstead February 1924 to April 1926; exhibited Goupil Gallery, 1927, and bought by the Contemporary Art Society for the Tate Gallery.

   Centre above: the porch with seated Christ; left: the negroes; right: the artist nude with arms resting on tombstones; centre below: Richard Carline nude with right arm raised; left below: Hilda in the ivy-covered tomb; right below: Sir Henry Slesser. (p. 165)

33. Burghclere Chapel, left-hand wall: (above) *Camp at Karasuli, Macedonia*; (arched panels, left to right) *Convoy of Wounded Soldiers Arriving at Beaufort Hospital Gates*; *Ablutions at Beaufort Hospital*; *Kit Inspection at Tweseldown Camp*; *Stand-to, Macedonia*; (predellas below, left to right) *Scrubbing the Floor*; *Kit-bags*; *Laundry*; *Tea-urns*, all at Beaufort Hospital. (pp. 178–9)

34. Burghclere Chapel, right-hand wall: (above) *River-bed at Todorova, Macedonia*; (arched panels, left to right) *Reveille*; *Filling Water-bottles at a Stream*; *Map-reading*; *Making a Fire-belt*, all of Macedonia; (predellas below, left to right) *Frost-bite*; *Tea in the Ward*; *Bed-making*; *Scrubbing Lockers in Baths*, all of Beaufort Hospital. (pp. 180–1)

35. *A Camouflaged Soldier*, pencil and wash, 19⅞ × 14⅝in (50.5 × 37cm), *c*. 1928; a sketch for *Stand-to* in Burghclere Chapel. Tate Gallery, No. 4245. (p. 187)

36. Working cartoon for *The Resurrection of Soldiers*, end wall, Burghclere Chapel, probably drawn in 1927. This photograph and another of the cartoon for the lower part of the picture were given to the author in 1928, probably the only record of the preliminary scheme. (p. 188)

37. *The Resurrection of Soldiers in Macedonia*, the end wall with altar, oil, 1928 to 1929. Burghclere Chapel. (p. 189)

38. Stanley Spencer, Hilda and Shirin at Cookham, 1929. (p. 201)

39. Stanley with Unity, Lindworth, Cookham, 1932 (p. 201)

40. Hilda with Shirin, Hampstead, early 1926. (p. 201)

41. *Hilda with her Hair Down*, pencil on several joined sheets of paper, 24 × 17¾in (61 × 45cm), drawn at Burghclere, signed and dated 1931. (p. 202)

All the work reproduced is by Stanley Spencer and in family possession, except where stated otherwise.

Plates 3, 4, 5, 6, 9, 10, 15, 16, 18, 19, 21, 22, 27, 28 and 31 are from photographs of the original drawings in family possession; the frontispiece and Plates 25, 26, 36 and 40 are from photographs which have been re-photographed; Plates 33 and 34 are from photographs taken in Burghclere Chapel recently. All the above, except for Plate 18 photographed by John Neale of Maidenhead, have been taken by Peter Spencer Coppock, who possesses the negatives and copyright on their further use.

The following reproductions are from photographs provided as follows: Plates 1, 32, 35, Tate Gallery, London; 2, the Slade School of Fine Art, University College, London; 11, 12, 13, 14 and 17 Imperial War Museum, London; 8, the Fitzwilliam Museum, Cambridge; 7, 20, 30 and 41 are from photographs taken by the Courtauld Institute of Art, University of London, from drawings and paintings in the author's possession.

Copyright of all works reproduced belongs to Stanley Spencer's heirs, with the exception of those belonging to the Imperial War Museum, as listed above, Plate 32 belonging to the Tate Gallery, and 7 and 30 belonging to the respective artists. The copyright of photographs Plates 23, 24, 38 and 39 belongs to the author.

Postscript. Since this text was written I have been indebted to Dr D. P. Waley of the British Library for showing me two letters (one dated 13 May 1917) addressed to the Raverats: 'Great storm clouds', he writes, 'are nearly always on the mountains, but they seem to hang there all day and cast great shadows from the side of the mountain. . . . But oh, I long for the sea. I feel when I am in land a good way as if I cannot breathe. . . . I loved it when the ship suddenly stops or the siren goes deep and long, and the flag flaps about the masts. The whole world seems to be "held up".' I am also grateful to the Librarian of the University of London Library for showing me a letter (26 April 1924) to Sturge-Moore, about the drawing he had made of his daughter Riette.

Index

INDEX

Beethoven, listening to, 85, 92, 141; 'Emperor' Concerto, 31
Behrend, George, author, 159, 199
Behrend, Louie (Louis), 150, 152, 158–9, 176, 204; drawing of, 151, 210
Behrend, Mary (Mrs), 152, 156, 158–9, 176, 194, 199
Behrends, the (Mr and Mrs), 47, 117, 150, 152, 155–6, 158–9, 160, 196, 204
Belfast, imagining a visit, 97
Belgrade railway, 71
Bell, Clive, Second Post-Impressionist Exhibition, 30
Bell, Vanessa, exhibiting in Second Post-Impressionist Exhibition, 30; visitor, 196
Benson, J. M. B., fellow student at the Slade, 31
Bentinck, Lord Henry, patron, 152
Berkshire School of Art and Design, 31
Berkshires, see Royal Berkshires
Betrayal, painting of, 138, 155
Bevan, 'Bobby', visitor, 143
Bevan, Robert, visitor, 119
Bible, the, reading of, 20, 23, 25, 36, 41, 108, 138
Biscay, Bay of, voyage in, 68
Bivouacs, see Macedonia
Blackbird, watching, 34, 36, 125
'Black Country', the, fellow soldier in Macedonia from, 97
'Black Prince', the, cook's nickname in Macedonia, 78
Blake, William, reading of his poetry, discussion of, 85–6, 166
Bleak House, reading of, 84
Bloomsbury 'set', 36, 197
Bone, Muirhead (Sir Muirhead), 46, 95, 130, 132, 143, 152, 159, 208
Bone, Mrs, 130
Bone, Stephen and Mary (Aldshead), visitors, 143, 197
Book of Life, Lamb, reading of, 136
Bosnia, reading about, 131; travelling to with the Carlines, 133; tray brought back, drawing of, 107
Boston, Lady, giving advice and lessons, 23
Bourne End, Berks, staying at, 117, 121, 123, 125, 128–30, 149, 209
Bourne End railway station, meeting at, 129
Bournemouth, municipal Art School, exhibition, 149
Bray, ambulance training at, 40
Brer Rabbit, quoting from, 36–7
Brett, Dorothy, visitor, 142
Breuil, Professor Henri, correspondence with, 38, 46
Bristol Hospital (see also Beaufort Hospital); Fishponds, imagining a visit, 96; asylum (see Beaufort Hospital); leaving for, arriving at, 48–50, 60; imagining revisiting, 96; orderly friend from, 210; recollections of, 70, 79, 208
British Army, 69; headquarters, Macedonia, 95, 105; objectives and offensive, 82, 97–8; serving in, 87, 111
British Museum, visit to, 194
'Brochure', proposed, about Burghclere

paintings, 194
Brown, Professor Frederick, 23, 26
Browning, Robert, reading of, 106
'Brughel', Peter van, work by, 121
Buden, Lionel, fellow orderly and friend at Bristol, 70
Bulgar (Bulgars, Bulgarians), contact at night, 94; feelings about, 70, 79, 82, 93, 104, 195; forces, 69, 98, 105; forces entrenched, 71, 103; lines, 79–80, 99; outposts, 92; positions on the front, 82, 99; shell-dumps, 82, 104; trench-wire, cutting of, 95
Bulgaria, participation in the War, 69; defeat, 105
Bulgarian peasants, meeting with, 100
Buna, source of the (in Herzegovina), visit to, 134
Bunyan, John, influence of, 172; Pilgrim's Progress, illustrating when a boy, 20
Burghclere, 182, 196, 198, 200, 205–6; Palmers Hill Farm, family moving to, 177; see also Chapel View
Burghclere Chapel, illustrations of, 178, 180, 187–9, 210–11; altar, plans for, 155, 176, 190–1; arched spaces and paintings, 155–6, 158, 176–8, 180, 185–6, 197; building plans and progress, 152, 154, 156, 159, 161, 177; canvas used in, 176, 186; cartoons for, 159, 161, 188, 190, 192, 211; cauldron of tea, painting of, 197–8; mosaics, plan to design, 176, 190; painting, drawing and working in, 177, 186, 191–2, 194, 196–8, 203, 206, 211; painting himself in, 182, 197–8; planning the paintings and compositions, 145–9, 150, 152–3, 155–6, 159–60, 212; plans and sketches for, 145–7, 152, 155–6, 158–9, 176; rashers of bacon, painting of, 197–8; scaffolding erected and removed, 186, 196–7; soldiers washing clothes, painting of, 189; stained glass window, plans for, 155, 176, 190; subscriptions sought, 152; visits, visitors, 16, 196–7, 207; work completed, 199
Burlington House, London, exhibiting in, 112, 128
Burn, Rodney, R. A., and Dorothy, visitors, 143
Burrell, Miss, student at Maidenhead Technical School, 20
Byrd, discussing music by, 86
Byways, Steep (the Bones' home), staying at, 130
Byzantine churches, 69, 158

Cambridge, Florence (sister), living in, 110, 117
Camden Town Group, artist members of, 144
Camouflaged Soldier, sketch of, 185, 211
Camouflaged Tent, plan to paint, 184, 186
Canadian Hospital, 4th Salonika, 74; 5th, Salonika, 79
Canterbury Tales, reading of, 66
Carfax Gallery, London, 46–7
Carline, Annie (mother), 46, 132–3, 135, 139, 143–4, 150, 155, 163, 167, 175, 196, 205, 210; drawing of at Burghclere, 198
Carline, George F. (father), 122, 144; death of, 129; paintings by discussed, 139, 144
Carline, George R. (eldest brother), 135, 137,

INDEX

INDEX

INDEX

Litter (rubbish, dustbins), visual interest in, 28, 58, 106–7, 197
Lives, Isaac Walton, reading of, 106
'Llandovery Castle', hospital ship, 67; on the Clyde, 67
'London Group', artists exhibiting in, members of, 45, 144
London University, 144
Lorenzetti, reproductions of work by, 38
Lorrain, Claude, work of, admiration for, 76, 81, 85–6

Macedonia, bivouacs, recollections and painting of, 72, 74, 78, 80, 83, 96, 98, 208; contemplating the future, 115; crosses in, painting of, 196; deprived of the opportunity to paint in, 96; dogs, wild in, 78, 80; dug-outs in, recollections and painting of, 91–2, 94–5, 100, 184–5; feelings about and reminders of home, 71, 191, 193, 195; goats in, 86; ideas based on experiences in, 184; limbers, travelling by, 78, 90, 96, 98, 112, 194; making comparisons with, 122; memories of, 131; mosquito-nets, use of, 98, 185; mountains in, impressions of, 88, 91, 96, 153, 208; mules, mule-lines, recollections and painting of, 72, 80, 90, 96, 153, 185–6, 193, 208; need for draughtsmen in, 86; outpost duty, outposts, recollections and painting of, 92, 94–5, 97, 185–6; permitted to draw, 86; sheep in, 86; sketches and notes lost in, 110, 209; stand-to, 184–5; storks in, 92; storms in, 81–2; subjects painted, 35, 73, 75, 89, 178–80, 183, 192, 207–9; summer heat in, 92; tortoises in, 78, 83, 195; travelling across, 80, 83, 98; wild geese in, 77
Macedonia Front, inactivity, 87, 91
Macedonia wilderness, 87
Macedonians, seen, 71
Macnamara, friend of Lamb, visitor to Hampstead, 142
McColl, D. S., art critic, Keeper of the Wallace Collection, 115
Maidenhead, by bus to, 118; civic guard, training, 40; Kidwell Park, 21, 40, 49; Marlow Road, 20; Mayor of, Town Councillor of, 20–2; mother pushed there in a bath-chair, 45; motorcar, and motoring accident in, 46, 135, 210; North Town Moor, 49; railway station platform, 49–50; Technical School, studying at, drawings of, 20, 22, 23, 31, 207; Governor of, 21; Technical and Art School (subsequently Berkshire School of Art and Design), 31, 118; Widbrook Common, *see* Cookham
Makikova track, Macedonia, 94
Making a Fire-belt, Macedonia, painting of, 180, 184, 186, 211
Malaria, attack of, recovery from, 74, 79, 105, 112, 116
Malta, 69, 74
Manchester, Henry Lamb trained in medicine at, 40
Mantegna, discussion of work by, 166
Map-reading, Macedonia, painting of, 180, 182, 211

Marchant, William, proprietor of the Goupil Gallery, 167
Mark Gertler, Selected letters (Noel Carrington), 32
Marriott, Charles, art critic of *The Times*, 43
Marseillaise, singing at sea, 68
Marsh, Eddie (Sir Edward), 31, 36, 39, 47, 123, 152, 159–60, 210
Marvell, Andrew, reading of, 85
Masaccio, work of, 39–40, 131–2
Masolino, work of, 40
Mass, the, order of, 92
Medici, Lorenzo, cast of drawn at Maidenhead, 21
Mediterranean, voyaging through, 96
Medley, Herbert, painter, Hampstead visitor, 143
Memories and Reflections (J. H. Badley), 143
Men and Memories (W. Rothenstein), 128
Mending Cowls, painting of, 44, 48, 158
Meninsky, Bernard, work of, 121
Mephibosheth, reading about, 108
Meredith, reading of, 109
Mesopotamia, troops for, 64, 66
Micawber, Mr, comparison with, 121
Middle East, Sydney and Richard Carline travelling to as war artists, returning from, 118, 128
Middlesboro', fellow soldier from, Tweseldown, 65–6
Milne, General, Salonika, 69
Milton, reading of, 88, 91–2, 106
Mirova Camp, Macedonia, 82, 87, 89, 209
Moby Dick, reading of, 193
Modern Painters, John Ruskin reading of, 74
Moggridge, Mrs, *see* Taylor
Mohammedan graveyard, Sarajevo, painting in, 133
Monastir, Serbia, 82
Monnington, Tom (Sir Thomas, P.R.A.), Hampstead visitor, 143–4
Montenegro, travelling to, 133
Morrell, Lady Ottoline and Philip (M.P.), 87, 105, 136, 152, 196
Mosaics, designs for, *see* Burghclere Chapel
Moses on Mount Sinai, reading about, 41
Mosques, 69, 131
Mosquito-nets, Macedonia, painting of, 96, 184–5
Mostar, travelling to, painting old Mostar bridge, 133–4
Mother and child, drawing of, 125
Motor-car, acquisition of, 46, 135, 196, 204, 210
Motorists, attitude towards, 34, 46
Mount Olympus, 70
Mozart, discussion of, 85–6
Muezzin's call to prayer, 133
Mules, *see* Macedonia
Munich, visiting, 133
Museum of Modern Art, New York, 175
Music, mutual interest in, 38, 74, 118

Nantucketers, *see* Resurrection of Soldiers, Whales
Narthex, proposed plan for, 158
Nash, John, R. A., teaching at the Ruskin School, 136

219

INDEX

INDEX

Shakespeare, carrying it, reading it, 66, 76, 78, 84, 88, 141
Shakespearian, 69
Signorelli, Luca, work of, dreaming about, 39
Slade School of Fine Art, Antique Room, drawing in, 25; arrangements to study at, 23, 31, 36; award of prizes, 26–7, 29, 31, 34, 119; Carline, Richard, at, 130; concentration on drawing, 29; general knowledge, examination in, 23, 26; influence of, 23; leaving, 31, 33; life room, 25, 27; return for drawing, 139; scholarship, award of, 26–7; Sketch Club, 23–4, 26, 207; social functions at, 29; students, contemporary and later, 25, 30–1, 46, 119–20, 141–4, 160; summer composition prize, 33
Slesser, Harry (Sir Henry) and Margaret, 117, 121, 123, 125, 149, 152
Smol, near Corsica Camp, Macedonia, 86, 110, 113, 209
Snakes (grass and rock), Macedonia, 80–1
Soap-suds, painting of, 176
Soldiers at a Well, Macedonia, sketch of, 75, 208
Soldiers playing cards in front of a camouflaged tent, idea for a painting, 186
Soldiers Washing in a Stream, painting of, 117, 197, 199
Solomon, Gilbert, war artist, fellow student at the Slade, 33, 120
Solomon, J., R.A., 128
Somerset (Taunton), visit to, 26, 49
Sorting and Moving Kit-bags, painting of, *see Kit-bags*
Sorting Laundry, idea for, painting of, *see Laundry*
Southampton, destination of troop-ship, 67; return home to, 110
Spencer, Annie, Cookham, 20
Spencer, Florence, Cookham, books sent to Stanley, 77, 84; letters addressed to at Cookham, 12, 15, 55, 58, 66, 67, 72, 74, 76–7, 79, 82–4, 86–8, 91–2, 95–7, 106, 108, 116, 207; letters to in Cambridge, 110, 122, 155
Spencer, Gilbert, attending the Slade School, and meeting Hilda, 119; attending the War Paintings Exhibition, 120; desire to enlist, opposed, 39–40; drawing of Henry Lamb, 42, 208; enlistment in the R.A.M.C., 48; transferred from Salonika to Egypt, 77; joining honeymoon at Wangford, 171; paintings by, 47, 121, 128; relationship with Hilda, 129; staying at Durweston, Dorset, to paint landscapes, 123; staying at Seaford with the Carlines, 122; swimming at Odney, 44; tea with the Slessers, 117; teaching at the Ruskin Drawing School, 136; together at Fernlea, 33; visits to Hampstead, 120, 141; writing letters to, 26, 132
Spencer, Harold, 20, 31
Spencer, Hilda, *see* Hilda
Spencer, Mrs (Ma), 92; bath-chair, pushing-in, 45, 58; enlistment, fear of, 40, 48; seeing her on leave from Tweseldown, 66; unwell, supper with her, 115
Spencer, parents, failure to say good-bye, and writing to, 49, 109
Spencer, Percy, enlistment in the army, 39

Spencer, Shirin (eldest daughter), photographs of, 135, 199, 201, 210–11; with the family at Burghclere, 177
Spencer, Stanley, acting charades at Hampstead, 141–2; 'after-life', discussion of, 76; art materials needed, provided, in Macedonia, 62, 77, 92; attitude towards women, sex, 14; autobiography, plans to write, 11–12, 15; carving, *see* sculpture; changes in the character of his work, 14, 123, 177, 206; classical literature, self education in, 12, 62; clothes, speech, behaviour, 25, 74; concentration on drawing at the Slade, teaching himself to paint, 29; confidence in being understood, 14, 166; contemplating a series of frescoes, anticipating Burghclere, 59; current affairs, political, social, lack of interest in, 39, 205; day's routine in Cookham outlined, 115; discontent with home-life in Cookham, 115–16; disposition revealed, frank, friendly, confiding, 25, 57, 204; sincere but stubborn, 140; tendency to be argumentative, critical, irritable, quarrelsome, 203; vitality, courage, 100–1, 203; drawing fellow soldiers, patients, 52, 74, 76–7, 79, 81; early inspiration, wish to recapture, 19; extra food needed in Macedonia, provided from home, 79, 84; foreground in painting, discussion of, 132; foreign travel, derided, 68; gardening, disliked, 204; general education, given by his sisters in Cookham, 20; Hilda as artist, admiration of, 119–22, 129; honeymoon, drawing and painting one another, 171; illness, operations, death, 12–13, 43, 74, 79, 86, 105–6, 108, 159, 203; illustrations made when a boy in Cookham, 20; landscape, concern with, inspired by, painting of, 33, 62, 67, 86, 123, 134, 154, 166, 196; permission to draw it in Macedonia, 86; repudiation of any wish to paint it, 37, 123; light, sunlight, discussion of, 137, 161–2, 172; importance of its position in the studio, 169; marriage, *see* Hilda; masterpieces, reproductions collected, seen abroad, 38, 133–4; method of painting, 29, 132, 163, 166, 186; money problems a source of irritation, 116, 204; musical career considered, 20; need for improvement or progress in painting repudiated, 170; nicknamed 'Cookham', 26, 31, 121; painting letter signs in Macedonia, 81; painting with Hilda in Sarajevo, 133–4; patriotism, patriotic, ardour, 49–50; places, feelings for, 28, 33, 37, 123, 125, 131, 138, 168, 200; plan to paint an epic of his war experiences, leading to Burghclere, 145; portraits, drawing and painting of, 154, 157, 196, 198–9; premonition of war, 39; proportions, size, considered, 33, 36, 162; proposal to re-marry Hilda declined, 200; pupils, acceptance of considered, 130; religious convictions uncertain, 63, 110–11, 117; religious differences with Hilda, 140–1; self-portrait, 197–8; separation, divorce, re-marriage, living alone, 13–14, 206; supervising the issue of beer, objection to alcohol expressed in Salonika, 83, 109;